RAMLEELA IN TRINIDAD

100 YEARS OF THE FELICITY OPEN-AIR, FOLK THEATRE TRADITION

RAMLEELA IN TRINIDAD

100 YEARS OF THE FELICITY OPEN-AIR, FOLK THEATRE TRADITION

Satnarine Balkaransingh
Ph.D

Vani Book Company
An imprint of Vani Prakashan Group

Vani Book Company
An imprint of Vani Prakashan Group
4695, 21-A, Daryaganj, New Delhi 110 002
Phone: +91 11 23273167 Fax : +91 11 23275710
India
Branch
Ashok Rajpath, Patna 800 004, Bihar
Coffee House Campus, Mahatma Gandhi Marg, Allahabad 211 001, Uttar Pradesh
Mahatma Gandhi International Hindi University, Wardha 442 001, Maharashtra
Motia Park Opp. Water Tank, Sultania Road, Bhopal 462 001, Madhya Pradesh
Goripur Taliya Para, 313, R.B.C. Road 24- Parganas (North) Kolkata 743 166, West Bengal

www.vaniprakashan.com
marketing@vaniprakashan.in
sales@vaniprakashan.in

In Association with

Ayodhya Research Institute

ESTD.-1986

presents

RAMLEELA IN TRINIDAD
100 Years of the Felicity Open-Air, Folk Theatre Tradition
by Satnarine Balkaransingh

Author's photo courtesy Mark Lyndersay
Photography (except those credited) : Edison Boodoosingh
Cover Design & Graphics : Jason Windsor

ISBN : 978-93-89563-26-9

Religion/Culture

First Edition 2021

Price : $ 25.99, £ 20.00, ₹ 2000

Based on a research project co-sponsored and partly funded by the Ayodhya Shodh Sansthan, an autonomous organization of the Department of Culture, Government of Uttar Pradesh, *Ramleela in Trinidad : 100 Years of the Felicity Open-Air Folk Theatre Tradition* is published by Vani Book Company An imprint of Vani Prakashan Group and copyrighted in 2021 to Satnarine Balkaransingh.

Printed at Thomson Press (India) Ltd.

Vani Prakashan's signature motif is created by Artist Maqbool Fida Husain

VICTORY IN FELICITÉ

Indentured Indians pioneering village theatre, Raghu's Leela,
Chanting and interpreting verses of this ancient saga
Of the legend of Prince Rāma of Kosala,
Battling demons and armies scattered all over India,
To rescue beautiful Sita from Raja Rawan of Lanka.

Today the staccato rhythm of the booming Tassa
Drowns out the audible roll of a distant thunder,
Cumulus clouds mingle with crimson nimbus, Ashwin weather,
Conjuring images of mystic lakes of molten lava
In the evening sky over the Felicité Ramleela.

Even the egrets in precise squadron formation
Glide overhead stealthy, like a dark bomber battalion,
Rāma's air force scanning the scene of today's conflagration,
Riding the air currents to their secret destination,
A foreboding omen of King Rawan's destruction.

T'is a tale of valour embodying an ancient culture,
An epic story that predates Christianity,
The legend of Sita and Prince Rāma of Ayodhya,
Brought by audacious adventurers across the Kali Pani,
And blossoming for a century in this soil of La Trinite.

S. Balkaransingh

DEDICATION

In memory of my mother, Rampiarie,
A devoted 'Ramanandi',
And to all those sewaks of Rām,
Past and present, of Felicity

CONTENTS

FOREWORD

Indian history informs us that in ancient times the area in India known as Ayodhya was the same place known as Kosala. From about the 6th century BC to the 1st century AD, Kosala formed part of the greater geographic, cultural and administrative region known as Bihar. Bihar or Vihara (the country of monasteries) then encompassed the countries of Videha, Vajji, Vaishali, Malla, Mithila, Magada, Anga, and parts of Jharkhand.

During the Mughal era, Emperor Akbar divided the whole of India into administrative regions one of which was Oudh or Awadh. Ayodhya became a part of Awadh with the bordering city of Faizabad being its capital city. Later Awadh was incorporated into the United Provinces or Uttar Pradesh (UP), with Ayodhya becoming a constituent part of UP. It continues to remain within this geo-political administration. But from ancient times, right up to the present period, waves of migration of the peoples of Bihar and Uttar Pradesh have taken place by road, sea and later by air, spreading India's vast treasure of learning and knowledge, including its rich literary and cultural heritage, traditions and life style, far and wide. While India has had a long relationship with the rest of the world, within recent times the Ayodhya Research Institute has been contributing its share in promoting the history, literature and tradition of our ancient civilisation. Established in 1986 as an autonomous organization of the Department of Culture of the Government of Uttar Pradesh, the Institute was set up to research and identify the significance and contribution of Ayodhya and this geographic region to Indian thought, philosophy, religion, literature, arts and overall culture.

Being in the forefront of research, documentation, archiving and promoting the role of the ancient story of Rama, the Institute commenced its relationship with The Caribbean in 2008. Research Scholar, Dr Satnarine Balkaransingh of Trinidad and Tobago arrived here in the month of Ashwin to pursue research on the history of the Rāma story, but with particular reference to Ramleela. His intensive field work in Ramleela was facilitated by the Institute. This resulted in his including a chapter on Ramleela in his recent publication: *The Shaping of a Culture : Rituals and Festivals in Trinidad Compared with Selected Counterparts in India, 1990-2014 (Hansib 2016).* That chapter was a comparative analysis of a Maidāni Ramleela of Ayodhya/ Faizabad with a Trinidadian counterpart.

With further encouragement from me, he undertook to continue additional documentation of the Rāma Story in Trinidad, but specifically its Ramleela. This new book entitled *Ramleela in Trinidad: 100 Years of the Felicity Open-Air Folk Theatre Tradition,* advances the Rāma tradition one step further. Dr Balkaransingh has not only mapped the existing Ramleelas in Trinidad but meticulously documented the history and the changes (the narrative, poetic and dramatic) that have taken place in the saga of the Ramleela in the village of Felicity in the central plains of Chaguanas where many indentured Indian immigrants went to work on its sugar cane plantations. He has also traced the influence of this long Ramleela tradition on the villagers and performers themselves. Writing from the perspective of not only an academic but also a performing artist, having earlier studied dance and music in India, he vividly captures in his book the religious, spiritual and secular influences of this open-air 'village theatre' tradition that still exist in our Indian villages. Written in an easy, flowing style, with much empathy, the book captures the interest and imagination of the reader. To a non-Trinidadian reader, his description of the Pandit's flawless chanting of the Rāmcharitmānas in Awadhi language, then translation of the text in English and further explanation in the Trinidadian English dialectic narrative, returning back to the Awadhi in a seamless transition, is very interesting. Moreover this is done simultaneously with the performers not missing a step in the enactment of the scene in the maidan. This publication is a work of immense historical and contemporary importance to the arts and particularly the dramatic arts. This is a valuable contribution to the body of existing literature on the Rāma Kahani (story) as perpetuated in this small country of Trinidad and Tobago in the Caribbean for more than 100 consecutive years. The Ayodhya Shodh Sansthan (Ayodhya Research Institute [ARI]) takes pleasure in identifying with this work of artistic and literary excellence.

On behalf of the ARI and in my personal capacity I commend this work and trust that it will find its place among the literature on the Rāma Katha.

It is also my fervent hope and prayer that the Felicity Ramleela, as described within these pages, will continue to attract audiences from far and wide and will continue to influence future generations for many more centuries.

January 2018

Dr Yogendra Pratap Singh

Director

Ayodhya Shodh Sansthan

Tulsi Smarak Bhavan

Ayodhya, Faizabad, INDIA

&

Ayodhya Shodh Sansthan

Ninth Floor, Jawahar Bhavan

Lucknow, Government of Uttar Pradesh, INDIA

ACKNOWLEDGEMENTS

The writing of a book - like works in other artistic mediums; whether it is a piece of sculpture, a painting or a script for a dramatic performative work - has a way of challenging its maker. It assumes a personality of its own, sometimes tugging the author in various directions. There were times when the script had to be left alone for a while and later revisited with a fresh eye and a clearer perspective.

It was also necessary to read expansively and discuss the Rām Story with many people; holy men, scholars and academics, performers, administrators, artistes, oral historians and a cross-section of audiences. Wide, deep and intense discussions were held on notions and views on spirituality, philosophy and religion – from the Marxist who saw Rām variously as 'a phantasm and mortal hero' to the holy men and simple village folk who saw him as 'God incarnate on planet earth'. Perseverance has been essential in this work. For that I express gratitude to many.

Between 1972 and 1976, Govind Vidyarthi, then a senior researcher at the Sangeet Natak Akademi, Delhi – and husband of my first Kathak dance Guru, the late Professor Reba Vidyarthi(Didi) of the Kathak Kendra, Delhi - had many conversations with me on the role of the Kathaks or story tellers and their influence on stories and religion in the Indian dramatic arts. Then in 1980 after one of these long rambling conversations at his home in Lakshmi Nagar, Delhi, he provided me with a copy of his original research manuscript on the 'Rāmayāna Tradition in India', saying, "Take this with you and keep it safely. You will have need for it in the years to come". In 2009, in Mumbai, I read some relevant parts of his unpublished biography courtesy the hospitality of Didi and their son, stage and screen actor Ashish Vidyarthi. Govind Dada's words were prophetic. I am deeply indebted to him and have quoted from his manuscript extensively.

Some of my views on the specific topic and then on the text of this book have also been discussed at three international, academic conferences in the UK, Trinidad and India. The first was at The University of Warwick in the United Kingdom; the second was at the First World Ramleela Conferences at the University of the West Indies, St Augustine campus, Trinidad and the third at the Second World Ramleela Conference, at the Indira Gandhi National Institute for the Arts (IGNCA), Delhi, India in November 2015. For these experiences I thank Dr. David Dabydeen, Prof Brinsley Samaroo, Mrs. Kamal Ramsubeik and Prof Molly Kaushal.

Thanks to Sahabir Naipaul who in 2014, and to my great surprise, informed me that my maternal grandfather, Belfie Boodramsingh had been a part of the Felicity Ramleela during the early days of its growth and development. He recounted incidents during the 1940s of this Ramleela and informed me also that my parents and elder siblings, then living in the nearby Perseverance Village, attended the performances.

The Ramleela performers and their families were supportive. The administrators of the First Felicity Ramleela and Cultural Organisation - especially Rance Kanhai, Gewan Nanak and Kelvin Saith - encouraged the writing of this book to mark the centennial anniversary of the Ramleela (some where between 2015-2017), providing the on-going support for the logistics of the research. Kelvin and Hardeo Ramsingh also gave interesting snippets of information, welding the histories of both Felicity and the Leela. Pundit Yankatessu supplied his narrator's script, read the manuscript and made useful comments. The Ramoutar family especially Sirju, Shivaram and Vikash have performed in the Leela for decades. They also gave useful advice and information.

Professor Prakash Persad brought his extensive knowledge of the various texts, the actual tellings of the story in Trinidad and the Caribbean and decades of the local folk theatrical tradition of Ramleela, to provide useful comments on the script and encouragement for the undertaking. Photographer and friend Edison Boodoosingh has spent over 9 years with me, many evenings dodging the open flames in fire scenes and trudging in the mud for hours during the performances of the Leela to get 'the right shot', capturing the mood of the 'play', to complement the narrative of this book. Jason Windsor enhanced the graphics in the images.

The research and writing of this manuscript took place in various locales and spaces; in airports, trains, buses, friends' homes, hotel rooms; in Ayodhya, Faizabad, Lucknow, Ghaziabad, Delhi, London, New York, Trinidad and in Tobago, spending many years in the process. For their hospitality and discussions, I thank Avijit and Dr. Anudha Dutta of the UK; Ashwini and Arvind, Ena and Anjali Parashar of Delhi; Kamini and Nimi Hart and Pundit Mitra Maharaj in New York. Kuntal Surana, Vibha Singh, and Dr. Arup Moitra provided technical and other support. Jassie Singh undertook the field work on the culinary aspect at the Ramleela venue, made useful observations and editorial comments throughout the manuscript stage. Yvonne Teelucksingh provided her editorial expertise.

Kama and Boysie facilitated the comfortable haven and support for me to undertake most of the writing while Pallavi provided comments on the manuscript, filial love and affection. There were several others who facilitated and encouraged this work, too many to list, for this publication has been a collective effort.

In 2008, I was introduced to and hosted by Dr. Yogendra Pratap Singh, Director of the Ayodhya Research Institute (ARI) of Ayodhya, Uttar Pradesh (UP). I was searching for an appropriate location to undertake research for a comparative analysis of a Ramleela in Trinidad with one in the Ayodhya/ Faizabad region of UP. I eventually selected the open-air (maidān) Ramleelas of Felicity and the Rām Janaki Mandir of Faizabad. In 2012 Dr. Singh encouraged me to proceed further with the documentation process and write a book on Ramleela in Trinidad. In 2015, he suggested that the ARI could facilitate the publication of the book. One year later he consented to write the *Foreword* for the book. This is the product of this nine-year collaboration with Dr. Singh and the Ayodhya Research Institute, to whom I am indebted.

Finally I thank my gurus and the divine graces for knowledge and the mercies of health and clarity of thought so that I could undertake this work and you the readers for your appreciation of this Ramleela performative tradition in Trinidad and Tobago.

INTRODUCTION

The folk theatre of Ramleela is the story of a hero warrior and King named Rām. This story, dating back into antiquity, long before the Christian era, has been told and retold for millennia in many countries and cultures of the south-east Asian region. Ramleela, literally translated means, 'the play of Rām'. The mortal hero Rām, over the centuries has been elevated to a God, Shri Rām. His story is told in epic proportions; his birth, education and training, marriage, exile, trials and tribulations, battles and triumphant return to rule the kingdom of Ayodhya in Northern India

The trend of the story is equally linear as its sub-stories which create detours, only to return in a circuitous way to the main narrative. The epic contains many key characters, each with their own sub story, all interwoven into the grand narration. It conveys messages on concepts of authority, leadership and management, morality and ethical issues in the quest for final freedom and release from the chains of human, earthly existence. It questions concepts of 'authenticity', whether classical, religious or secular.

To the Brahmin caste in India who kept the Sanskrit language and the knowledge that was written therein as their sole preserve, Tulsidas's rendering of the Rām story in the Dev Nagri script - the dialect of the common man of north India - was blasphemy. But it has endured. It opened up more vistas of opportunities in other languages also, for India's far-flung off-springs to sup from this and others cups, which contain the essence of her ancient civilization.

This story found its way to the New World within modern times, beginning with the export of contract immigrants from India to the Caribbean during the nineteenth century. In Trinidad and Tobago, the story arrived through several texts and in the folkloric medium, thanks to the saint-poet Tulsidas. Since its introduction in the landscape of Trinidad it has been told and retold through various mediums; as story, chanted as poetry, narrated as the word of God, presented through sculpture, paintings, sung as devotion to

God and enacted as Ramleela or 'the play of God'. Today one does not hear of, or read the Rām story in Trinidad for the first time. People are already familiar with it or know of it. Its presence, like a gentle mist wafting over the physical landscape, has enveloped and influenced our cultural and religious outlook for over 170 years, or 6 generations. It has become indigenous.

The Ramleela is this same story of the warrior-prince Rām, presented in a folk, dramatic format. Currently there are over thirty-five Ramleela groups performing annually in Trinidad - so far it has not been performed in Tobago - during the annual Ramleela 'season' usually held during the bright half of the lunar month of Ashwin (September–October). Many of them culminate at the period of Vijay Dashmi - victory on the tenth day - or the Sunday closest to the Vijay Dashmi of the month.

One of the most popular Ramleelas in Trinidad is the First Felicity Ramleela. According to oral history[1] this Ramleela was introduced in that locale by the Indian indentured workers during the early part of the 20th century, somewhere between the years 1915-1917. Today it is a village event observed by the entire community. Members of the Felicity community who stage and support this Ramleela have traditionally been, and continue to be mostly of East Indian origin. Despite the many religious persuasions of its people; its culture remains basically Indo-Trinidadian, influenced by a traditional Indian value system, ethos and practices. In quick succession of the Ramleela is the annual Divali celebration, the national festival of lights. Felicity remains in a stage of heightened animation. During this Divali festival the entire village of Felicity - households, business places and roadways - presents an Indian visage, celebrating the occasion as a community, attracting great numbers of both local and foreign tourists.

But what had initiated this Ramleela folk performative tradition in Felicity? What kept it alive for over 100 years, when many other folk dramas, such as 'Indar Sabha' (Indra Sabha) and 'Harichand' (Harish Chandra), which flourished in earlier years in the local environment, have all disappeared? Even the Felicity Hosay or Muharram has disappeared. And what has kept this village drama alive, even as it maintains such a difficult production format - running for eleven consecutive days, each year, continuously, without break, for a century? The epic dramatization of this story as village theatre - staged by supposedly unschooled, migrant, village folk, initially living apart from colonial 'civilisation', on the borders of virgin swamp and even within the swamp itself and eking out a livelihood from the surrounding sugarcane plantations and the swamp as they built a village community - is a story worth documenting and telling.

And even as the socio-political and cultural environment changed, how have the annual Ramleela celebrations in this village of Felicity in the central plains of Trinidad survived the ravages of time and their ever changing environment? The answer lies partly in the fact of it being a performative tradition. Our traditions to a great extent reflect our values, norms and patterns of behaviour, our work ethic, our rituals and festivals. In our plural, mosaic society our traditions help us to understand one another's histories, creative and performative urges, lifestyles and ambitions. The Ramleela falls under the definition of being both a 'performance' tradition and a 'performative', faith-based tradition. In this regard a 'performative tradition' is defined as: "Relating to or being an utterance that performs an act or creates a state of affairs by the fact of its being uttered under appropriate or conventional circumstances."[2] These performative traditions are educational, conveying information and sentiments of our past, telling us about our heritage, our ancestry and the legacy being left for this and future generations. When these events take on dramatic dimensions the impact is even more forcefully felt and 'hammered' home.

The Evolution of the Leela

The Leela has undergone many changes in its evolution. While the text has not changed, there have been changes in the social criteria and guidelines used for the selection of performers. Changes have been effected in the costuming, funding of the production, the performance timings, use of technology, female involvement and management of the performance. Even the selection of the script and the contextual interpretations of the script, relating these to actual happenings and contemporary influences in the community and society have undergone changes. It is a study in village mentoring of its youths and in the dynamics of village relationships. In this annual village 'happening' or *mela,* the religious and the secular morph into a seamless flow of community camaraderie. This Ramleela is thus part of our living, subaltern culture which has been integral to our country's modern, socio-economic and cultural history.

This book contains the faithful recording of aspects of the planning activities and the narratives and events as they unfold in this rural setting over

11 consecutive days of the festival. This includes the narrative of the story teller, the *Vyas, Sutradhār* or Pundit, the actions and dramatic interpretations of the performers in interpreting the pundit's narrative and the reactions and moods of the audience to the overall daily presentation. It also deals with the annual event from the perspective of Leela, folk theatre and *mela* or festivity.

As one consciously read and studied the story of Rām in order to appreciate and grasp its narration and interpretation as Ramleela in Trinidad, the epic took on different faces. Saint Tulsidas's version of the Rām story, his Rāmcharitmānas of 24,000 metric verses, is no less daunting, comparatively speaking, than the narrative works of Shakespeare, who interestingly enough was writing, though oceans apart, around the same period as Tulsidas. Then, as I attended the First Felicity Ramleela and other performances (from 2006 to 2016) and began to grasp the full impact of the story on village life and on the people dramatizing it, its extraordinary complexity emerged with multiple levels of meanings, also allowing for contextual interpretations.

The story of the Felicity Ramleela as much as the Felicity story itself is multifaceted, multidimensional and porous, yet it is amorphous. The presentation reflects both synthesis as well as that element of catharsis. Similar to the Leela, the lives of the villagers of Felicity are as much reality as perception, and *maya* or illusion. It was therefore important to capture for posterity, the magic of the village performers, their faith and their lifestyles as demonstrated by their dramatic performances, both visually and textually.

There was also the need to capture and record the spirit of those devout spectators, Rām's devotees who come day after day, year after year to be submerged in the multiple layers of the story, chanted daily in the musical language of the poet author. They come to be transported over space and time as they witness the unfolding of the Leela. For them, this is not just village or street theatre. It is Leela, God's play. It is faith contained in their very consciousness, embellished and infused with its own energy. Each day's performance delivers an electrically charged atmosphere; of melodious chanting by the Pundit cum narrator combined with music, movements and moods, costuming and lighting. These deliver emotions, flavours of actions and reactions or *rasa*, all accentuated by dance and music which themselves create dynamic, ever expanding actions and reactions.

In doing the research for this publication, the various accounts of the history and current views and explanations of events of the Felicity Ramleela, as told to me were repetitive, disjointed and sometimes contested. Some, however, contained new snippets of relevant information. Even the dialogues in my interviewees varied from one telling to the next, one version to another of the same historical events or series of connected events. I never attempted to analyse the veracity of each individual's oral version except to verify historical linkages and events in chronological sequence. But within it all, there appeared a thread of fluidity and consistency within the dozens of tellings.

Out of the numerous interviews and actual viewings of the Leela, over a 10-year period I have been able to structure a narrative that contains the strands of many stories and the oral histories of the people who lived in Felicity, initiated and developed the Felicity Ramleela and the subsequent generations who have kept it alive. The story is not always delivered 'word for word' but sometimes coloured with the narrative and poetic license of a story teller, a Sutradhār or Kathakar. These stories are histories even as they are myths based on local legends, perpetuated orally. It is their language. The aim was to make the people of Felicity and their Ramleela convey that dramatic tension of a dynamic community living through their beliefs, their folk theatre, marrying the religious and the secular without a clearly defined beginning, middle and certainly no ending. This allowed for the structuring of this work in a form and format that was relevant to the community. The writing conveys both factual, oral history, village theatre and the meandering lives of the villagers and the Ramleela people.

While this book seeks to capture the theatrical aspect of the Leela, it is also a socio-economic, anthropological, ethnographic and overall cultural insight as to how the Rām Story has been and continues to be portrayed in Trinidad. It identifies the changing dimensions of the 'maidān' or 'open-air savannah type' village Ramleelas in Trinidad, but specifically the 'maidān' Ramleela as performed by the First Felicity Ramleela and Cultural Organisation. This Ramleela as a living, theatrical heritage in Trinidad, and specifically in the village of Felicity, is used to examine the role and function of this folk tradition in building community cohesiveness, advancing artistic and aesthetic pride and providing good, wholesome entertainment. It examines how cultural identity and general positive values are formed even as the production underwent many incarnations since its commencement in Felicity at the turn of the twentieth century.

The evolution of the First Felicity Ramleela is very much like the evolution of its script, adapted from the Tulsidas's text. In 2006-2007 Pundit Budharat Yankatessu, the current narrator cum director and prompter of the Ramleela, revealed that the first written script for this Ramleela was prepared by Pundit Lalchan Balroop. Pundit Yankatessu's 2007 'script outline' has been edited by me - yet keeping to his version – to maintain the dramatised flow of the story over the period of its narration.

The Language and use of local jargon

Language is a broad term that essentially comprises stories, rituals and symbols which are heard, seen and performed. Language plays a significant role in establishing, maintaining and passing traditions (which includes our myths and mythologies) on to subsequent generations and to the society at large. It records history and literature. It conveys the philosophy and religion(s) of a culture; the truths and wholeness of the culture. The phonetic sounds, inherent in its linguistic style, create the moods, unique flavours and characteristic gestures of the culture it conveys or represents. It is always dynamic, always producing new expressions and explanations, given the soil or environment in which it is growing and functioning. Language thus represents the identity of a culture at any particular time. It easily merges into new environments but its success in this new terrain depends on its adherents and the importance that they place on their own sense of identity, selfhood and value to their everyday existence.

Words and expressions that are conveyed by language and uttered in different environments or cultures carry their own cultural baggage and when transported to, or being transposed in another culture they can be easily misinterpreted.

Words are never innocent. They exercise their own nuances and even tyranny; and a writer has to be very aware of this when adapting a text from another culture. One has to be wary of words and expressions when they are transplanted to new and unfamiliar environment. These words can betray and even violate the text because they are too culturally 'loaded', since they exert their own exclusivity. The reverse is also the case. They may even erase certain original ideas and images and conjure up others, contrary to the original intent and purpose. During these years of viewing the Leela and observing the unfolding of the daily episodes I remained merely a spectator, recording the language, absorbing its intent, purpose and the impressions it conveyed.

Many of the words and phrases in the Rām story have entered the local vocabulary and their phonetic accentuations have also produced unique and different connotations and meanings. For instance, referring to someone as *Rawan* (instead of the textual name of Rāwan), stressing the syllables differently, carries its own derogatory meaning, locally. The word Rām is pronounced here as Ram, as in the name Ramnath. Lakshmana is spelt and pronounced as 'Lutchman' as in 'Lutchmansingh'; Bharata is also spelt as Bharat or Bharath, and even anglicised into Barat.

Care has been taken to ensure that words and expressions used to convey the appropriate meaning of the story are maintained so that the thoughts expressed are not mistranslated and misinterpreted. Some of the words and expressions used in the original text(s) have therefore been retained. Pronunciation of names and places using the phonetics of the 'Bhojpuri' dialect are still a common feature of Indo-Trinidadian and general speech. As such, the spelling of many of the words (both places and character names) has been kept as close as possible to the actual Bhojpuri pronunciations used throughout the actual Leela performance, by the interviewees, the Pundit cum director and by the audience.

Symbolism in the Ramleela

Symbolism plays an integral role in the religious and cultural life of man. Symbols are conveyed through written language, oral traditions, the creative, performing and other dramatic arts, through architecture and archaeology. It appears in literally every aspect of a civilisation. Indian culture and its various religious persuasions, especially Hinduism, is replete with symbolism. The Hindu sees all aspects of creation, and creation itself, as a divine act of God, present in all things, animate or inanimate. Just add a pair of eyes and hands to an image; rock, metal, wood, clay etc., infuse it with energy and it becomes an icon or symbol of the divine, potent with energy. The eyes represent the sense organs; the hands symbolise the organs of actions. A water course, being potent with energy is accorded divine status. Symbols are thus used to bring home the point or create the impact on its audience that was intended.

In the dramatization of the Rām story, a simple act of the clothing change; from crown and rich apparel to being bare headed, with beaded garland and orange-coloured dhoti symbolises his change of status. He has moved from being crown prince to that of exile and forest wanderer. This is equally the case with the change in attire of Lakshman and Sita. The touching of the elder's or pundit's feet symbolises respect and humility on the part of the toucher. During the actual performance of the gesture, the Pundit, teacher or elder in turn stretches his (her) right hand, palms facing the bent person. This is a symbolic gesture of blessing. The physical presence of four hands on an image of God (Shiva) or the female aspect of divinity (Lakshmi) represents the multi-facetted capabilities attributed to the male or female being. Similarly the physical presence of the ten heads on the effigy of the evil King Rawan symbolises that he had the intelligence, knowledge and prowess of ten persons. This is also the case with the Panchmukhi, the five physical visages of Hanuman as he goes to Patal Lok, the underworld, to rescue the brothers Rām and Lakshman. The Ramleela is replete with such symbolism and therefore the uninitiated has to be cautious of according literal interpretations to some of the physical images that appear periodically in the scenes in the drama.

Scope of the book

Ramleela in Trinidad is not only a study in ethnography, in how people i.e. the people of Felicity, live their lives and in so doing create meaning and significance in the lives of others. It is also about micro economics, small-scale business enterprises and village commerce, within the community and between communities. It is part of the promotion and propagation of their values and practices, their artisanal crafts and culinary traditions. It is about congregation, community togetherness and camaraderie. It is a living example of mentoring, with the Ramleela being used to foster and impart knowledge from adult to juvenile and child and, in so doing, enhance community development in a holistic way. It is a living example of the child being guided and brought up by the collective support of and training by the elders and other older members of the village. It is a study in identifying, recognising and documenting the work of these village role models in providing selfless service during this annual on-the-job training programme which reflects overall village life.

This book records the efforts of the performers, the scores of technical Ramleela artistes and the artisans in other related fields. They range from the bamboo cutters, wire benders and effigy fabricators, costume designers and makeup artistes to the Ramleela administrators and the audiences who trek annually to enjoy the village folk theatre festival. There is much to satisfy the curiosity of the readers and encourage them to attend the village folk theatre, to even work with the various members of this community in experiencing the Felicity Leela and promoting its work.

The book is divided into three parts with 11 chapters, a glossary of technical terms, end notes, appendices and a bibliography. Part I of the Table of Contents identifies the psychological and anthropological issues associated with a migrant, multicultural, multi-religious society searching for and establishing its identity in a new landscape. It examines the role of traditions, folklore and the arts in this process of identity formation. It traces the history of the story of the legendary hero, Rām and the variations of the tellings of the story in the Indian diaspora from ancient times, right up to the modern period. It also explains the methods and formats adopted in the presentation of the narrative of this epic poem.

Part II is centered in the village of Felicity, located south of the central Borough of Chaguanas in Trinidad with its unique history, geography and demography. It also traces the history of the Felicity Ramleela, (later renamed the First Felicity Ramleela) as presented by the First Felicity Ramleela and Cultural Organisation. The section identifies the various elements that are integral to the development and implementation of this annual Ramleela ritual cum festival.

Part III documents the entire performance of the Leela on a daily basis. This involves the narration on the form and format used in the telling of the story; the use of costuming, props, sets and décor and the work that is involved in their design and fabrication. It also contains recommendations for the role of the Ramleela and other similar performative traditions in national policy planning, in reconfiguring our education curriculum, in training and in our collective approach to achieving social cohesion and an all-inclusive national identity. These issues are integral to the diversification of the national economy and to its attainment of self-sustaining growth and development. This work may also pique the interest of others, especially our young people, to visit and enjoy similar Ramleela celebrations in their own communities in Trinidad and Tobago. It may even help them to discover our other existing dynamic and vibrant subcultures, and in so doing promote local tourism.

Orthography

Many of the words used in the story have originated from Sanskrit, Hindi and other Indian languages brought by the East Indian immigrants. Those words that have entered current usage in the Trinbago English language (dialect) are written in normal English script. Those of different languages i.e. Sanskrit, Hindi, Awadhi, Bhojpuri, Bundeli or other Indian language, and not readily familiar or easily translatable, are written in *italics* and appropriate translations are given in a Glossary. An attempt has been made, as far as possible, to render technical terms in a sort of standardized way. While many technical terms have gone into local Creole usage through the oral medium, those technical terms that do not enjoy current common usage in Trinbago are explained. For instance, for all words in which the syllables are stressed as in the name 'Raama', an accent is written above the stressed syllable. The letter 'a' at the end of the word is also dropped as in 'Rām'. The name 'Rāvana' is similarly spelt 'Rāvan' or 'Rāwan' or 'Rawan'; 'Lakshmana' is written as 'Lakshman'. 'Maidaan', the open air savannah stage, is written as 'maidān'.

January 28, 2018 **Satnarine Balkaransingh** PhD.

ENDNOTES

1. While oral history seems to indicate that the Felicity Ramleela began in the year 1915, there is no documentary evidence to justify this. This Ramleela has been performed solely in the Green Park Savannah, which was originally a coconut grove. The Savannah came into existence approx. 7 years after that date (1915). However there was a Ramleela performed before that date, in East Chaguanas. This moved to the grounds now occupied in part by the Chaguanas Borough Corporation and part being the grounds of the former mud *Sewalla*, which is today's Chaguanas Sai mandir, abutting the Borough Corporation on Cumberbatch Street. P.I with Septuagenarians Bhagan Singh and Pundit Krishnadath Naipaul, both of Longdenville, Chaguanas in 2014-15. Pt. Naipaul was intimately connected with the Cumberbatch St Ramleela prior to the 1970s.
2. The American Heritage® Dictionary of the English Language, Fourth Edition, copyright ©2000 by Houghton Mifflin Company.

PART : I

The Rām Story as a Performative Tradition

Chapter One

THE RÃM STORY: IT'S DEPICTION IN VARIOUS MEDIA IN INDIA AND ASIA

It is common knowledge, documented and oral, that wherever people migrate to new places whether for economic, commercial, trade or other reasons in the long history of migrations, they carry their cultural baggage with them. This is equally so with the peoples of the Indian subcontinent starting from antiquity. From the medieval period into modern times they travelled into the Far East, Africa, South East Asia and Europe where they introduced their art-forms, literature and folk traditions in those new environments, significantly influencing the landscapes of their adopted countries. Simultaneously foreign travelers who arrived in India took aspects of its culture - spices, fabrics, religion, literature and life style - and introduced these abroad.

The Rām story

The story of Rām, the heroic Prince of the pre-Christian era epic has been told and retold for millennia in many countries and cultures of the south-east Asian region. It is told in panoramic proportions of his birth, education and training, marriage, exile, abduction of his wife, trials and tribulations, battles and triumphant return to rule the kingdom of Ayodhya in Northern India.

In the Rāmayāna, the hero Rām is assisted by one of his trusted brothers and constant companion, Lakshman and later, by his friends - Hanuman (his devotee) and Sugrīv and his army - in his quest to achieve his goal. The hero Rām experiences a series of trials and tribulations and finally battles with Raja Rāwan, the King of Lanka. Rāwan had abducted and imprisoned Rām's wife, Sita in retaliation for the humiliation and disfigurement of his sister Shurpanakha by Rām and his brother, Lakshman. These events test his (Rām's) valour, his virtue and the righteousness of his actions and hence his life style, his *dharma*.

The heroine Sita is also of divine birth, a woman of great virtue and beauty who is abducted, dishonoured, released, and honoured again. Much later she is dishonoured again, stripped of her rightful role as Queen and cast out of the kingdom (while being pregnant) only to be invited once again to her legitimate home. This is too much for her. She vanishes.

The trend of the story is linear while its sub-stories create detours, only to return in a circuitous way to the main narrative. This long story contains many key characters, each with their own sub stories, all interwoven into the grand narration.

The Rām story as Epic

Among world literature, the story of Rām of the Rāmayāna stands out as one of the great epic poems of all times. The Rāmayāna is possibly the oldest known and consistently extolled epic of modern times. It predates the other Indian epic, the *Mahabharata* and is equal to or possibly better known than the other, providing the story material and inspiration for later poems and dramatic works in modern Indian languages.

The Oxford dictionary defines the term 'epic' as being 'a long poem narrating the adventures or deeds of one or more heroic or legendary figures.'[1] An epic is a simple story delivered in an elevated style of rendition. In the epic's narrative, the hero usually encounters great difficulties and hardships in his quest to claim the heroine so that he or rather 'they' can finally live 'happily ever after'. In his quest to achieve his goal the hero goes through extended periods of tribulations, battling superhuman and negative forces, settling disputed titles of rule between warring kingdoms, and establishing strategic alliances while he searches for and defends the character and personage of the heroine. The heroine may herself be the product or progeny of unusual circumstances or even divine birth, with glowing qualities, virtues and beauty. The story strings together many smaller stories or sub stories. In its telling, the plot makes large and circuitous detours to narrate many of these sub stories within the main story, with each one connected to this main storyline.

The *Rāmayāna* as an epic poem has been variously referred to as *Adikavya*, the first poem, and *Mahakavya*, a great poem. It also falls within the Indian literary classification as *Itihaas;* history and legend, a story with moral and ethical values, extolling the philosophical principles of living. It conveys messages on concepts of authority, governance, leadership, strategic alliances and warfare, management, magic and metaphysics in the final quest for freedom and release from the chains of human, earthly existence. It questions concepts of authenticity, whether classical, religious or secular; hence its messages are worthy of emulation.

In an epic, the mortal hero is also accorded super human qualities or sometimes divine status. The Rāmayāna explains the concept of the supreme, divine consciousness or God, taking various forms in the long history of mankind to destroy unrighteousness and restore a sense of righteous living or *Dharma.* In the telling of the story of the hero Rām in poet Valmiki's Rāmayāna, he is first portrayed in the original narration as a mortal hero with a semblance of divine characteristics. Much later, after millennia and scores of tellings, with variations of the original, the saint poet Tulsidas finally portrays Rām as having all of the characteristics of divinity.

There is a non-linear narrative style in composition, almost adopting the cyclic process that is so common to Indian philosophy of life, and hence contained in all of its artistic expressions, music and dance, and indeed all Indian life. There are stories within the main story; the stories move along from one episode to another, making large detours, jumping from one story into another story, meandering and sometimes digressing from the story proper to an elaborate description of nature and the environment. There are flashbacks to the main story, diversions into cosmology, philosophy, governance, morality, ethics, genealogies, the environment and advice on daily living; and finally a return, in a circuitous route, to the main story for a satisfying conclusion.[2] In this way the epic poem unfolds with the subtle majesty of a mighty river or rather a vast ocean of inexhaustible wealth, defying all analysis at the psychological, historical, thematic or structural levels and sometimes - while they seem to contradict - they intertwine and move on.

Other known epics are the *Iliad* of Homer, Milton's *Paradise Lost, Valmiki's Rāmayāna* and the longest one in the world, the *Mahabharata* comprising 100,000 verses, narrated by sage Ved Vyas.

History of the Rām's story: The dating of Rām's birth

In order to place the Rāmayāna in proper context it is necessary to ascertain the period of the birth of its hero on planet earth. Ancient Indian scholars of mathematics and science have devised a method of dating time into distinct periods or ages, eons, or yugas of which there are four - Sat yuga, Treta yuga, Dwapar yuga and Kalyuga. Each Yuga or eon contains specific characteristics. Based on an established mathematical formula for calculating these yugas, scholars are divided in their opinions as to whether mankind is currently in Kalyuga or on the cusp, between Kalyuga and Sat Yuga. What they do not dispute however is that Rām's birth is traced to the Treta Yuga.[3] His successor, Krishna of the other epic, the Mahabharata, was born in Dwapar Yuga, thousands of years after him. This dating of time does not negate the currently accepted concept of the present era subdivided into ancient, medieval and modern time, for indeed all the yugas would be so divided and classified according to time.

The genesis of the Rām Story therefore stretches way into the unknown past. Through the ages, even in the country of its birth, it underwent many tellings and retellings in multiple forms and formats. In the various tellings, Rām has been represented variously as a virtuous, ideal man or as godhead.

The expansiveness and variants of the story

Over the years, scholars and authors identified numerous versions of the Rāmayāna which have been popular in different Indian languages and dialects. Authors have narrated and interpreted it in the original language of Sanskrit and their own regional language.

In Sanskrit alone there are at least five versions. These include the *Adhyatma Rāmayāna*, the *Ānanda Rāmayāna*, the *Adbhuta Rāmayāna*, *Yogavasishta Rāmayāna*, and the *Tatvasamgraha Rāmayāna*.

In addition to the above five major versions in the Sanskrit language, there are at least 25 major, recorded versions of the Rām story across India alone, in 11 separate regional Indian languages. These are:

i. *Rāmcharitmānas* of Tulsidas written in Hindi/Awadhi
ii. *Rāmavatar* in Punjabi
iii. *Kamban* or *Kampan Rāmayāna* and *Uttarakanda* by Ottakuthan in Tamil
iv. *Ramcharitra* by Rāma Kannasi Panikkar's translation of Valmiki, and Vallattol's translation in Malayalam
v. Narasimhachari's *Torve Rāmayāna*, *Rāmayāna Darshana* of Kuvempu, *Ramchandra Charitra Purāna* by Nagachandra (in Jain tradition) in Kannada

vi. *Ranganatha Rāmayāna*, *Molla Rāmayāna* and Bhaskara's Rāmayāna in Telugu

vii. *Katha Rāmayāna* by Raghunatha, *Geeti Rāmayāna* by Durgavara and Madhava Kandaliya's translation of *Valmiki Rāmayāna* in Assamese

viii. *Krittivasa Rāmayāna* and *Chandravati Rāmayāna* in Bengali

ix. *Saptakand Rāmayāna*, Balaramadasa's *Dandi Rāmayāna* and Saraladas's *Vilanka Rāmayāna* in Oriya

x. Ramacharitra Balana's *Ramavivaha* and Giridhardas's *Rāmayāna* in Gujarati and

xi. Eknath's *Bhavartha Rāmayāna* and Sreedhara's *Ramavijaya* in Marathi.

The most important among these are the 10th century, *Kamban Rāmayāna* and *Ramanatakem* of Arunagiri Nadar in Tamil; the *Rāmcharitmānas* of Tulsidas in Awadhi /Hindi; *Kunnassa Rāmayāna*, *Ramakatha Pattu* and *Adhyatma Rāmayāna* in Malayalam language; *Pampa Rāmayāna* and *Torve Rāmayāna* in Kannada language; *Krittivasa Rāmayāna* in Bengali language; *Ranganatha Rāmayāna, Bhaskar Rāmayāna* and *Molla Rāmayāna* in Telugu language.[4] These works, over the centuries, have supplied the story and spoken-word material to the widespread *Rāmayāna* theatre tradition in different regions of that country.

Researcher Govind Vidyarthi noted that 'some of these are translations and adaptations of the ancient *Valmiki Rāmayāna* or of the medieval *Adhyatma Rāmayāna*, and others, though greatly influenced and inspired by them, were more or less original works of great poetic beauty written in various languages.'[5] Since many of the tellings are considered 'original works', there are differences in the telling of the stories.[6] These versions of the Rām story, told in many of India's sub-cultures thus carry their own and differing narratives, many conflicting with one another. Even within the story itself there are conflicts in the interpretation of the story when these are taken from different angles - as simple drama, as faith, as moral and ethical aspects of actual life, as the word of God versus simply as an epic told in a lofty way.

For instance the ancient tale of Valmiki, the *Rāmayāna*, varies in many parts from the sixteenth century version, the Rāmcharitmānas of Tulsidas. There is also controversy as to whether the first part or book and the last book of the *Rāmcharitmānas* are actually integral parts of the original text or later additions to the text. There are other debatable issues. For instance there are the issues of Rām's humiliating treatment of Shurpanakha, the sister of

King Rāwan; of his treatment of his wife Sita; of Rām's role in the battle between King Bali and his brother Sugrīv, and the moral and ethical nature of a warrior hiding behind a tree in ambush to kill another warrior. These supposedly controversial issues of the texts, the types of texts, the varieties of issues contained in the texts that are contentious or spur debates of a moral, ethical or sociological nature are not addressed in this book.

The Rām Story as a performative tradition

The Rām story is considered as a performative tradition. Performative traditions, according to the American Heritage Dictionary of English language, refer to these 'religious, folkloric, heritage and other traditions which are transmitted or performed through various mediums or combinations of mediums, whether in recognisable or unrecognisable, structured or unstructured form or format.' These include the oral (narrative, verse and lyrical) musical, dance, pantomime, and other ritualistic or dramatic performative activities, whether on the proscenium or other stages - the open air, the street or village theatre - or other community gatherings in various environments inclusive of 'power spots', water courses or other sanctified areas.

A tradition would have begun, been told, recited, narrated, sung, seen or heard and perpetuated long before writing was invented. Therefore, it encompasses the oral and aural, the one who delivers and the one who receives the message. Performative traditions are not static but are subject to change: old stories are reconstructed, reformed and retold so that the new tellings or narratives seem or sound somewhat similar to the old ones. A really living tradition has no need for "preservation" because it is always being preserved by a truly traditional singer or story teller, with every new telling sounding like the same traditional performance. In this way a tradition establishes continuity between past and present, incorporating aspects of the present within the past.

There is, however, a fine line of difference between a performance art and a performative tradition. A performance art involves a number of elements. These include a performer or group of performers establishing a relationship between themselves and an audience in a particular time frame and a space. In this regard, 'Performance artists often challenge the audience to think in new and unconventional ways, break conventions of traditional arts, and break down conventional ideas about 'what art is'"[7]. Some kinds of performance art nevertheless can be close to or be easily confused with the performative tradition which would have developed over a long period of time, using a fictitious setting, with a script (whether linear or circular), and follow conventional theatrical dynamics whether of a folk, contemporary or classical nature.

Such performative traditions include a textual script or contextual work or both interlocking devices. They can both transport their audiences into other realms of consciousness and transform them into new worlds of consciousness. In looking at the drama, one can be absorbed and led to 'see' what other members of the audience cannot perceive. These performative traditions usually contain individual and community involvements.

The material of this great epic has been made familiar through the performative traditions not only to the literate but also to the unlettered through constant recitation, through dramatic presentations and through folk songs and other folk arts. Oral history narrates the traditions of singing or reciting Rāmayāna right from the time of Valmiki. The legend has it that Kusha and Lava, the estranged sons of Rām, sang the story of Rām, as taught by Valmiki, in the presence of Rām himself which brought about the family reunion. From then onwards, *Kushilavas* or performing artists - (this term probably had its origin from this legend) - continued this tradition. Numerous versions of the Rām story have been popular in different Indian languages and dialects. Vidyarthi noted that: 'This tradition continues to the present time in Hindu households in India in various languages' of that multilingual subcontinent. Whether it is *Rāmcharitmānas* in Uttar Pradesh and Bihar or *Adhyatma Rāmayāna* in Kerala or *Krittivasa Rāmayāna* in Bengal or *Pampa-Rāmayāna* in Karnataka or the *Giti Rāmayāna* of Assam or *Dasarathi Sutakamu* in Andhra Pradesh, the tradition of singing Rāmayāna has been an unbroken one among Indians.

Rāmayāna in dramatic forms: Classical and Folk Theatre – Ramleela

There is a considerable volume of dramatic representation of the Rām story in ancient classical theatre, in Sanskrit literature, and in India's regional folk theatre. In the Mahabharata (the other Indian epic) it is written that the first (dramatic) presentation of this story - commonly referred to as Ramleela - was made 'at the time of Dharmaraja Yudhishthira-sponsored Rajsooya Yagna.

The presentation was made by Sri Krishna, his brother Balarama and their Yadav friends' with all the theatrical appurtenances that were thought necessary to enhance its audio-visual quality. According to this textual evidence, the presentation faithfully followed the rules of stagecraft, as later enunciated in Bharata's *Natyasastra* the ancient treatise on dramaturgy (3rd century BC-2nd century AD).[8] Vidyarthi indicated that:

> *In this era the earliest dramatic presentations of Rām Katha were the Pratimanatakam and Abhisheka Nataka by Bhasa, written in the 4th century B.C. That these dramas on the theme of Rām were regularly staged is evident from the fact that they form part of the repertoire of Koodiattam, the oldest Sanskrit theatre tradition extant in the country. Koodiattam, with an unbroken tradition of at least two thousand years, is still staged by Chakyars in the Koothampalam theatre attached to the temples in Kerala. Two of the plays popular with them are the Abhisheka Nataka of Bhasa and Ascharya Chudamani of Shakti Bhadra.*[9]

From Valmiki's Rāmayāna to Tulsidas's Rāmcharitmānas

As the story is elucidated in its innumerable retelling over millennia, Rām in the Tulsidas' opus magnum, the Rāmcharitmānas (The Holy Lake of the Acts of Rām) has evolved into Shri Rām, God incarnate, an avatar. The Rāmcharitmānas was written by Tulsidas (1532-1623) between the years 1574-77 A.D.

Speaking of the Rāmcharitmānas, R.C. Prasad, Professor and Head of the Department of English of Patna University in Bihar, India, in his "Introduction to the Tulsidas's *Rāmcharitmānas*" (edited and translated into Hindi and English by him, in 1990) states that: "Tulsidas borrows a great deal from the *Valmiki* and *Adhyatma Rāmayāna* and the *Hanumannataka.*" Prof Persad elaborates on Tulsidas' text as follows:

> *Lest, however, the reader should form the impression that the Rāmcharitmānas is merely a Hindi impression of the Sanskrit epic, it must here be pointed out that while Tulasi follows the course of Valmiki's story, dividing it into seven Kandas bearing the names that Valmiki has given to his sections, the Hindi Rāmayāna is essentially different from that of Valmiki.*

Persad provides examples of his explanations of Tulsidas' deviations in his sixteenth century writing:

The Uttarakanda (section– author's insertion*) in the Hindi epic, for instance, bears no resemblance whatsoever to that of the Sanskrit work. Nor does the reader find anything in the latter resembling the conversation between Garuda and Kakabhushundi.*

Tulsidas' Rāmcharitmānas however maintains the epic proportions of Valmiki's story. While Valmiki's Rāmayāna was divided into 5 parts but 7 sections, Tulsidas' Rāmcharitmānas is divided into 7 books or Kandas. These are as follows:

Bala Kanda	-	Birth, adolescence and marriage
Ayodhya Kanda	-	Proposal for Rām's coronation, his banishment, Bharata's arrival in Chitrakoot, his failed plea to Rām to return as King and Dasarath's demise
Aranya Kanda	-	Rām's ascetic life in Chitrakoot and Panchavati, the abduction of Sita by Rāwan and the beginning of the search for Sita
KishkindhaKanda	-	Rām's meeting with Hanuman, his alliance with Sugrīv, slaying of Bāli, coronation of Sugrīv and resumption of the search for Sita
Sundara Kanda	-	Intensified search for Sita, Hanuman flies to Lanka, converses with Sita, his capture and dialogue with Raja Rāwan, the burning of Lanka and Vibhishan meeting with Rām
Lanka or Yudh Kanda	-	Construction of a bridge to Lanka, war and casualties, Rāwana's defeat and demise, installation of a new King in Lanka and Rām 's return to Ayodhya, and
Uttara Kanda	-	Rām's coronation and rule, dialogues on various topics of religion, virtue, learning and love life in the mundane world and finally disappearance. It also deals with the expulsion of the pregnant queen Sita; the birth of her sons, Lava and Kush and their return to the royal court in Ayodhya to read the story of Rām to their father, the King.

The epic contains a staggering number of 84 stories*or kathas*. These are stories within the main story. The epic deals with the whole gamut of human emotions and life, ranging from mysticisms, sorcery and illusion to farce, transcending time and space. Like a mighty river from source to finish, the stories, like tributaries, cascade from one into the other.Some are swift flowing,with fast forwards and flashbacks to the main story and with countless diversions, even as the main story navigates large detours, meandering on its free flow towards the ocean.

In the Valmiki's epic, there is a relationship established between the hero and the gods. Here the hero is transposed. He takes physical birth, from the metaphysical to the physical realm, through a special blessing; 'between cosmic order and human destiny: the cosmic plan of the gods becomes the human hero's fate'. He is constantly wondering why he has to bear such trials and tribulations. The Gods' divine plan has cast one of their own in the form of a mortal, Rām, to fulfill a destiny, their purpose. In the Valmiki story, he is informed that he is God incarnate after his battle with and the death of his arch enemy, Rāwan, and the return of his abducted wife, Sita.

This is what gives Valmiki's story such poignancy. Ram is an avatar; an incarnation of God, born on planet earth to achieve some stated purpose; the restoration of liberty, equality, righteousness, where peace and harmony reside. There is the interplay of karma or cause and effect;of destiny, dharma or righteous living, and *kaala* or time. These forces operate in such a way that they determine what the hero can do and what would be the repercussions of his actions. Within the complex of these countervailing forces there are the 'boons' and 'curses' meted out to the mortals by the gods.

The divine maiden, Sita takes birth herself in mystical circumstances, appearing to Raja Janak out of a jar from the furrow - the word 'Sita' in the Sanskrit language means 'furrow'- of the earth, marries Rām and, while sharing his tribulations is abducted and transported far away, while they both pine away for each other. Even when they are reunited her troubles are not over. She leaves the hero in equally mystical circumstances when she is called upon, not once but twice, to prove her chastity as wife. This is a classic case of the patriarchal nature of the Rāmcharitmānas. On the second occasion, she disappears into the earth forever.

The entire epic is written in an elevated poetic style and as such, it is narrated by chanting the metric stanzas. In the Tulsidas' version of the Rāmayāna epic, these stanzas include: *Chowpai* or 4-line verses of which there are 980, 18,200 *Dohas* or Couplets, 24,000 *Shlokas* or 2-4 line verses, *Sortahs* another type of couplet, *Chhand* or 6-line verses; and *Stuti* which are 2 or 4 line prayer-couplets. The epic contains a staggering total of 168,000 words.

This story has deeply influenced the social, cultural and moral life of the Indian people and their progeny wherever they have been scattered, for more than two thousand years while considerably enriching their literature and arts. It has also enriched the life of those societies which have been influenced by India through the ages.

The Rām Story in Folklore and Tradition

In India

Rām has been depicted by the writer Valmiki as an ideal man among men. As such, early dramatic representations emphasised this aspect of Rām as a mortal hero. However, from the 12th to the 13th century onwards there appeared a gradual but noticeable change in the portrayal of Rām. From the ideal man, the writers began depicting Rām as a man with divine attributes and finally, as an incarnation of Vishnu. This noticeable change commenced with Rām as the Supreme Being in the *Kampan Rāmayāna* of the 10th century, followed by the Adhyatma Rāmayāna of the 14th century. The *Rāmcharitmānas* of Goswami Tulsidas elaborates this aspect of the Rām story, and the Ramleela performance initiated by him in Varanasi cast Rām as God. This version of the story later spread all over Northern India.

The decline of the Sanskrit traditions in India's history was a result in part of the recurring religio-political upheavals in the country which threatened the age-old religious and cultural foundations of the society and its traditions. But beginning from the 10th century to about the 16th century, the medieval period, a new and powerful wave of worship emerged, the *Bhakti* period. It was the worship of God, a personal God, through absolute, uncontaminated and pure devotion or *Bhakti*. This was the introduction and establishment of a new tradition known as *Vaishnavism*. As a part of this new wave of worship, the stories of Rām and Krishna were retold through literature, in a spate of books in almost all of the languages of the vast Indian subcontinent. It appeared in sculpture, painting, fabric designs, handicraft, pottery and other artisanal arts. It was being propagated to both the literate and the unlettered through the oral tradition and the medium of music, dance, puppetry and drama. There was constant recitation through dramatic presentations and through folk songs and other folk arts. It stirred the minds of the masses. The *Kampan Rāmayāna* of south India, the Irāmāvatāram (the incarnation of Rām) written in Tamil in the 10th century is attributed by scholars to the period of the commencement of the change in the story from Rām being portrayed as a god-man in *Valmiki's Rāmayāna*, to him being god incarnate in Kampan's version of the telling of the Rām story. Kampan's version added to the promotion of the Bhakti form of worship. The Tulsidas' Rāmcharitmānas provided further source material to this wave of literature and the tsunami of the Bhakti movement that continued.The Rāmcharitmānas of Tulsidas, written in the 16th century, was therefore an important landmark of this cultural revival in north India.

Vidyarthi noted that the tradition of staging Rām Katha as a drama had been popular in the Mithila region in the state of Bihar since the 13th or 14th century.[10] The Ramleela, in an operatic form, was performed not as an annual ritual, but as a living drama by organised groups all over the Mithila region. There is evidence that this tradition continued into the 7th decade of the 20th century.[11]

Vidyarthi however noted that:

> *The tradition of Ramleela performance did not originate with Tulsidas. A great devotee of Rām called Megha Bhagat, a contemporary of Tulsidas, had initiated the staging of Ramleela performance in Kamacha. That performance attracted vast audiences. That Ramleela was drawn from the Valmiki Rāmayāna.*

In this interesting history of Varanasi and its Ramleelas, around the mid-16th century, Vidyarthi continues:

> *In those days, Varanasi was divided into two sectors, known as Kashi Khand and Kedar Khand. While Megha Bhagat stayed in Kamacha which was in Kashi Khand, Tulsidas stayed in Kedar Khand. Since there was already a Ramleela in Kashi Khand, Tulsidas started his own Ramleela in Kedar Khand. In course of time … Megha Bhagat (also called Narayan Das) became a good friend and admirer of Tulsidas and later adopted Rāmcharitmānas as a text for his Ramleela. Thus these two Ramleelas became very popular. Although today Ramleela is performed at almost two dozen places, in Varanasi the original two traditions still attract the largest crowd.*

He also identifies differences in the 2 versions of these Ramleelas as late as 1975:

> *While the famous Bharat Milap of Kamacha is reminiscent of the original Ramleela of Megha Bhagat, the Ramleela started by Tulsidas flourishes under the princely patronage in Ramnagar across the Ganga.*[12]

This Ramleela was introduced in Ramnagar by Maharaja Udit Narayan Singh (1796-1835). Anuradha Kapur in her book, *Actors, Pilgrims, Kings and Gods* (1990) justifies this date by referring to 'drawings by James Prinsep of the Ramnagar Ramleela' entitled *Benares Illustrated in a series of drawings.*[13] Ramnagar is situated on the eastern side of the River Ganga flowing through Benares.

There are many stories on the transfer of this dramatic presentation to Ramnagar. One such story, according to Vidyarthi, goes as follows:

> *The young son of the Maharaj Uditnarain Singh of Kashi fell seriously ill. When there was no hope of his recovery, the desperate father was advised to seek the help of Rām at the Ramleela performance. The Maharaj went to the Kedar Khand Ramleela and prayed to the Lord. The son recovered.*

The son later succeeded the throne as Maharaj Ishwarinarain Singh. The Ramleela, introduced in Ramnagar, has been performed there annually,up to today, under the current Maharaja's patronage.

Tulsidas' Rāmcharitmānas was also used as one of the effective tools against the Muslim juggernaut which, for over 8-10 centuries had been converting via the Quran or by slaughtering the Hindu resistors of conversion, the 'infidels'.[14] It functioned as a social and religious response to this onslaught of Islam. India's Muslim rulers were later replaced by British successors who for over 200 years used more sophisticated methods of keeping the Indians under socio-economic, political and military subjugation. Tulsidas used the theme of the story - of denial of lawful right to property, of complicity in unethical, immoral and dishonest decision making, banishment, suffering and eventual return - to claim ownership over the rightful property. It was a familiar theme being experienced by the masses of India. It resonated within their psyche. It gave moral and spiritual sustenance and hope for a better future.

The Tulsidas's version of the Rām story rapidly spread to other regions of India viz the villages in the State of Avadh (Oudh) –Ayodhya, the outskirts of Benares, Lucknow, Gorakhpur, Faizabad, Bareilly and the Mithila region of the State of Bihar. Village Ramleela sprung up in and around Uttar Pradesh and

Bihar, the Bhojpuri and other Hindi speaking regions.No doubt the indentured Indian immigrants who originated from those Ramleela-performing areas would have experienced the Tulsidas version of the Ramleela prior to their departure from India and so would have introduced it within their communities as worship, as a divine play to be performed, its music soothing to the restless minds and a balm to the tired souls of sugar and cocoa plantation workers. Moreover, the lofty ideas and ideals contained therein were worthy of constant repetition and emulation.

Tulsidas, however, gave new dimensions to the Ramleela performance by introducing the pattern of staging different scenes at different locales in the Kedar Khand sector of Benares. The sites were named to correspond with the names in his Rāmcharitmānas book. Thus, the area north of the River Assi was known as 'Ayodhya' and the one to the south as 'Lanka', and so on. These places are commonly referred to, even today, by these names. The staging of different scenes at different venues - moving from venue to the other - within the overall production involves long processions. This aspect of Ramleela, referred to The *Nakkataiya Ramleela* or processional theatre, is also common in Benaras and its surrounding regions. *Nakkataiya* which takes its names from '*nak kat*' or nose cut, referring to the cutting of the nose of Shurpanakha, usually has Shurpanakha at the head of the procession. It is a nocturnal event. They stop periodically, perform several scenes and move on.[15]

Rām story as folk theatre in India

Turning to the folk and ritual theatre, the story of Rām provides the thematic content to these myriad, colourful theatrical forms existing in India and its diaspora. They all fall under the generic name of Ramleela or Ramleela as we know it in Trinidad and Tobago. They are presented in various forms and formats such as shadow theatre, processional theatre, *jhaki* theatre, puppet theatre, stage or *manch* theatre and *maidān* or open-air savannah-type, theatrical presentations. There is the shadow theatre of the southern state of Kerala, in India, from where some of our Indo-Trinidadian citizens trace their lineage. This shadow theatrical form of presentation, known as the *Tolpavakoothu*, draws its theme from the 10th century *Kampan Rāmayāna*. This presentation is a totally temple-based, ritual tradition, performed in Rām temples. The entire Rāmayāna is performed in 21 days.

Then, in Andhra Pradesh - the state from which our late musical icon Narsaloo Ramaya traced his ancestry - there is the shadow theatre, the *Tholu Bomalattam*. The Rām story is narrated through an on-screen projection of multicoloured images. The *Bomalattam* performances have also spilled over into the state of Tamil Nadu of which Chennai is its capital city. This presentation draws its theme from the *Dwipad Rāmayāna,* also known as the *Ranganath Rāmayāna*, both of the 12th century. The presentation is embellished by songs from the *Molla Rāmayāna* of the 16th century. This shadow theatre tradition later crossed over into the Karnataka or parts of the southern regions previously called Mysore, where it was known as *Thogalu Gombeyatta.* The shadow theatre of Orissa, from where the classical Orissi or Odissi dance derives its origins, is known as *Rāwanchaya.* The Rām theme of this tradition is drawn from the *Vichitra Rāmayāna* of the 16th century. In Bengal, the rod puppets or *Putul Naach* are the characters used to tell the story of Rām.

There is also a processional form of Ramleela known as the *Terayattam* folk drama tradition of Kerala. It is probably one of the oldest living traditions of processional theatre in India. The cast of players move in procession and stage different episodes or scenes at different times of the day and at different locales. "The entire male population of four villages in the jurisdiction of the temple (which is staging the production), form the army of Rām, and they march bare-bodied with him up and down the procession, carrying a stick symbolising the bow..."[16]

Prof. Molly Kaushal also identifies an array of lesser known processional theatre traditions, other than that of the Ramleela of Ramnagar. These combine *Jhankis*, effigies, masked performances, dance-drama, martial arts and devotional singing...'[17] There are also *Swang* and *Rasdhari Khayal* in Rajasthan. There is the *Jhanki* Ramleela and *Nukkad* Ramleelas all across north India, the Madhubani Ramleela from Bihar, *Rām Jātra* from Bengal, *Daspalla, Bisipada* and *Boudh Ramleela* from Orissa and *Chho/Chau* dance-drama from Bengal and Orissa which weave popular episodes from Rāmayāna into its repertoire. The Northeast part of the country has preserved forms of both Vaishnava and Buddhist traditions: *Ankiya Nat* from Assam, *Khamti* Buddhist tradition and *Aji Lamo* performances from Arunachal Pradesh.The Rām story pervades several performing traditions of Southern India: *Koodiattam* and Kathakali from Kerala, *Yakshagana, Doddatt*a and *Sonnatta* from Karnataka, *Bhagwatmela* from Tamilnadu and Kuchipudi from Andhra Pradesh. In northern India the theme of the Rām story has been a part of the Kathak Classical dance performance tradition.

Arts and crafts associated with Ramleela and Rāmkatha manchan range from set designs, backdrops, costuming, makeup, masks, effigies, crowns and umbrellas to richly decorated and ornate tableaux, props and décor, including pyrotechnic displays integrated within the drama.

Different communities and professional groups bring their skill and expertise in the staging of Ramleela, making it a unique experience of a composite tradition spread over anywhere between three days to four weeks. The Ayodhya Research Institute, under Director Dr. Yogendra Prasad Singh has established a record of Ramleela, running continuously for years.

ENDNOTES

1. The Concise Oxford Dictionary of Current English, R.E. Allen. Ed. (Delhi: OUP, 1990), 393
2. Satnarine Balkaransingh, *Trinidad Space Speaking through Indo-Trinidadian Rituals and Festivals: 1990-2009*, Ph.D. Dissertation. University of Trinidad and Tobago, 2010.
3. The Treta yuga has been calculated to be 1,296,000 earthly years. See Rajendra Pratap Singh's Rāmayāna Quiz Book, (Delhi: Ocean Books Pvt. Ltd., 2003)
4. Govind Vidyarthi, *Ramleela of Ramnagar, (Unpublished Manuscript, 1975*) 3.Also see *Sakshi Vol.5,* Ed. K.G. Srivastava et al (Ayodhya: Ayodhya Shodh Sansthan, 2012)
5. Govind Vidyarthi was a Senior Research Scholar of the Sangeet Natak Akademi, a constituent body of the Ministry of Culture of the Government of India during the period 1960-1980s. Many of my quotations have been taken from his original research (unpublished) manuscript of 1975.
6. Vidyarthi 3.
7. (https://en.wikipedia.org/wiki/Performance art).
8. Rajendra Jain, *Ramleela in Ballet* (New Delhi: B.R. Publishing Corporation, 1994) ix.
9. Vidyarthi 2.
10. Vidyarthi.
11. Vidyarthi 3.
12. Vidyarthi 4.
13. Anuradha Kapur, *Actors, Pilgrims, Kings and Gods: The Ramlila at Ramnagar* (Calcutta: Seagull, 1990), 5 The drawings are those of Benares as it appeared to Prinsep in 1825. So the Ramnagar Ramleela based on the Rāmcharitmānas was already, logically well established by the 1820s.Moreover, the Ramleela established by Megha Bhagat - a contemporary of Tulsidas - in Kamacha of Kashi Khand sector of Varanasi and performed simultaneously with the Tulsidas

version, annually in the Kedar Khand sector of Varanasi was also in existence. See Vidyarthi, (1975) 4.

14. K.S. Lal. *The Legacy of Muslim Rule in India* (New Delhi: Aditya Prakashan, 1992).
15. Maruti Nandan Pd Tewari, "Living Traditions of Ramleela in Varanasi with Reference to Nakkataiya". Paper presented at an International Conference on Ramleela, 'Epic Processes: Mobility, Patronage and Aesthetics'. IGNCA, New Delhi, India, 2015.
16. Vidyarthi 3.
17. Molly Kaushal, "Concept paper for the Second *International Conference on Ramleela. Epic Processes: Mobility, Patronage and Aesthetics.*" (Unpublished).The Conference was held at the Indira Gandhi National Centre for the Arts, New Delhi, November 22-27, 2015. Dr Kaushal was then Professor, Performance Studies, IGNCA, New Delhi, India.

Chapter Two

THE RĀM STORY ENACTED AS RAMLEELA IN ASIA AND THE INDIAN DIASPORA

The Rām Story in Asia and the Indian Diaspora

Ramleela in Asia

Commencing from antiquity, Indian merchants, settlers and migrant workers have established a rich legacy of commercial, economic and cultural ties with various parts of the world, near and far. The earliest recorded history of oceanic migrations from India took place long before the birth of Jesus Christ. By the 3rd century BC, Emperor Ashoka, the third ruler of the Mauryan dynasty then ruled most of India from his kingdom of Magadha. Magadha is a constituent part of today's Indian State of Bihar. Bordering Magadha there was the large and powerful maritime kingdom of Kalinga. Kalinga comprised today's States of Orissa/Odisha, parts of the Deccan, East Bengal (now Bangladesh), and some surrounding areas. Its army then comprised 60,000 foot soldiers, a cavalry of 1,000 horsemen and a regiment of 700 elephants. With an expansive coastal boundary on India's eastern frontier the Kalinga kingdom had already established significant maritime trade with neighbouring colonies, including 'Burma and South East Asia'. The Kalingas were also known to be 'Nagas (pirates) of the sea, robbing jewels and making (Emperor) Ashoka angry'.[1]

Ashoka continued his Mauryan predecessors' expansionist policy to achieve a complete political integration of the country. In the eight years of his reign (256 BC) - and with his capital city of Pataliputra in Magadha so close to the Kalingas - he invaded and conquered this mighty, independent kingdom. It is contended in the ancient text, *Dīpa Vamśa,* that 'the war was waged for economic and commercial reasons'.[2] That was however a defining period in the history of India. The war created major changes in the geo-political and

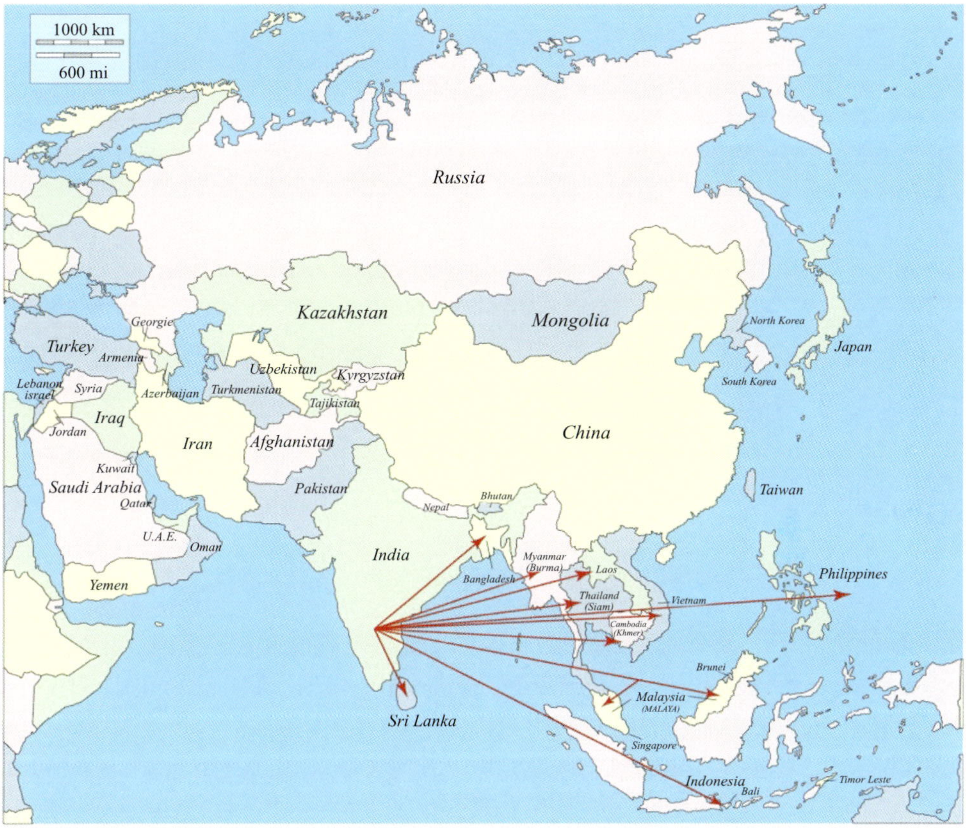

Map 1: The movement of the Rām tradition from India to the Far East, circa 300 BC – 300 AD

cultural landscape of the Indian subcontinent. The Mauryan Empire had expanded to include parts of Afghanistan, the Himalayan regions (including Kashmir) up to the borders of Nepal, Tibet, China, the Arabian Sea in the west of India, and the Bay of Bengal,down to Southern India. Only Assam, Madras, Kerala and Ceylon were outside Asoka's empire. [3]

The war also created significant repercussions. The carrying away and slaughter of over 300,000 people and the sight of the 'rivers of blood' which flowed on the battlefield caused Asoka such revulsion to war that he terminated his expansionist policy, consolidated his gains and accepted the religion of Buddhism. Shortly thereafter he propagated the Buddha's philosophy of Ahimsa or nonviolence and engaged in the humane governance of his vast empire, propagating a national policy of *Dhamma* -

peaceful co-existence with other nations, economic gains, and provision for the overall welfare of his subjects, 'using minimum force and no vindictiveness in governance.'

This war also resulted in large migrations from the Kalinga and others neighbouring territories, through already established sea routes into the foreign ports of the Indian and Pacific oceans, to Africa and the Far East. These migrants, who were living and practicing an already advanced form of philosophy, religion, artistic expressions and culture, went east. Over a period of time they had settled in Siam (Thailand), Champa (a portion of today's southern coastal region of Vietnam of which Indrapura was its capital city from 875 to1000 C.E.)[4], Khmer (Cambodia), Vietnam, Malaya (Malaysia), Sumatra, Borneo, Java and Bali. As part of that migration the Rām story and other aspects of India's rich artistic expressions, including its architecture (e.g. *Angkor Wat* temple in Cambodia, the largest temple complex in the world) were introduced and integrated into the new landscape.The presentations of the Rām story were not only narrated in various languages of that region but dramatized in various forms and formats. In some instances it was even reinterpreted to accommodate local customs.

Today, India's neighbours of South–East Asia record no less than eleven versions of the Rāmayāna Tradition.These include Cambodia - the *Reamker;*Thailand - the *Ramakien;* Laos - the *Phra Lak Phra Lam*[5];Burma (Myanmar) - the*Yama Zatdaw;* Malaysia - the*Hikayat Seri Rama*; Java/Indonesia - the *Kakawin Rāmayāna* or *Rāmayāna Kakawin* and Philippines - the *Maharadia Lawana.*

In the Sinhalese language of Srī Lanka it is called '*Jaanakeeharana*'. In Japan, it is referred to as the *Hobutsushu.* The story is popular in Singapore, Bāli, Mauritius and Fiji.The Ramakien (Sanskrit *Ramakeerti*) of Thailand is said to be derived from the Sanskrit version from Bengal, the VishnuPurāna and Hanumannataka and some indigenous sources in India. It is said to differ from the Valmiki Rāmayāna in many episodes. King Rāma I, the first king of the present dynasty (AD 1782-1809) of Thailand, compiled the first poetic form of the Rām Story. King Rāma II (1809-1824) gave a much smaller version suitable for theatre performance. The story is narrated entirely through shadow theatre (play) and masked, folk dances which are still performed to popular local acclaim.

In Malaysia, the *Malay Hikayat Seri Rāma* does not consider Rām as an incarnation of Lord Vishnu who is one of the three aspects of the Hindu Trinity. However, the principles of truth, dharma, dedication to family and the interests of the kingdom are retained within the story. In many western Malaysian towns the shadow puppet shows depicting the stories from the Rāmayāna are common forms of entertainment.[6]

In Singapore, Rām is treated as synonymous with Dharma (Dhamma of Buddhism); Sita is synonymous with Truth and Hanuman with dedication. Rāwana's ten heads are symbols of ten vices, with Shurpanakha symbolising desire.

The Indonesian islands of Java, Bāli and others have the rivers Sarāyu and Praaga (derived from Prayāg). Puppeteers still narrate the stories of the Rāmayāna in these islands. There is even a temple for Valmiki in Indochina, constructed more than 700 years ago.

The Nepal Bhasa version called the *Siddhi Ramayan*[7] was written by Mahakavi Siddhidas Mahaju Amatya during the Nepal Bhasa renaissance era. The Khas language (later called "Nepali") version of 'Bhanubhaktako Ramayan' marked the first epic written in the language. In Tibet, it is found in several manuscripts from Dunhuang.[8]

The overland 'silk road' routes which included Asia and Europe also facilitated trade, commerce and the transfer of labour from India.Through these routes, many versions of the Rām story were further scattered on foreign soil and blossomed in their new environments. The Rāmayāna has been translated into the Persian language by several scholars, including Abdul Khader Badouni (a scholar in the court of Mughal Emperor Akbar), by Mullah Saadulla, and by Giridhardas, a Hindu scholar in the court of the Mughal emperor Jahangir.

There are Rāmayānas where Rāwan has also been glorified. The works in the Jain tradition do not mention that Rāwan was killed by Rām. It is Lakshman who performs the act. Here, Hanuman is married and Rām has several wives. The Bengali work by Madhusoodana Dutta rejects the Hindu principles and portrays Rām in a derogatory manner while he glorifies Rāwan.

The Rām Tradition in the West: South America and the Caribbean

The countries of the South American continent and the Caribbean, prior to the 15th century, were virgin territory for European and Asian cultural traditions.

Over the last 500 years they have been populated by migrants from ancient and medieval cultures. East Indians have ventured into the new world,travelling into Europe and across the Atlantic. Commencing the nineteenth century, crossing the *Kala Pani* (black waters) and the *pagal samundar* (crazy seas) around the Cape of Good Hope, they went to South America and the Caribbean territories.

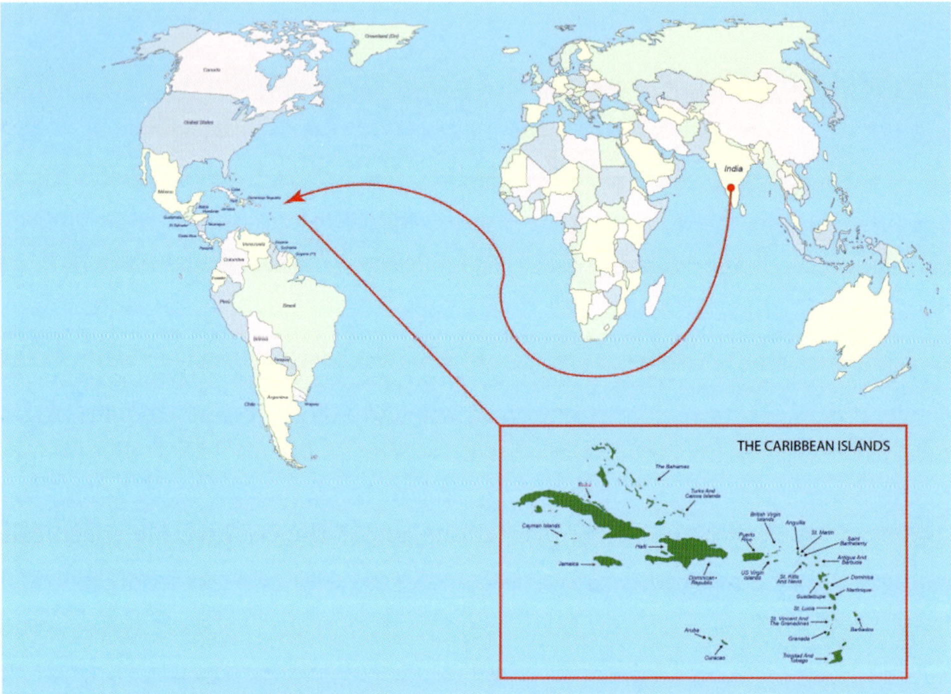

Map 2: The Rām story travels from India to the Caribbean

Today these societies reflect aspects of the rituals, festivals, artistic pursuits and traditions from those old societies. The structure of the Caribbean society, and more so the southern Caribbean with its unique population dynamics, thus reflects a composite culture; the influence of the Amerindian, African, Middle Eastern, European and Asian heritage and tradition of the Indian subcontinent and China. The East Indian population in the southern Caribbean comprises a sizeable and inextricable part of this milieu.

The Rām Story, in the form of Ramleela, arrived in the 'jahaji bandals' of the East Indian contract immigrants. The story arrived at various times, through several texts and was read and chanted as Holy Scripture. Its theme was also manifested through the folkloric medium. The two most important texts on the story to arrive in these parts were the ancient Valmiki Rāmayāna and the sixteenth century version of this original story, written by the saint-poet Tulsidas. This latter text, referred to as the Rāmcharitmānas, was read, recited, chanted and rendered in songs on this theme.

Guyana

The Rāmayāna tradition arrived in British Guiana (Guyana) with the indentured workers from India, commencing 1838. This was followed by similar arrivals to Trinidad and Jamaica in 1845, and to Suriname in 1873. Indian indentured immigrants landed in several other islands of the Caribbean during this period. By the end of East Indian indentureship in 1920, the Caribbean islands and the lands around the Caribbean basin had been populated by approximately half a million East Indians, the vast majority of whom were familiar with the Rāmayāna tradition.

The Rām story enacted as Leela or 'the Play of Shri Rām' was part of the Indo-Guyanese folk tradition in the early days of East Indians arrival to that country. The Anglo-Indian Christian missionary H.V.P. Bronkhurst in *The Colony of British Guiana and its Laboring population(1883)* indicated that Ramleela was performed in the plantations across the country. He specifically identified the plantations of "Enmore, Great Diamond, Farm, Cane Grove and in Georgetown, Essequibo and Berbice." Rampersaud Tewarie indicated that: "The Gossai minstrels in Guyana continued the tradition of singing verses of the Rāmayāna in the country.[9] From Tewarie's personal observations, Ramleela was performed in: "Paradise, the second and third were staged in the mandirs at Non Pareil and Annandale... Ramleela performances seemed to have declined in importance after 1966."[10] Prior to 1966 both Indian and African performers took part in the Ramleela in Guyana, as they did in other Indian dramatic productions.[11]

Ramleela in Guyana was resuscitated at the beginning of the 21st century. Shri Ravindra Nath Maharaj (Ravi-ji) of the Hindu Prachar Kendra of Trinidad assisted Pundit Hardish Tewarie in the training of Guyanese students for the staging of maidān Ramleela in 2006 in the Lusignan area in Guyana. Then in 2009 a Manch Ramleela was staged by The Guyana Hindu Dharmic Sabha with choreography by Dr. Vindhya Persaud.[12] It was performed on the proscenium stage at the National Cultural Centre in Georgetown where

President Bharat Jagdeo of the Co-operative Republic of Guyana delivered the keynote address.[13] It was also performed in 2015 by the students of the Guyana's National School of Theatre Arts and Drama.[14]

Suriname

The Ramleela festival was introduced in the Suriname landscape around the year 1905, approximately 32 years after the first arrival of Indian immigrants to those shores, according to researcher and Ramleela activist, Dr Gangaram Pandey. Speaking at the First International Conference on Ramleela in 2013 at the University of the West Indies, St Augustine campus, Dr Pandey indicated that the festival was introduced by Indian immigrants to those shores to meet a shortage of agriculture labour which had developed in that colony after the abolition of slavery in Suriname by the Dutch colonialists in July 1863. In order to fill that void, a total of 34,304 British Indian immigrants landed there between 1873 and 1916. Approximately one third of the'coolies' who went to Suriname, through indentureship, returned to India. The rest were assigned to various estates throughout Suriname, only to introduce their age-old tradition of reciting Rāmayāna and performing Ramleela.

Pandey (2013) indicated that the first grand Ramleela performance in Suriname was held around1905 in Janboiti (Half Flora) in Paramaribo. This area 'later became known as the Ramleela centre' of Suriname. By the year 1915, the Ramleela celebrations had spread to other localities in Suriname, wherever the Indians had been domiciled.These areas included Kronenburg and Meerzorg in the district of Commewijne, in Welgedacht B in the district of Wanica, and in Heritage and Pontbuiten in the district of Paramaribo. Much later, with growing interest and audiences, this folk theatre spread too many outlying districts, such as Saramacca and Nickerie. It was staged in'5 of the 10 districts' that comprise the Republic of Suriname.

With its strong folkloric character, the Leela attracted whole neighbourhoods, especially the youths. People of all ethnicities and social standing attended the folk festival. During the 20th century the selection of the performers in Surinamese Ramleela was both caste and gender bias, in conformity with the immigrants' north Indian, patriarchal, village Indian tradition. It was an all-male cast with Brahmins performing the main roles of Rām, Sita, Lakshman, Bharat and Shatrughan. Males also performed all of the female roles. Currently, however, the festival is dwindling in popular appeal and participation. Pandey indicated that: 'Only in few places the tradition of an annual performance has been continued.'[15]

An interesting feature of the current celebrations is that its annual period of performance continues with the established local tradition of being staged during the holiday period of August, instead of the period of September-October that was traditional in the grandmother country of India. The daily episodes run from 5.00 pm. to 8.00 pm.

A flying Hanuman in Ramleela, Suriname. Photo: Pundita Indrani Rampersad, 2009

Tradition has also changed with respect to cast selection, both in terms of caste and gender. Currently the cast of the production comprises mainly young people, males and females, with no caste bias and with the dialogues spoken in 'Hindustani', one of the four spoken languages of Suriname.[16]

Europe & USA

There are many countries in both North and South America and in Europe where members of the Indian diaspora observe the Rām tradition. Moreover, significant numbers of the 2nd and 3rd generations of Indo-Caribbean peoples have also migrated to North America, UK and Holland and are carrying on the tradition.

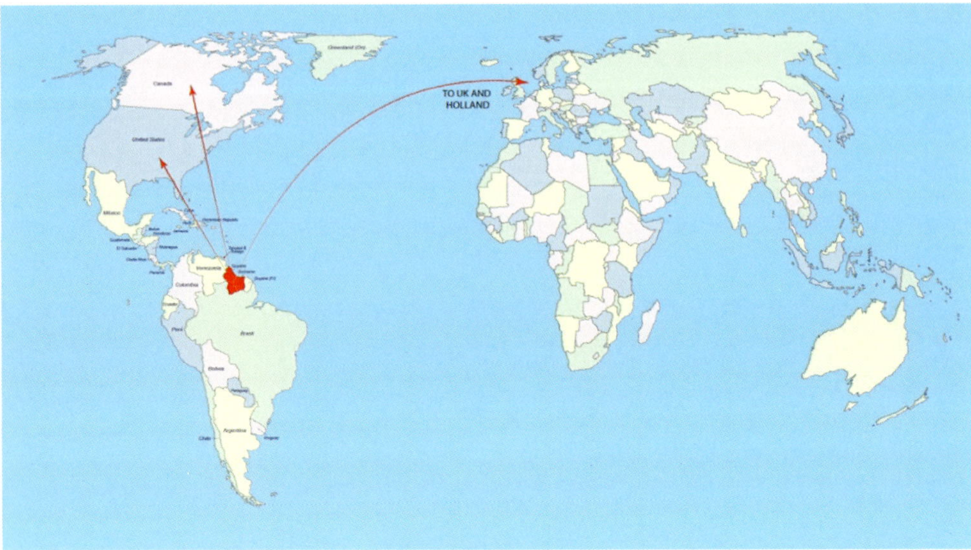

Map 3: The movement of Indo-Caribbean peoples to Europe and the America

ENDNOTES

1. *A Comprehensive History of Bihar. Vol 1.Part 1*. Ed. Bindeshwari Prasad Sinha (Patna; Kashi Prasad Jayaswal Research Institute, 1974) P 439-440.
2. Dīpa Vamśa, VI. 24-27 quoted in *A Comprehensive History of Bihar. Vol 1.Part 1*. Ed.Bindeshwari Prasad Sinha (Patna: Kashi Prasad Jayaswal Research Institute, 1974) 421-500.Also refer to *Raghuveera; A Global Journey of Rāmayāna* (Ayodhya: A Research Presentation of Ayodhya Research Institute, India. N.A) 5-7.
3. Sinha (ed.*) (1974) 441.*
4. Coedès, George (1968). Walter F. Vella, ed. *The Indianized States of south-east Asia.* trans. Susan Brown Cowing. (Hawaii: University of Hawaii Press.).*ISBN 978-0-8248-0368-1.*The site is close to the modern city of Da Nang, Vietnam. See Https://en.wikipedia.org/wiki/Indrapura (Champa).
5. The word is also spelt, 'Pha lak pha' Lam in Laos. See Gisa Jähnichen's, *The Phalak Phalam Dance Drama in Laos.*Manuscript for the 2nd World conference on Ramleela, Nov 2015, IGNCA, New Delhi, India.
6. Also see C.M. Bandhu's, "Ram Katha in Nepali with special reference to Balun Performances."Paper presented at the 2nd World Conference on Rāmlīla, Delhi India. Nov 2015.
7. The Siddhi Ramayan was written by Mahakavi Siddhidas Mahaju Amatya during Nepal Bhasa renaissance era, and the Khas language (later called "Nepali") version of Bhanubhaktako Ramayan by Bhanubhakta Acharya marked the first

epic written in the language. Refer to Vidyarthi. There is also a version called 'Raamaaswamedha' in Nepali ; https://en.wikipedia.org/wiki/Versions_of_Rāmayana Wikipedia Dt: 2013812

8. Rampersaud Tewari, *Ramleela in Guyana, 1838-1966.* Paper presented at First World Conference on Ramleela at The University of the West Indies, St. Augustine, Trinidad and Tobago, July 12 – 14, 2013. P6-9

9. Rampersaud Tewari, *Ramleela in Guyana, 1838-1966.* Paper presented at First World Conference on Ramleela at The University of the West Indies, St. Augustine, Trinidad and Tobago, July 12 – 14, 2013. P6-9

10. Tewarie 7&9.Nalini Mohabir however feels that Ramleela in Guyana died after 1966. See Nalini Mohabir, "Colonial and Post-Colonial Ramleelas in Guyana: Implications for the Diasporic Archive." Unpublished. Paper, presented at 2nd International Conference on Ramleela in India entitled, *Epic Processes: Mobility, Patronage and Aesthetics,* November 22-27, 2015.P1-19

11. Tewarie 7-8.

12. Mohabir 10.

13. Mohabir 10-13.

14. Mohabir 12.

15. Gangaram Panday. Extracts of a Paper delivered at the First World Conference on Ramleela in Trinidad, June 2013. Performances of the Ramleela in Suriname are continuing. The last recorded one being in October 2015.

16. The other 3 languages are Papiamento (taki taki), Dutch, and English to a lesser extent.

Chapter Three

THE RÃM STORY AND RAMLEELA IN TRINIDAD

The Rām story in Trinidad

The story arrived in Trinidad through several texts and in the folkloric medium. The Rāmayāna as text and oral tradition began arriving on these shores from 1845 - Tobago was not yet part of the twin island union - and continued to do so right up to 1917. The waves of migration to Trinidad resulted in a total of 147,592 East Indians landing on these shores, of which approx. 80% chose to make this country their home.[1] Of that number who chose to stay, approx. 80% were Hindus, approx. 11% Muslims and the rest belonged to several other denominations, including tribals from the jungle regions (*janglis*) of India who were outside of the religious stream. After over 172 years the Indo-Trinbagonian community has carved out its own presence in the local landscape, contributing in a significant way to the creation of a unique society with a rich cultural mosaic of traditions. An integral part of this culture is its dynamic folk forms.

One of the traditions introduced was the reading, chanting and performing of religious cum literary texts of the Indian epics of the Mahabharata and the Rāmayāna. The influence of the Rāmayāna was, however, more potent in the forging of a new society on these shores since three known texts on the story had arrived in Trinidad. They were the Valmiki Rāmayāna, the ancient story of a mortal hero Rām. The second text was the *Sukh Sagar*, said to be written by Ved Vyas; and a third text, Tulsidas's Rāmcharitmānas. There were two other supporting texts written by Sant Tulsidas which also arrived in the 'Jahaji bandals'. They were the *Hanuman Chālisa* and the *Sankat Mochan Ashtak*.[2]

From these texts, the Rām story has been told and retold through various mediums - as story, sung, chanted as poetry, narrated as the word of God, presented in literary discussions, danced as devotion to God and enacted as Leela or 'the play of God'. It helped to centre and 'brand' successive generations of Indo-Trinidadians. The main stories and their various sub-stories contained within these texts, which were introduced here over a period of time, in turn stamped their imprint on our cultural landscape.

Today, one does not read the Rām story in Trinidad for the first time: people are already familiar with it or know of it, especially those of Indian origin. The Rām theme is a part of everyday life, pervading almost all aspects of community and especially Hindu life. It is manifested in paintings, sculpture, and the performance of vocal and instrumental music, dance and drama, literary discourse, religious and spiritual development. It is reflected in name places, performative traditions and relationships. It has influenced people's names, using unique Trinidadian dialect spellings viz Ramkissoon, Rambissoon, Parasram, Lutchman (m), Lutchmin (f), Barat, Chattergoon, Hanoomansingh, Sitaram and Sirju (the River Sarāyu in Ayodhya). It has influenced street names such as Ramnath Terrace, and even pervaded our local politics.[3]

There are birth, marriage and festive songs ('chautāl' songs in Phagwa include some of the lyrics of the local 'Chutney music'). Some Hindu funerary rituals are accompanied by the chants: "Jai Ram, Jai Jai Ram" and "Ram naam sat hai" (Rām's name is eternal). It has influenced temple names. The tellings of the Rām story are enacted annually across the country. Moreover, given the close proximity of the races and religions, the Rām legends have become part of Trinbago's socio-cultural landscape so much so that in 1995 Trinidad was referred to as 'Rāmayāna Country'[4]

Even the standardised greeting for callers to one of the local 'Indian' radio and television stations in the country, 'Jagriti', is 'Sita Rām'. This greeting is said, regardless of the caller's race, religion or social status. In this socio-cultural milieu, there is no clearly demarcated boundary between fiction, legend, myth and reality. Men have made the myths and these myths now determine the reality of our daily lives.

The Ramleela, the 'play' of Shri Rām falls under the definition of being both a performance tradition and a performative, faith-based tradition. It is highly likely that many of the indentured immigrants prior to their arrival in Trinidad would have either seen or been part of this annual, village, folk theatrical performance of the Ramleela. However, the exact date of this first staging of a village Ramleela, or a Ramleela on one of the plantations on which the immigrants lived, is a matter of conjecture.

The first documented dramatized Ramleela was in 1880 at Dow Village in California, approx. 35 years after the first arrivals of Indian immigrants to Trinidad. This Ramleela folk theatre performance was staged as a 'maidān' Ramleela (an open-air, savannah Ramleela), and was performed in the central, sugar-cane growing plains, in a clearing in the cane fields, at Dow village in California. This Ramleela continues annually at the same venue.

Dow Village Ramleela in 2012 with its male and female participants doing ārti before the daily performance

The Ramleela was an ideal tool which the immigrants used for keeping the memory of the legacy and traditions of their homeland alive. It provided education and training for imparting moral and ethical values, for theatre and for entertainment. It represented India's literary tradition, possibly at its highest level. It was more so a source of religious sustenance to India's far flung children. The Rāmayāna and the Rāmcharitmānas provided that religious and psychological prop to these simple village folk (peasantry) - India's children who had been weathering, in their homeland, the constant onslaught of foreign dominance on many fronts; socio-economic, political, artistic, military, religious, cultural and psychological. The East Indian immigrants in the Trinidad environment - so named as to differentiate them from the indigenous, Amerindian (American-Indian) peoples - found themselves in similar circumstances as their homeland counterparts. They looked for religious succour and spiritual survival.

The majority of these immigrants originated mostly from Northern India and the vast physical expanse of land mass that comprised the Indo-Gangetic plains. This included the Brij, Awadhi, Bhojpuri, Bundeli and Maithili regions, with others coming from the southern region of the then Madras Presidency, now renamed Tamil Nadu. These regions were centreed within the Indian States of Uttar Pradesh, Bihar, Rajasthan, Madhya Pradesh, Punjab and Tamil Nadu. This northern region had just a few centuries earlier spawned a new wave of religious and spiritual awakening, the Vaishnavite form of worship, or service to a personal God through Bhakti or devotion. Bhakti was practiced by worshipping God through the creative, performing and literary arts viz. sculpting, architecture, vocal and instrumental music, dance, literary and dramatic works.

The moral, ethical, religious and spiritual teaching of the Rāmcharitmānas as exemplified by its heroes (Shri Rām, Lakshman, Bharat, Sita and Hanuman) again came to the assistance of the East Indian immigrants, fueling the Bhakti form of worship. It provided moral and ethical support, religious faith and their spiritual sustenance. The Rāmcharitmānas embodied in its pages the visions and hopes of the East Indians struggling for justice, righteous leadership, self-identity and self-determination in these far-flung lands away from home, beyond the 'Kala Pani' and the 'pagal samundar'. Having been part of this surging wave of the Bhakti tradition for around six centuries, it was naive to think that the indentured immigrants and their offspring would have cast out its spell within the short span of a few decades. They clung to the Rāmayāna, studying its contents, recognising its intent, purpose and value to community building and God realisation.

There was another aspect of the story that resonated with the early Indian immigrants to Trinidad. They equated themselves with the hero Rām, the heir apparent of the kingdom of Ayodhya, who willingly accepted the instructions for his banishment from the kingdom for 14 years. He underwent significant trials and tribulations, pain and sorrow and finally returned triumphantly to claim his kingdom.The Indentured Indians, living in meagre circumstances on the sugar and other agricultural, cocoa and coffee plantations, and later on other menial tasks in Trinidad, equated their current socio-economic situation to those circumstances. They considered their life as similar to that of a form of banishment. They lived in anticipation that someday they would return to India in more favourable circumstances.

There were also the parallel circumstances experienced much later and in different, though somewhat similar circumstances; i.e. the trials of Imams Hassan and Hussein, grandsons of the Prophet Muhammad (P.b.u.h.) during the embryonic stages of Islam which were no less different. They experienced pain and suffering within the Islamic fold, experiencing even martyrdom, fighting to uphold righteousness within the early stages of the religion. These similarities of circumstances welded the Indian Muslims and Hindus in this new environment and gave them common platforms from which they continued to mold their relationships of *jahaji bhais* and *bahins* and celebrate their village Ramleela festival while jointly commemorating their Muharram or Hosay rituals annually.

In this common environment, the text of the Rāmcharitmānas was read, debated, sung, chanted, and enacted. Its dramatic presentations with their music and accoutrement further enhanced the appeal of the story and breathed life into the characters that were contained within its pages. It became the Leela, or 'play' of God, the Bible of the common village folk, presented in a living and tangible form. It became pain, collectively experienced, faith personified and worship dramatised.

Historical trends and features of the Trinidad Ramleela

The Ramleela tradition in Trinidad did not develop as a common and unified festival. Each community or group within the village approached the story and its actual presentation from its own perspective. While the story, adopted from the text (basically the Rāmcharitmānas), remained the same, the selection of the portions within the main story, the length of the full production (3-11 days), its daily episodes and its aesthetic presentation varied. The success of the production also depended on a number of inter-related factors. These were based on the availability of the proposed cast of performers, the availability of a pundit or translator cum narrator who had the time, the capability and willingness to undertake the project, and access to the financial resources to stage the production. The Pundit invariably assumed the role of *de facto* guru and artistic director.

Given the circumstances of the Indian immigrant to Trinidad, living in unhealthy conditions in the plantation barracks, overworked, underfed, malnourished and ill-treated, it was an audacious attempt and a significant achievement to have commenced the staging of this epic of over 24,000 verses over a 10- day period. Still much of this initial staging has either changed or is changing. For instance, the form and format of the actual physical presentation have changed. So, too, have the physical stage and its features. The initial village, open-air maidān Ramleela has now incorporated combinations of several types of stages but remain within the village setting. The text of the story of the Ramleela remains more or less intact while the presentation of the folk drama has evolved. The open-air or maidān drama, which was initially performed by amateurs and villagers, has evolved to include several aspects of theatrical presentations. Each village presents its version of the story using different casts, design concepts and different stages, props and décor. The intent and purpose of the Leela continues to be in keeping with its original aim, telling a story with spiritual, religious, moral and ethical values, and presenting a theme for all to follow and emulate.

Prior to the 1960s, some texts in the Ramleelas were chanted directly in the Awadhi language (the language in which the Rāmcharitmānas was written) without any translation in English. The older generations were still *au courant* with the languages brought from India, the main ones being Bhojpuri and Hindi. However, as the young Indo-Trinidadians started to lose knowledge of the Indian languages, translations in English became necessary. The actual presentation then began to take on a different format: The relevant portions of the texts selected were chanted in the Hindi script and then translated by the narrator into English. This allowed the performers to mime the actions of the story while the audiences simultaneously listened to the chanting, to the narrative of the story telling, and viewed the actions on the ground.

Socially, there have also been changes in almost all aspects of the production. Initially cast selection was dependent on social 'caste' consideration. Today there is no exclusion of people from the actual performance whether on grounds of gender, race, language or socio-economic considerations. This is particularly so for the selection of the main characters of the Leela; Rām, Sita, Lakshman, Bharat and Shatrughan. Formally, females performing female roles were taboo. Women are now included among the players. Children play several roles. There is now an equal number of youths as there are of mature persons.

They participate in the drama as part of the process of both individual and community development. Their involvement is an actual rite-of-passage in their transition from youth to maturity. They learn through or under the direction of seniors. As such, they invariably inculcate subconsciously, the traditions and values of their positive cultural traits. The Ramdilla ground remains, more or less, the central focus of village life for that period. It has become an excellent training ground for character development, identity formation, religious and cultural development.

While the story line remains basically the same, there has been much innovation within the production i.e. in the costumes, props, sets and performances in the Ramleela season during the month of Ashwin (September

Map 4: Map of T&T showing geographic locations of Ramleela performances

- October). Many of them culminate at the period of Vijay Dashmi -victory on the tenth day - of that month. Each of the groups operating in Trinidad presents its own unique production; this includes the form, format, time of performance and length of performance.

Types of Stage Designs and Presentational formats

Indian theatre, like its civilisation, has its history in antiquity. Stage designs in Indian theatre evolved over time from tribal and folk presentations, flat on the ground, to variations of sizes, heights and shapes. The *Natya Shastr*a or treatise on dramaturgy (compiled by Bharata muni between the 2nd century BC and the 5th century AD) speaks of the evolution of stage designs. Initially the performance was undertaken on a stage with the audiences sitting or standing in the open air. The stage area was a raised platform of approximately 4'-4½' high. Then as the performance shifted to the temples' grounds and then to the royal courts, the entire stage and audience area was covered. There were basically three types of stage designs. One was the triangular stage (*Tryasra*). 'If it was a square in the centre of the (identified performing) space the stage was *Caturasra*; if the space was a rectangle, with the length greater than the width, the stage could be at one end of the rectangle - the *Vikrsta*'.[5]

The evolution of the stage design continues. The physical stage designs for the performance of the Leela in Trinidad include combinations of open-air, ground-level, savannah stage or *maidān,* to open-air raised stages or *manch* and open-air. The manch stage comprises combinations of theatre–in-the round, where audience and performers are at ground level; arena stages, plus apron stages, thrust stages, and full indoor, proscenium stages.[6] Currently there are over 37 Ramleela groups performing annually using variations of these stage designs.

ENDNOTES

1. Shamshu Deen, *Solving East Indian Roots in Trinidad (*Trinidad: H.E.M. Enterprises Ltd., 1994) 281.Other historians quoting statistics from various sources have put the number at 143,939. These include Bridget Brereton in *Calcutta to Caroni.* Ed. John La Guerre, (Trinidad: St Augustine, UWI, 1985 [1974]) and Walton Look Lai, *Indentured Labour, Caribbean Sugar* (Baltimore: John Hopkins Univ Press, 1993) 276.

2. This information was confirmed by Pt. Dr. Rampersad Parasram in a tel. interview with author on 23, September 2016.
3. A former leader of the Opposition party in Trinidad and Tobago in 1995 (Mr Basdeo Panday of the UNC) publicly referred to the leader of the ruling party and the then Prime Minister, of African descent (Mr Patrick Manning) as a 'Rāwan'. The subscript here was that the Prime Minister's behaviour was equated with that of Rāwan's.
4. This description was attributed to Rabindranath Maharaj (Raviji) of the Hindu Prachar Kendra, Chaguanas, Trinidad.
5. Adya Rangacharya, *The Nāṭyaśāstra*. Trans. in English (Bangalore: IBH Prakashana, 1986) 230-231.
6. In the 1990s and again in 2001, performances were done on the Rām Katha in balletic form on the proscenium stage, at Queens Hall, Central Bank Auditorium and in several other parts of Trinidad. The first local production was choreographed by Kathak guru, Pradeep Shankar based on the choreography of Pundit Birju Maharaj, while the second set of stage performances were choreographed by Ashok Chakravarty and Mondira Balkaransingh for the Nrityanjali Theatre and directed by the author.

PART : II

FELICITY AND ITS RAMLEELA

Chapter Four

FELICITY AND ITS RAMLEELA

Felicity

Felicity is a village situated approximately three kilometres or two miles, west of the town centre of the Borough of Chaguanas in central Trinidad. It is sandwiched between the Chaguanas main road to its south, Charlieville in the north and north east, and the mangrove swamp leading to the sea coast in the west. Felicity has been a major target area for anthropological research and analysis of the changing dimensions of the Indo-Trinidadians' society and its cultural life styles.

History of Felicity

The village of Felicity got its name from one of the many estates which were amalgamated into the present township. The estate was named Felicité, a French word meaning 'Happiness'. Former school principal and researcher Hardeo Ramsingh, in his informative book, *The History of Felicity Village (1838-1996)* 1996, conjectures that the estate might have been owned by a French Planter who received it as a Crown Grant under the Spanish *Cedula de Poblacion of 1783*. This Spanish law provided handsome grants of virgin land to people who were willing to settle in Trinidad, provided that they were of the Roman Catholic faith and were prepared to swear allegiance to the Spanish Crown. Many French planters in the Caribbean, facing uncertain futures in their respective islands, took up the offer and resettled in Trinidad, establishing new estates, including Felicité. Ramsingh (1996) notes that:

> *Though the French version of the name Felicité was used throughout the 19th and early part of the 20th century, the English version (Felicity) has now replaced it in all legal documents.*[1]

Legal documents on the land ownership are dated up to 1848, so the history of Felicity can be traced back to this date. Over the years, many smaller adjacent estates, with their own names and identities were purchased and amalgamated into this larger estate.[2] From 1907 to 1914 this larger estate changed hands no less than 7 times. In 1937 it was sold to the British sugar magnate, Tate and Lyle. The Tate and Lyle estate was finally acquired in 1975 by the government of Trinidad and Tobago as a State Enterprise and renamed Caroni (1975) Ltd.

The village has been historically and intricately tied up with the sugar industry and those who played a major role in its growth and survival. East Indian migrant workers, under a contract system of indentured labour - and subsequently their descendants - played crucial roles in this aspect of the country's socio-economic development. Following the emancipation of slavery in 1838, the majority of the freed slaves departed the estates. Many efforts were made to recruit suitable labour for the sugar industry, the mainstay of the then plantation economy of Trinidad. Tobago, at that time being a separate entity, became a Ward of Trinidad in 1898.

Indentured workers were brought from Europe, Madeira and China to work the plantations but with limited success. The planters turned to India whose workers were found more suitable for this type of labour, and so the bulk of indentured workers were recruited from that country. Workers were recruited for five year periods with fixed contractual obligations, one of which included a promise of a return passage at the end of the contract. During the period of indentureship, each worker performed not less that '280 nine-hour days or tasks per annum (task work was not measured in hours but by the quantity of work allotted)' to fulfill the contractual obligations.[3]

From 1869, British Governor Gordon varied the contract stipulations and sanctioned instead, the granting of parcels of lands to male immigrants who wished to remain in Trinidad at the end of their indentureship period. This was in lieu of the return passage to India. Land was sold at £1 per acre. This 'commutation' grant varied as the years progressed until lands were no longer provided in lieu of the return sea passage, only money. The same treatment could not be said of women.They suffered significantly during the entire 'bond' period. They received a mere £5 sterling at the end of their indentureship period.

By 1878, East Indian indentured immigrants were already living in

Felicity. The Registrar-General's office records the birth of the first offspring of an indentured immigrant on the estate as Gunness, born on the 2, April 1878, the son of Gildhary (father) and Pajroo (mother). The first registered marriage in Felicity by East Indians was that of Rassa (the groom) and Kinderia (the bride) in 1882. This marriage carried the registration number: 159 of 1882.[4]

Felicity really began developing into an Indian immigrant village when a former indentured worker named Cacandee received the first Crown Grant in this area in 1886. He brought his pioneering entrepreneurial skills into effect. He subdivided the land into housing plots and sold them, then purchased other lands, further subdivided them into building plots and provided these to interested settlers.[5] Other plots were similarly either sold or leased in this area to immigrants through 'commutation'. As the demand for housing plots increased and available lands became scarce, the estate made additional plots available along a thoroughfare that ran north to south through Felicity. These plots were either leased or sold. A ribbon-like settlement of adobe houses developed on both sides of this thoroughfare which was later named Cacandee Road.

These adobe houses or ajoupas were built either flat on the ground or on stilts with wattled walls, plastered over with a mixture of mud and grass (tapia) and covered either by the leaves of the carat or the timite palm tree or by 'needle grass'. The floors were slightly upraised with compacted dirt and plastered over with *gobar*, a liquid mixture of cow dung and dirt. Ventilation windows and doors were wooden. Lighting was provided by open flames of a kerosene lamp or flambeaux - a wick inserted into a bottle filled with kerosene and lit. Cooking was done on *chulha*s – earthen fireplaces fueled by dry wood, Roseau twigs from the swamp, coconut husks or dry cow dung. Cris-crossing, dirt traces connected the village. There were mosquito and other insect infested, open drains. It was spartan living. This village cluster would have undoubtedly resembled the adobe houses of rural India.

In addition to working on the sugar estate, the villagers supplemented their incomes and supported their families by performing a number of allied agricultural tasks such as rice cultivation and vegetable farming. Some were involved in sea fishing, oyster and crab harvesting from the adjoining swamp. Former tradesmen gradually returned to their previous, pre- indentureship professions. Micro entrepreneurs diversified into retail dry goods. The village gradually developed. The first mandir, a *jhopry,* referred to alternately as *kutiyah*, and '*sewalla*' (Shivala or Shivalaya) was built along the Cacandee Road in 1911 to cater to the needs of the predominantly Hindu village. It was constructed on lands donated by the Capildeo family. Its first pujari was Pundit Kalloo Maharaj. The *sewalla* later became the Shiv Shankar mandir. The first primary school, the Felicity Canadian Mission Indian (CMI) on Cacandee Road, opened its doors in 1921 and was formally opened on 16, January 1922.[6] During this period the Hon. Lionel Ramsarran ('Sarran') Teelucksingh, the first elected Member of the then Legislative Council (which became today's Parliament)[7] for Caroni, and the Chaguanas Local Road Authority paved the Cacandee Road with asphalt.

The materials used in house construction in Felicity began improving gradually from the 1920s, but accelerated from the late 1940s. In 1948, the Soulbury Commission Report on the state of housing for sugar workers prompted positive effort by the Colonial Government of Trinidad and Tobago to provide adequate housing and, where necessary, financial assistance through soft loans for home construction for its sugar workers. Consequently the Sugar Industry Special Funds Ordinance No. 12 of 1948 - now referred to as the Sugar Industry Special Funds Act Chap. 64:04 of the Laws of Trinidad and Tobago - mandated the then Comptroller of Accounts to establish three funds, one of which was The Sugar Industry Labour Welfare Fund. The Sugar Industry Labour Welfare Committee (SILWC) was subsequently established in 1951 by an Act of Parliament (Sugar Industry Special Funds Act Chap. 64:04) to give loans from the 'Fund' to sugar workers for housing development. This Sugar Industry Labour Welfare Fund was funded by a levy of $2.40 placed on every ton of sugar exported from Trinidad and Tobago. Felicity's sugar workers benefitted.

The physical image of the village and its housing infrastructure changed significantly. Simultaneously, the transport and public utilities infrastructure improved. From the 1950s, the mud traces connecting the village and other works and transport infrastructure began to be upgraded. Some minor and connector roads which were still mud traces were paved, thanks to the commitment and indefatigable spirit of the local government representative, Chunilal Saith. The development expanded on all sides.

The free East Indians and their immediate off-springs invested their time, labour and finances in their properties and in the education of their children. Simultaneously, they commenced the building of strong spiritual and religious bonds within the community. They developed and consolidated community spirit, perpetuated their rituals, festivals and other performative traditions and integrated and managed their communities, based on a mixture of traditional values of their village India and the circumstances presented in this new landscape. The development of Felicity, as a village within the evolving milieu of Trinidad and Tobago's society, continued. From 2010, Felicity received another major facelift under the Peoples Partnership political administration and its Parliamentary representative Mr. Jack Warner. Its road network and other physical infrastructure were significantly enhanced.

Geography

Physically the village of Felicity is divided into four blocks; the union block to the north, a central block, the third or Casecu block and the fourth block that includes the settlement, south of Boundary Road, including the Cacandee settlement. The settlement incorporates the Green Park Recreation Ground where the First Felicity Ramleela is staged annually. Felicity is approximately two miles in length from north to south along the Cacandee road and approx. one mile from east to west at its widest part i.e. from the Tahadille Road/ Pierre Road junction on the East to the now abandoned sugar cane fields on the Western periphery of the village. The village is approx. two square miles in area[8]. See Map 5.

Cunupia River at Northern boundary of Felicity. Photo: S. Balkaransingh, 2011

This expanded village lies parallel to the Solomon Hochoy Highway; an arterial road which links the industrial South of Trinidad to the financial centre and Capital city in the North. The village is bounded on the east by rice and now abandoned sugar cane fields; on the west and north-west by the same abandoned fields, merging directly into the mangrove forest of the central part of the Caroni swamp with its evergreen arbours, brackish waters and teeming swamp flora and fauna.Its northern boundary is the Cunupia River which runs through thick marshy reeds of the Caroni swamp. The southern extremity of the village is bounded by the Chaguanas Main Road which initially connected Chaguanas to a pier, three kilometres away, on the Perseverance Bay on the coastal Gulf of Paria.

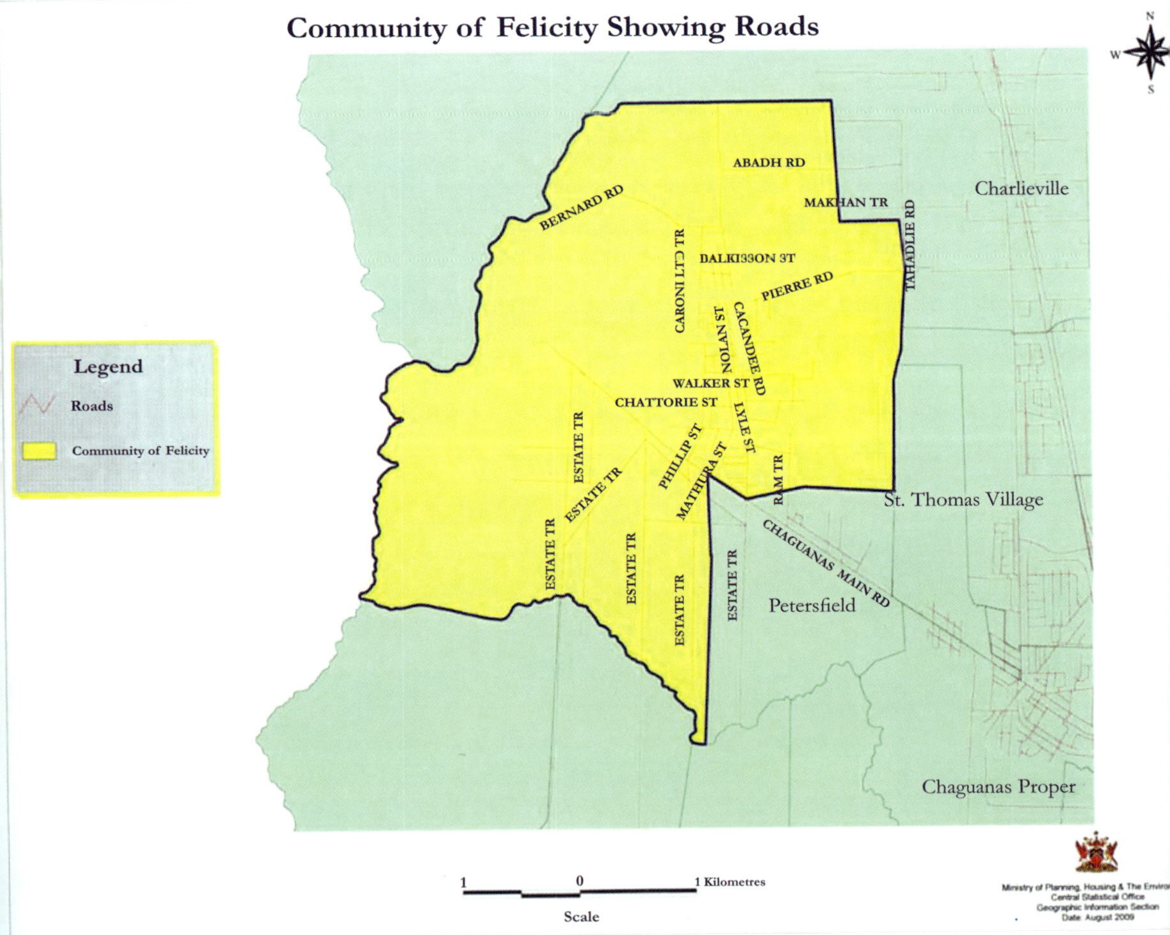

Map 5: Geography of Felicity

An "old tramway began from this pier and near which 'the Madame Espagnole River, skirting the Caroni swamp on the south, enters the sea'."[9] In the 1870s the British travel writer, Charles Kingsley, in the company of the British Governor to Trinidad, Gordon, alighted from this pier to visit Chaguanas and Longdenville.[10]As one drives east along this Southern main road one notices the abandoned sugar cane fields to its south being converted to new housing developments. Houses are being planted on fertile soil where sugar cane was once cultivated.

Demography

In 1946 the population of Felicity was 2,943. In the 1990 census of population, Felicity reflected a population of 6,191. The disaggregation of this 1990 census of population, according to ethnic distribution, showed that the Indo-Trinidadians accounted for 97.11%, and Afro-Trinidadians were 1.32%. The mixed race distribution in Felicity was just 1.08%; and the rest (Whites/ Caucasians and Chinese, including 'not stated') were less than 1 %. In 2000 with the population of the Borough of Chaguanas increasing dramatically to 67,433, Felicity, being a part of Chaguanas, its population increased marginally to 6,625. In 2011, Chaguanas continued to grow. Its population was 83,516[11] but Felicity's population grew marginally. The racial composition of Felicity, reflecting the historical development of the village, remained basically the same, with Indo-Trinidadians still being in the majority, followed by Afro-Trinidadians and other mixed races.

In all of these changing demographics, one thing has remained steady. The village was still a predominantly and uniquely Indo-Trinidadian village when compared to the rest of the country which reflected population statistics (in 2011) of 34.22% Afro-Trinidadian; 35.43%, Indo-Trinidadians; 7.66% Mixed-African and East Indian; with 22.69% being a mixture of Caucasian, Chinese, Indigenous, and Mixed-Others (Portuguese, Syrian/ Lebanese and others).

Socio-religious setting

Felicity today is emerging from a basically agrarian background of peasant farmers into a business and professional class in the manufacturing, industrial and service sectors of the country. Notwithstanding the demographics of its population, the village has a demonstrated history of socio-religious understanding and tolerance. This is possibly because of the cultural background, the closely-knit village life and overall education. There are three preschools and two primary schools: The Felicity Presbyterian, formerly named the Felicity Canadian Mission Indian (CMI) primary school established in 1922, and the Felicity Hindu School, established in January 1953. These schools are managed by Boards of Directors of the respective religious bodies. Students access secondary education just a few kilometres away in Chaguanas and tertiary education from two universities, The University of the West Indies, a few km away in St Augustine and several campuses of the University of Trinidad and Tobago (UTT) and other foreign franchise universities, located within close proximity.

The villagers belong to several faiths. These are mainly Hindu, Muslim and Christian. The Hindu sects are Sanatanist, Arya Samajist, Aghore Pant, Bharath Sevashram Sangha (started in 1950)[12] and devotees of Shri Satya Sai Baba. The Muslims belong to the Anjuman Sunat-Ul-Jamaat Association (ASJA), Trinidad Muslim League (TML), the Tackveeyatul Islamic Association (TIA) and the Ahmadiya Association. The Christians are Presbyterians, Roman Catholics, Seventh day Adventists, Baptists, Methodists, Pentecostals and Jehovah Witnesses.

The religious and cultural needs of the village are intricately interwoven into the fabric of this community. The Hindu segment is supplied by seven community mandirs. There is one masjid, five Christian churches, one cemetery and one cremation ground or burning *ghat*. Yet within this plethora of religious persuasion there is no evidence of religious intolerance. In terms of performative traditions, Felicity has a long history of celebrating Ramleela, Divali, and Phagwa, Eid- Ul- Fitr, Eid- Ul- Adha or Bakra Eid and, until the late 1950s, the Indian folk dramas of Indra Sabha, Harichand (Hariścandra), and the commemoration of the ritual of Hosay or Muharram. It also celebrates Christmas and other Christian holy days.

Despite the many mandirs, masjids and Christian churches, over 80% of the people are influenced by the Indo-Trinidadian thought, values and practices or Indian culture. There is a saying in Felicity that even though those who have moved away from the ritualistic practice of mainstream religious belief, Hinduism, into the evangelical, 'smaller' Churches and other persuasions - leaving Indian (read Hindu) cultural practices behind- when they are faced with domestic crisis, they return to the fold. They visit the Indian chiropractors, seeking refuge in the ancient Ayurvedic medicinal practices and other natural healing remedies; using neem, ginger, turmeric or haldi accompanied by the incantation of mantras, invoking the gods as these home-made ointments are applied for various ailments. Indianness then returns.

ENDNOTES

1. Hardeo Ramsingh, *The History of Felicity Village -1838-1996.* (Trinidad: Self-Published, 1996) 1-2.
2. Ramsingh 2. Some of these estates were *L'Amitie* and *L'Amatie Barrancou,* all French appellations, suggesting that they were land grants to planters under the 'Cedula of population'.
3. Ramsingh 11.
4. Ramsingh 14.
5. Ramsingh14-15.
6. Hardeo Ramsingh, The History of Felicity Village (1838-2008).Rev Ed. (Trinidad: Self-Published, 2008)26.
7. Hon. Sarran Teelucksingh was elected as the representative of Caroni district/ constituency to the Legislative Council of Trinidad and Tobago in 1924. Ramsingh 25.
8. Satnarine Balkaransingh, *Trinidad Space Speaking Through Indo-Trinidadian Rituals and Festivals: 1990-2009* (Ph.D. Dissertation, Arima, University of Trinidad and Tobago: 2010) 60-61.
9. Anthony deVerteuil, *Eight East Indian Immigrants* (Trinidad: Paria Publishing Co. Ltd, 1989)132.
10. Hardeo Ramsingh.
11. Central Statistical Office, Government of the Republic of Trinidad and Tobago (web).
12. Krishen Singh. P.I. August 14th, 2012.

Chapter Five

HISTORY OF THE FIRST FELICITY RAMLEELA

The staging of the Ramleela: Calendric period, venue and time

The majority of the Indian immigrants who arrived in Trinidad were from northern India; the bulk of these originating from the Indian states of Uttar Pradesh and Bihar. The Ramleela in India was traditionally held during the month of *Ashwin* of the Hindu calendar which equates with September-October of the Gregorian calendar. The enactment in Felicity and in other venues in Trinidad therefore conformed more or less to this same period of Ashwin, just after the observance of *Pitra Paksh* which is the period that is dedicated to the memory of the ancestors. The drama begins in the bright half of the moon, or *Shukla Paksh,* of *Ashwin.*

The Felicity Ramleela has traditionally been an 11- day folk pageant or village drama enacting the epic story of Rām. It captures the various episodes of his eventful life and those associated with him during this period. Traditionally, the 11 consecutive days of performance are so chosen that the day of *Vijay Dashami,* or the victory of Rām over Rāwan (on the 10th day), and the final immolation of Rāwan is scheduled for a Sunday so that audiences can view this annual spectacle in all of its splendor and excitement. On the 11th day, Rām and his victorious army return from Lanka and he is installed on the throne of Ayodhya as its King. The destruction of Rāwan always ends before the annual Divali celebrations which are held in the succeeding, auspicious month of *Kartik* (October-November).

From an employment point of view, the Ramleela celebrations were originally, and coincidentally so, scheduled to coincide with the lean period of work on the sugar plantations in and around the Chaguanas area, particularly the nearby Woodford Lodge estate. Those who had already left the plantations worked in close proximity to, or within the commercial area of the agricultural township of Chaguanas. This town and its environs were then part of the catchment area for both the performers and the audiences.

The History of the First Felicity Ramleela

Just when did the First Felicity Ramleela begin and when did it acquire its present name? While there seems to be no formal existing documented evidence of the actual date of the first performance of the First Felicity Ramleela, some oral folk historians date it to around the year 1915.Others date it between 1915-1917, more towards 1917 but before 1922.[1] Formal history, however, establishes the Felicity Ramleela as being first performed on the Green Park recreation ground around 1921-1922. Ramleelas were being performed in Chaguanas. Later on, another one was established in Felicity, carrying the same name, 'Felicity Ramleela'. In order to differentiate this one from other Ramleelas in the area, the administrators of this Ramleela organisation named it the 'First Felicity Ramleela and Cultural Organization'.

Durgan Balgobin, a former President of the organisation indicated that: "Based on oral history, the Leela was first performed outside of Felicity, in present-day Chaguanas East, on a piece of empty land at the point where Chaguanas main road merges with the Montrose/Longdenville road in the vicinity of what is today the Chaguanas overpass."[2] The area between the Chaguanas/ Montrose link and the Caroni Savannah Road was then the Endeavour Estate owned by DeVerteuil. This estate comprising cocoa, citrus, toncabean and coconut was later surveyed, subdivided and sold in parcels.[3] One parcel was cleared and the Chaguanas market was constructed. Other buildings were constructed in the vicinity of the market. Another parcel was donated to the Roman Catholic Church on which was established the Pamphilian College, later renamed the College of St Phillips and St James and eventually renamed the Presentation College.[4] The town gradually moved westwards. West of the Caroni Savannah Road was the Woodford Lodge Estates Ltd., then owned by Sir Harold Robinson. It stretched westwards towards Felicity.

The important roads into Chaguanas were the Caroni Savannah Road, connecting Charlieville with Chaguanas and the Eastern Main Road leading east from Felicity into Montrose, just before it merged into the Longdenville road, where the petrol station stands today. The Solomon Hochoy Highway, formerly the Princess Margaret Highway, was constructed later. It bisected Chaguanas from Montrose. Then a flyover was constructed on the Solomon Hochoy Highway, bypassing Chaguanas. This highway connects the southern, industrial, port city of San Fernando to the bustling, commercial, capital city of Port of Spain which nestles between a scenic hillside to the north and north-east and the waterfront with a deep - water harbour to its south.

The first staging of a Ramleela in Chaguanas east lends much credibility to this oral history since the families who were associated with and who played Ramleela then were the Mathuras who lived in Montrose, the Seereerams who lived on the border of Chaguanas and Montrose, and the Naipauls of Montrose.[5] The Chaguanas Ramleela later moved from this area to Perseverance Village which was then the western periphery of Chaguanas. The Leela was enacted on an empty parcel of land of the Woodford Lodge sugar estate, along Cumberbatch Street, bordering the village *Sewalla* - a tiny hut with mud walls and a thatched (leaf-covered) roof, north of the Chaguanas Main Road in the Perseverance Village.[6]

Somewhere in the early 1920s the organisers of that Chaguanas Ramleela were unable to secure the venue (the sewalla ground) from the estate management for the performance. The villagers who worked on the Felicity estate had recently received a cleared space from the sugar estate for village recreational activities. This venue was initially covered with coconut trees and termed 'the coconut'. Some of the coconut trees had been felled and the 'savannah' was created for village festivities and sports. It was named the Felicity Recreation ground and was being used as a venue for cricket by the 'East Indian cricket team'.[7]

Mr. Chatoorie, an influential member of the then growing Felicity community, was approached by the Chaguanas Ramleela organisers, among who were Baboo and Pundit Hargobin, to secure the use of the Felicity Recreation Ground and to help stage the Chaguanas Ramleela there. Mr. Chatoorie who lived in close proximity to this recreation ground obliged and the Chaguanas Ramleela performance was shifted temporarily to this open space so as to maintain continuity.

When the Chaguanas Ramleela organisers returned to their Perseverance village venue the following year, the Felicity Ramleela continued on this ground. The Perseverance village 'ground' was a stone's throw, approximately 300 yards, from the iconic Lion House, the ancestral birth place of Nobel Laureate, Sir Vidya S. Naipaul. With Chaguanas then being a hub of Indo-Trinidadian residential and commercial activities, many within the extended Naipaul clan, the Sitahal clan and other influential people who resided in that area were part of the organisation and the running of the Ramleela.[8] Ramesh Naipaul recalls that he, "played earlier in the grounds of present-day Chaguanas Borough Corporation. That Ramleela was later run by a committee which included Mr. Ramcharitar Rikhi," (teacher Lally) a former Headmaster, School Supervisor and later a manager of the West Indies Cricket team. Mr. Rikhi left the administration of the Ramleela in 1950s when he took up residence in Tacarigua. The Ramleela moved to other locations, depending on the availability of space; to the 'Invincible' Recreation Ground, off Taitt street and then to Saith Park, Chaguanas. This former Sewalla Ramleela ground is now a part of the south-eastern section of the compound of the present-day Chaguanas Regional Corporation's administrative headquarters.

Much later the Chaguanas County Council took charge of the Felicity 'Coconut' ground, providing the general maintenance while the annual Felicity Ramleela festival continued there. The ground was eventually surveyed and renamed the Green Park Recreation Ground of Felicity. By the 1950s this recreation ground was recognised as the Felicity Ramleela ground.[9] It is rumored that the appendage 'Green' was the name of a senior manager of the estate, which had changed ownership to Tate and Lyle Company of UK, and later acquired by Caroni (1975) Ltd. Notwithstanding its current official name, the Green Park Recreation ground still remains an open savannah, a *maidān*, instead of a developed park.

The Evolution of the Performance and its Management Committee

In the early days of its operations, the Felicity Ramleela production was organised and managed by a 'Committee' comprising villagers such as Sookdeo Bandhoo, Harry Persad, Phagoo, Tahalsingh, Baboolal, Paran Narine, Gobin and Mahelal Singh. The Organising Committee also arranged for the performers to be recruited and housed in one venue so that they could be collectively taught and instructed spiritually, intellectually and materially during the period of the extended production. In other words their life styles were guided and supervised during the entire period of the Leela. The Vyas-jis or officiating pundits during the production runs were Hargobin (Hargovind), Deo, Samlal

Mathura and Sonny Jangali. Pundits Hargobin Maharaj and Baboo Maharaj chanted the verses, explained the literal and spiritual significance, instructed the performers and generally directed the evening's episodes.

The annual performance ended with the 'Bharat Milap' on the 11th day. In this episode Bharat, the brother of Rām, welcomes Rām and his entourage back to Ayodhya and installs him on the throne. When this scene ended, a *Bidai* or farewell ceremony was usually performed in which the performers each received a small token of appreciation for their involvement in the Leela, which traditionally included clothes, money and some food item.[10] The Pundit also received his *cēdhā,* or gift, which also comprised clothes, money and some uncooked food items. From the 1930s to the 1960s the Ramleela performers lived temporarily, for the entire period of the performance, within the confines of the Shiv Shankar Ashram and Mandir situated on Cacandee Road. This ashram and mandir, the "first Hindu place of worship in the area" grew out of a tiny "*Kutiah* built somewhere around 1910-11, on lands donated by the Capildeo family."[11]

While living in the Ashram, the performers were not permitted to visit their families. As *bramacharis* or students, they lived a spartan, ashram life of purity; no meat, alcohol, tobacco or sex. Pundit Kalloo Maharaj functioned as the guru or spiritual guide and tutor of the performers. He was succeeded by Pundit Hargobin Maharaj and thereafter by Pundit Baboo Maharaj. The wives of these two pundits (the daughters of the Patriarch, Pundit Capildeo),[12] prepared all the meals, washed the clothes and had the costumes of the main characters, the swarūps, prepared at the ashram for the daily performances. Pratap Sahabir, a former performer with the Ramleela, vividly recalls that the Swarūps and the major Pātras took up communal residence at the Shiva Mandir on Cacandee Road, Felicity. Each afternoon of the Leela, they did the appropriate pre-performance rituals in the mandir, dressed in the costumes of the respective characters and went from the mandir directly to the performance venue, returning to the mandir after the evening's episode, for prayers, dinner, further guidance on the day's performance and then to sleep. Sahabir concurred:

> *Right from the 1950's, up to the 1960's, the performers used to live in the Shiv Shankar Mandir, on Cacandee Rd., next to the Devi Mandir. They took up residence for the entire period of the production, in the ashram of the mandir .... Living*

together as a unified, consolidated group allowed the players to bond, learn from their elders and contemporaries, plus practise their simple folk steps so characteristic of the folk theatre. It also kept them in check to maintain the strict rules of celibacy for the designated period of the play, viz no alcohol, meat eating or sexual relations with spouses.

During this period, fabric was bought in bulk for costumes for the entire cast of players. All costumes were stitched by the village tailors, Hiraman and Deo who doubled up as costume jewelry fabricators. Mr. Deo then lived on Chatoorie Street, adjacent to the maidān. Other village seamstresses were co-opted to assist in making costume jewelry and other décor so as to meet the deadline for the opening night's performance.[13] The two ashram ladies also helped to apply the makeup to the faces of the Ramleela performers. The mandir and ashram functioned as a temporary hermitage, an ashram, for lodging, boarding and training of the cast and crew for the period of the Ramleela, plus a mini production site for props and costume decorations and finishings.

The performers - these included Lutchman Maharaj, Baboo Maharaj, Bale Maharaj, Kayakoo, Jadoonanan Bhagwandeen, Ramsahai, Ramjass Maharaj, Ramsubhag Maharaj, Bhola Persad, Dass Bhagwandeen, Kanoon Ramkhelawan, Kumar Dasrath, Sankar Bharose, Khedar Maharaj, Dhanraj Rampersad and Atmaram Maharaj[14] - also assisted in making some of their own costume jewelry. No doubt some of the designs of the jewelry and even the costumes, their colours and fabric selection would have been influenced by the new wave of religious movies that were coming out of the Indian film Industry. With the introduction of the first Hindi film Bala Joban, in 1935, followed by a rush of Indian films in other genres, a young consumer industry of Indian films had become a great source of attraction for Trinidad audiences, but more so Indo-Trinbagonians and their first and second generation's off-springs whose umbilical cords were still metaphorically attached to India. The religious films, some of which were screened at the Jubilee cinema in nearby Chaguanas would have certainly influenced changes in the evolving 'look' of the Felicity Ramleela production.

The ashram was converted in 1953 to the Cacandee Road Hindu School, following the period of Hindu primary school expansion throughout the country under Bhadase Sagan Maharaj, the visionary leader of the newly established Sanatan Dharma Maha Sabha. Bhadase Maharaj had consolidated several small and sometimes combative Hindu organizations into one unified body which was incorporated by Act (No 41) of Parliament in 1952. Like many temple compounds, some being only sheds; the Shiv Shankar Ashram and Mandir became the location for a primary school cum village mandir. The Ramleela performers were gradually eased out of the ashram and Mandir through attrition. Today, the mandir serves the dual function of being both mandir and the Felicity Hindu School.

Shiv Shankar Mandir, Felicity

In the decade of the 1960s-1970s there was a new group of players who joined the First Felicity Ramleela. Pratap Sahabir continued to be a member of that cast. During that period, he remembers that "Dhanwant Lutchman performed as Rāwan. His elder son Khedar Lutchman played the role of Rām and Harry Lutchman played Rām's brother, Lakshman. Roy Santoo played Bharat. Latchman's younger son, Kesho (Krishendath) played the role of Sita." Other performers included Roopdial Ramnarine, Shanie Balgobin, Mulchan Paltoo, Omaram Ramkissoon, Richard Agard, Wayne Reds, Roland Lochan, Dinesh Bachew and young Sirju Ramoutar[15] (who in 2016 was still performing as Rāwan). The drama then was an all-male affair. The lead 'players', the 'swarūps' Rām, Lakshman, Bharat, Satrughan and Sita were all played by young

Brahmin boys. This selection of the main character roles in the production was undertaken on the basis of caste. This was ironical, especially at the dramatic level, for unlike what was being done, Rām and his brothers - according to the original text - belonged to the Kshatriya caste. From a socio-economic standpoint, the Kshatriyas were classified into the category of fighters or protectors, the rulers of the kingdom or Maharajas (Great Kings). This is the caste of Rām's lineage. The Brahmins traditionally performed the societal roles and functions as advisors, ministers of the King, religious persons, the performers of rites and rituals, gurus or mentors and guides of music and dance.

While everything appeared to be good superficially, there were also other existing problems under the surface of the production. For instance, in terms of casting of the players, men were cast and played the same roles for years, without changes. These roles included that of Rām, Janak, Rāwan and Hanuman. There was little room for upward mobility of new performers and many potentially very good performers became disillusioned and disgruntled.

Female performers were also not included as part of the production cast. The obvious elimination was justified on the grounds that their inclusion in the ashram life would have created many problems for separation of the sexes. Moreover, during their menstrual cycles they were considered unclean and unfit to perform the roles within the sanctity and 'purity' as required of the production period. Moreover it was taboo to have females doing female roles since they were excluded from doing public performances for male audiences. This selection of persons to perform specific roles in the Ramleela applied, across the board, to all Village Ramleelas, including Felicity Ramleela, possibly up to a far as the 1970s. Female participation in this village theatrical was later included due to relatively recent changing societal developments, possibly from the 1980s.

From the 1960s the Organising Committee was expanded and reinforced. Messers Mathura and Jangali were joined by Lochan and Dolly Heeraman, Sonny Mykoo, Dindee Tirbanie, Boney Ram, Laloo Bissoon, Rampersad, Goolcharan Dass, Lal Bahadoor, Ramnarine Manik, Harrynanan Jogie, Goomansingh, Vas Seenath and many others. They assumed the mantle of leadership and took up the task of continuing the planning, implementation and management of the Leela. "From the late 1970s, celebrations temporarily ceased, until 1982." In 1984 Mr. Lalchan Balroop assumed chairmanship with Mr. Sumair Sookdeo joining the Organising committee.

No one, however, could change the march of time and the changes taking place in the society. By the 1990s, the national economy had undergone radical changes. There was increased socio-economic activity. Many of the audiences and performers had moved out of the agricultural sector and taken up employment in the manufacturing, industrial and service sectors outside of the Chaguanas area. Per capita income when adjusted by Purchasing Power Parity had improved significantly from 1990, averaging 21,140.42 USD from 1990 with a dip in 1993 to 13,158.01 USD and then a steady rise up to 2013, reaching an all-time high of 30,874.91 USD in 2008.[16] The country reflected the characteristics of a society of conspicuous consumption. There was rural to urban migration. Vehicular traffic had increased significantly, resulting in major traffic management problems. Community and household lifestyles changed. So, too, did value systems.

It became difficult for the players and the technical crew to conform to initial performance timings. More performers, assistants and technical crew working with the production had full-time jobs. They worked outside of the Chaguanas area and its environs. Performers could neither get time- off from work during the Ramleela days nor reach the performance venue and be fully costumed for the initial 3.00 pm. commencement time. Even the audiences whose presence and patronage are so important to the success of the play could not arrive in time for the start of each afternoon's performance. A solution had to be found to accommodate this changing scenario and the requirements of the performers, administrators and audiences. The daily starting time of the performance was shifted to a more realistic time to cater to all those involved. It moved from the original 3.00 pm. to 6.00 pm. to a 6.00 pm. to 9.00 pm., the current performance schedule.

This single change in performance timings rippled throughout the production, resulting in a series of changes. There was need to illuminate the maidān for the performers and audience, so a limited lighting system was rigged up; bare white lights. This resulted in innovative changes to the props, weapons and sets: Reflective materials were attached to head pieces, battle weapons and other appropriate sets. Even the costume designs experienced changes. Imam Ali, a costume designer for carnival band leader Peter Minshall assisted in designing and fabricating some of the costumes and props. These included the full-bodied costumes of the birds (Jatayu, Sampati and Garud) the golden deer and the horse (Burroquite) to be used for the Panchavati scene where Rawan kidnaps Sita. A new sound system was also introduced. The original old P.A system was replaced by a 'surround sound' which significantly enhanced the performance.[17]

Oral history informs us that since its inception in Green Park Recreation Ground, the First Felicity Ramleela has maintained a continuous annual run, save for two interruptions; the first in 1956-58 and the second between 1971-72. These were due in the first instance to internal conflict caused as a result of the direction that the organisation should pursue. It also had to do in part by a fight for control of the organisation. The second interruption was due to internal administrative problems. In the post 2000 period the Organising Committee was reconstituted. It comprised Mr. Durgan Balgobin (President), Jivan Kissoon (V.P), Kelvin Saith (Treasurer), Ms. Stephanie Pysadee (Sec.) and Omkar Balgobin (PRO), with Suraj Mathai and Sitaram Balroop as trustees. The membership of the current organising committee is at Appendix 1.

Funding of the production in the early days

Prior to the achievement of Independence of Trinidad and Tobago in 1962, the organisers used to be responsible for the sourcing of funds for the annual production. They undertook this through a series of activities. These initially involved house-to-house visits, requesting donations for the event. Then, as the period of the Ramleela approached, members of the Committee would go directly to the paymaster's office of the Felicité estate on the 'pay-days' and solicit donations directly from the sugar workers of the village. This was done with the support and approval of the paymaster. In this way the sugar workers helped to fund their Ramleela. Actual and anticipated short falls in expenditure were solicited directly from small business houses in the area.[18] Other charitable donations were also received, both in cash and kind. These varied from food stuffs - uncooked vegetarian staples of rice, peas, fresh garden vegetables to be prepared for the artistes - and fruits during the actual days of production.

After 1962 another maidān Ramleela was established at the Invaders Recreation Ground, about a half mile away from the Green Park venue. Rance, the former president of the Ramleela recalls that: 'From this period the method of sourcing of funds for the annual event changed'.[19] The Committee of the First Felicity Ramleela organised fund raising events. The financial shortfall for the production was met by individuals and business sponsors in and around Felicity. Gradually funding for the Felicity Ramleela was expanded to include a number of sources viz. some fund raising projects, individual donations in cash and kind, donations from business establishments and rental of booths around the periphery of the performance space during days of play. Kelvin Saith recalls that in 1992 the administration of the Leela experienced a major setback. Three of the key members of the executive accidentally drowned. The community banded together to support the Leela with both their presence and their personal financial contributions, donating handsomely, according to their ability, when the arti was passed each evening of the performance. Literally, buckets of notes and coins were collected.[20] Later, government's annual grants were provided for the festival.

In an attempt to bring all Ramleela groups in the country under one umbrella, the National Ramleela Council was formed in 1989, with support from the Sanatan Dharma Maha Sabha of Trinidad and Tobago Incorporated (SDMS). The First Felicity Ramleela and Cultural Organisation was a founding member of this Council. While this Council achieved limited success in uniting all the existing Ramleela Organisations under a national umbrella in the country, it had made a breakthrough by bringing a few major Ramleelas under one umbrella.The SDMS National Ramleela Council sought and received government's financial assistance and distributed these funds to its members, including the First Felicity and other Ramleelas. This Council lasted until 1994.[21] The 'Grant' from the Government of Trinidad and Tobago was of varying sums annually. This 'Grant' invariably arrived after the event and satisfied only a small fraction of the funding requirements of the annual production.

In 2001, the First Felicity Ramleela and other similar groups applied to the then Ministry of Culture and Human Resource Development for financial assistance for undertaking their annual 10- day Leela. The Minister, the Hon. Ganga Singh advised them that their application would be considered if they came as an umbrella organisation. This resulted in the establishment of The National Ramleela Council of Trinidad and Tobago (NRCTT) in 2001, with a membership of seventeen groups. First Felicity Ramleela was a member which had benefitted from government's promise of financial assistance for its folk theatre. In 2003 following the ratification of the rules, regulations and Constitution, the NRCTT's first general election of officers of this umbrella Ramleela body was held. The NRCTT in collaboration with the Ministry of Culture and Tourism, under its new Minister the Hon. Penelope Beckles hosted a successful, historic 'Awards' function. Convened at the Rudranath Capildeo Learning Resource Centre, the function honoured pioneers of Ramleela in

Trinidad and Tobago since 1880. The First Felicity Ramleela was honoured in several pioneering fields.[22]

Hon. Minister of Culture and Tourism, Penelope Beckles, Presents award of 'Pioneers of Ramleela in T & T' to First Felicity Ramleela Committee member, 2003'

That year (2003) the Felicity Ramleela received possibly its largest grant from government, up to that time, the sum of TT $10,000.00. In total, the sum of $330,000.00 was distributed that year to the 33 functioning Ramleelas in the country, by the Hon. Penelope Beckles, Minister of Culture and Tourism.

ENDNOTES

1. Hardeo Ramsingh, P.I. 17th April 2015. While Ramsingh was born in Felicity on 12th September 1929,and later became the Principal of the Felicity Presbyterian School (formerly CMI - Canadian Mission, Indian - established in 1922) he learnt of the oral history of the area from his elders.
2. Durgan Balgobin, former President of the First Felicity Ramleela. P.I. 16 Jan 2015
3. Kenneth Subran, former employee of the Valuations Division, Ministry of Finance, Gov't of Trinidad and Tobago. Tel Interview 24th, August 2017.
4. Rampiarie Balkaransingh, neé Boodramsingh. Author's discussions with mother on their family history over the period 1960-1970.

5. Balgobin. P.I. 16 Jan 2015.
6. This *Kutiyah* of thatched roof and galvanized walls, housing a Shiva Lingam and other mūrtis was later converted to the present-day Sai Temple. The author's parents and siblings lived during that period on Greaves St, Perseverance Village. P.I. with septuagenarian Bhagan Singh on 20th November 2014.
7. Hardeo Ramsingh (2008)88-89. Also P.I with Ramsingh, 17th April 2015.
8. Ramesh Naipaul. P.I in October 2014, during the Ramleela celebrations at the Green Park Recreation Ground, Felicity.
9. Sundar Singh. Tel. Interview, 3rd April 2012.Sundar recollected that in 1950 he began living on Cacandee Road, Felicity and the Ramleela was already being performed on the 'cricket ground', referred to today as the Green Park Rec. Ground.
10. Ramsingh. P.I. 17th April 2015.
11. Ramsingh.P.I. 17th April 2015.
12. Pundit Capildeo, the grandfather (nana) of Nobel Laureate V.S Naipaul, arrived in Trinidad from Gorakhpur district, U.P. India in 1894 as an Indentured immigrant. He had his contract bought out, married in 1895 and had 14 children. Eleven of them survived (2 boys and 9 girls).The boys were Rudranath and Simbhoonath. He married his seven daughters to men 'of Brahmanical descent'. One was Hargovind Deepan from Carapichaima, (See De Verteuil [1989] 126-137). Ramsingh referred to 'Hargovind' as 'Hargobin Maharaj' (Ramsingh, 2008).
13. Ramsingh P.I. 17th April 2015 and Balgobin, P.I. October 2014.
14. Ramsingh 74-75, and verified with him in P.I. by author in April, 2015.
15. These names are verified by Ramsingh (2008)75 and Sirju Ramoutar.
16. The GDP per Capita, in Trinidad and Tobago, is equivalent to 166 per cent of the world's average. Source: http://www.tradingeconomics.com/trinidad-and-tobago/gdp-per-capita-ppp. 1990-2014 figures.
17. Kelvin Saith. P.I. with author on December 16 2017.
18. Ramsingh, P.I. 17th April 2015
19. Rance Kanhai. P.I. during Ramleela celebrations in October 2014. Kanhai was President of the Executive Committee of the First Felicity Ramleela and Cultural Organisation in 2014.
20. Rance Kanhai and Kelvin Saith in October 2015, and reconfirmed by Saith. P.I with Saith in Dec 2017.
21. K. Ramsubeik, "National Ramleela Council of Trinidad and Tobago", *National Ramleela Council of Trinidad and Tobago 2007: Commemorating 127 years of Ramleela in Trinidad and Tobago* (Trinidad: Self-Published, 2007)10-11.
22. *National Ramleela Council of Trinidad and Tobago 2007: Commemorating 127 years of Ramleela in Trinidad and Tobago (Trinidad, Self-Published:2007). Photos on pages 38-39.*

Chapter Six

ELEMENTS OF THE RAMLEELA PRODUCTION

Felicity Ramleela: Selection of text, script and language for delivery of the narrative

Given the region from where the majority of the early East Indians originated in India - Uttar Pradesh and Bihar provinces - it was natural that they would choose a north Indian version of the Rāmayāna, one that was easily readable and with which they were familiar. This was Tulsidas' version of the Rām story, the Rāmcharitmānas, written in Awadhi, the familiar language of the common north Indian man. Moreover, this text was already being used by Tulsidas himself when he staged his first Ramleela in Banaras during the seventeenth century.

Interpreting the Rāmayāna in Trinidad for Ramleela: The text

The familiar text in Trinidad, those that the immigrants brought with them, was the Rāmcharitmānas of the Gorakhpur Press. As a matter of fact, almost every group who performed Ramleela in Trinidad, their pundit or Vyas adhered to the north Indian tradition of the Bhakti movement and used the Gorakhpur Press version of the Rāmcharitmānas. Periodically, references were made to the Valmiki's original version of the Rāmayāna which also came as part of the Indians' 'jahaji bandal' of traditions and literary heritage.

The text of the Rāmcharitmānas has presented many possibilities for interpretation. There is the audience interpretation that arises from the very act of listening to or hearing the rhythmic and melodious chanting of the selected verses in current or contemporary time. These include recitation of the various types of verses - the *dohas, chaupais, sorthas* and *chands*. The very act of listening to the words of God constitutes worship or *shravan*, to those who are part of the bhakti movement or are devotees of Shri Rām. Bhakti is worship of the divine being through pure, selfless devotion (bhakti), usually through music and dance.

Then there is the act of looking or 'seeing'. From the physical, secular perspective the spectator looks or views the theatrical event, simply as a pageant, with all of its costuming, colours, hues, music and drama unfolding before the eyes. However, from the spiritual perspective, the devotee's act of 'seeing' the scene unfold before the eyes provides the concept of 'darshan', the perception or recognition of the inner meaning of the physical actions that are being enacted in the Leela. It involves a method of 'seeing' or perceiving the higher reality of life; of receiving the 'vision' of the thing, its inner meaning, the hidden meaning. It involves both the 'vision', the 'darshan', and the 'seer's' response to the 'vision', This response may take the form of being shocked, crying, or a total psychological transformation, of being 'cleansed' or 'washed', of experiencing *anand* or bliss. On the other hand, it may cause confusion in the mind, going mad or out of one's logical mind; going mad with bhakti or devotion, or becoming very peaceful and just waiting in anticipation for the next 'darshan'. In other words it deals with one's relationship with their ritualistic and religious inclination.

Another interpretation comes from the act of participation, of preparing the ground for consecration, the fabrication of the costumes, the application of the make-up to the faces of the ordinary village boys that transforms them into *swarūps* in this Leela or divine play. Then on each night of the Leela there is the act of performing ārti to these *swarūps*, Sri Rām and Sita, while bhajans and other sacred verses are chanted. The text also caters to the audience becoming pilgrims, following the entourage from Lanka to Ayodhya, through the streets of Felicity, or just being a devotee who bows to the earthly forms or *roop(rūp)* of Shri Rām and Sita as the entourage passes on the streets of Felicity, back to Ayodhya. These acts are really a number of phenomena that can only be witnessed. They cannot be dissected for clinical examination and interpretation. Ritual worship transcends the boundaries of physical interpretation.

Selection of script

The selection and physical presentation of the script for the Felicity Ramleela has been a very important factor in the success or failure of the annual event. This script has traditionally been the responsibility of the Pundit selected to function as the Vyas or narrator for that year's programme. The Vyas initially begins his detailed selection of the specific portions of the Rāmcharitmānas a few months before the commencement of the actual performance. Basically, he follows the main story format, selecting and linking abridged dramatic portions sequentially, from the various books or *Kandas* that comprise the full story, from Rām's birth to his return from exile and final coronation on the throne of Ayodhya. He would then select the most suitable episodes from each book or section in the life of Shri Rām - commencing with his childhood to his reign as King of Ayodhya. The story, an abridged version of these seven books or 24,000 verses, moves flawlessly from the period preceding the birth, into his return from the eventful years of his banishment.

From this perspective there was no clearly established or written script identifying which particular episode was going to be recited and dramatized for any particular day. The guiding principle was the maintenance of the flow of the story in a logical sequence as written in the Rāmcharitmānas. However, the pundits who chanted the verses were so familiar with the story and the dramatic aspects of the Leela that they would extract the most riveting and message-bearing parts of the Leela and deliver these to the audience in a seamless unfolding that usually kept the audience glued to the performance.

Over the years many pundits were engaged by the First Felicity Ramleela Group to be the *Vyas* or director of their annual 11-day Ramleela productions.[1] Traditionally, the production has always been performed annually during the month of *Ashwin* or September-October, ending during its auspicious period of *Vijay Dashami*, or the 'tenth day' (Dashami) signifying the victory (Vijay) of Rām. The occasion of *Vijay Dashami* is a long-established and recognised date on the Hindu calendar. Sometimes, the Ramleela began in *Ashwin*, and ended in *Kartik*, the succeeding month in which two major events occur - Divali the festival of lights and *Kartik Snaan* (Nahan), the ritual of having a sea bath during the month of Kartik.

Since after the 1950s there was no ashram life and hence no formal training or training period for the performers, the major roles were repeated annually and understudies for the main roles, if any, were similarly costumed as the identified character to be studied. The understudy entered the maidān, following and learning from the specific character by an imitative process, during actual performance. This performance format resulted in the script, more or less remaining the same annually. Being versed in Hindi at that time and in the chanting of the Rāmcharitmānas, the Pundit also prepared minimum 'script notes' references. The script comprised two purposes; the first being that which was sung, or rather chanted to explain aspects of the story, or the respective mood or emotion that was being highlighted. The other purpose was for the simultaneous dramatization or portrayal by the actors of that part of the text that was chanted.

By the 1950s there was a distinct evolution of an abridged version of the original story; a story within the major story, a script within the overall script that came to be adopted as the story to be narrated from year to year. But as the years rolled on, successive Pundits found it necessary to write brief scripts for their own guidance. These were more notes, rather than scripts. These scripts consisted of blocked or marked areas that were identified in the text of the Rāmcharitmānas as suitable for dramatization. The actual text and lyrics were delivered straight from the singhasana - the area where the pundit sat, chanted and generally directed the Leela. The delivery took the established form of chanting to the accompaniment of live music - harmonium, majeera, dhantaal and other supporting vocals. This chanted portion was then translated by the Vyas as the performers enacted the translated narrative through gestures of the body, limbs and props – *mukdar* (*Gadda)* or mace, *talwar* or sword and *Dhanush* or bow. These gesticulations were supported by appropriate *rasa* or emotions such as love, hate, valour, anger or forgiveness. The performers never delivered dialogues.

As the years passed, the Pundits or *Vyas(s),* the *swarūps* and *Pātras* and the *rasikas,* (the audiences who identified and empathized with, actually lived for the moment and thus enjoyed the flavour or emotions that emanated

Vyasa Mayawatie Maharaj

Vyasa Geeta Ramsingh in 1993

from the play) came to strike an understanding on the specific parts of the Rāmcharitmānas which would be selected for dramatization each day for the eleven days.In 1993 with the departure of the then in-house Pundit, Ravi Maharaj, there was a void. A new one had to be identified to continue the Leela. The group sought help from Ravindra Nath Maharaj, a Trinidadian who had studied religion and Indian philosophy in Banaras. He returned in the early 1980s, commenced the teaching of religion and Indian philosophy and established the Hindu Prachar Kendra in Longdenville, Chaguanas. 'Ravi-ji sent two of his students, Mayawatie Maharaj and Geeta Ramsingh to undertake the role of Vyāsās...'. These ladies being Rām's devotees, or Bhaktins of *Rām*, were part of a group at the Kendra who had been undergoing formal training in the Ramcharitmanas. They brought a refreshingly new approach to the text selection and script presentation of the Leela.

Maya and Geeta were the first Panditas or female narrators (Vyāsās [f]) in Trinidad to select the text, prepare a script (in English) and jointly, figuratively, sit on the *singhasana*, to both deliver the lyrics of the script and direct the production.[2] This was a significant deviation from the existing norm of occupying a *singhasana*, the seat of the lion. Prior to their ascension on the *singhasana,* this role was traditionally reserved only for males, Pundits of the Brahmin class. The First Felicity Ramleela and Cultural Organisation, Raviji and the two ladies together shattered this glass ceiling of Hindu, religious, upward mobility and social ostracism that publicly prevented females from functioning as Ramleela director(s) - chanter(s).The Vyāsā-jis returned to the Hindu Prachar Kendra a few years thereafter and another Vyas was identified and dispatched by Raviji to the First Felicity Ramleela organisation.

Pundit Budharat Yankatessu, the replacement to Geeta Ramsingh and Mayawatie Maharaj, was also part of that group in training at the Kendra. He has been functioning for over 20 years in this capacity. Pundit Yankatessu spends much effort in researching and preparing his script. On any given day of performance, the Pundit always has two documents next to him as he delivers the story. One is the Tulsidas Rāmcharitmānas and the other is a personal script containing the specially selected parts of the long story and the sub stories within the main story that he will narrate during the succeeding days (nights) of the performance. This personal script is a combination of the appropriate verses: *chaupais, dohas, chand*

and other dialogues as contained in the text, the Rāmcharitmānas. These verses are linked with his translated and interpreted narrative. Unlike other contemporary Sutradhār(s) or narrators or Vyas-jis who relate the text in a context of contemporary issues, Sutradhār Yankatessu deviation from the text is restricted only to his linkages of the verses.

The guiding principle of the text selection is that the dramatic content of the episodes must be integral parts of the story. The Pundit sticks doggedly to the main story line, only touching on some of the sub-stories or Kathas. In this way the audience's attention is held and maintained throughout the 11-day period of the Leela. This does not mean that there are no comic moments or satire or burlesque in the presentation. The performers add sumptuous portions of these in their daily, dramatic interpretations of the text.

Pundit Yankatessu adopts a combination of Indian languages and local dialects in his stand-up delivery of the evening's episodes. He chants the verses in Sanskrit and Hindi. Then he interprets and delivers them through a combination of *Trinhinglish*. This potpourri of reading and narration is delivered in a combination of languages and dialects: Hindi and Awadhi, Bhojpuri and English languages, with the English being delivered in a combination of Standard English and the Trinidadian, colloquial dialect. At the beginning of each day's play, he commences by chanting the opening prayers or mantras in Sanskrit. This is followed by him leading the live musicians in singing, in Hindi, the verses of the bhajans selected for that evening's commencement of play. There are, however, some bhajans which are repeated, especially the ones that accompany the performance of the ārti. The other musicians follow with the chorus, as the full cast assembles in the 'sanctum sanctorum', the consecrated spot in the middle of the ground, at the foot of the tallest Jhandi. This is the locus of the performance. For this Ramleela, this spot is the symbolic centre of the world - its *axis mundi*. They perform the ārti here. Then they perform ārti to the Pundit ending with the familiar greeting, 'Sita Rām '. This procedure is repeated at the end of the day's play. The scripts of the days' episodes are read and chanted in Awadhi, the language of the Rāmcharitmānas.

Casting

The identification and selection of the cast of players have always been important aspects of pre-performance planning. A small 'Ramleela

Committee' controlling the actual performance traditionally identified and approved the casting and selection of the artistes. The cast of performers were initially pre-selected by this Committee, well in advance of the actual commencement date of the Leela. This Organising Committee for the annual event simply identified the persons and negotiated with their parents or guardians for these individuals to be enrolled in the production. It was more of a family affair. There was, and continues to be, no formal village audition. This tradition continues, with some variations.

In the selection of the cast, two categories of performers are established, the Swaroops or *swarūp*s and the *Pātras.* A *swarūp* represents the form, the appearance and the physical features of the earthly manifestation of God. He or she is a person who becomes the character to be portrayed. He moves from being the simple, village young boy or girl in ordinary life, living village lifestyle; riding bicycle and playing with friends, to one playing the part or the role of the respective aspect of god. This swarūp, however, is really a miniscule representation of the vastness of the divine being within the Indian concept of omnipotence and omnipresence. God is indescribable; being explained by all negative attributes or characteristics - not this, not that, not the other, with no form, *arup*, or no characteristic, *nirgun*, yet God is also described as having all forms, *sarvarup,* and all characteristics or features, as *sagun.* Using this concept the swarūp can easily be conceived as a drop in the ocean of this inexplicable phenomenon. In this regard, the assumption of the role of God, or a tiny aspect of God on earth, is acceptable within the concept of Hindu philosophy and its physical interpretation within the orbit of Indian aesthetics.

The Swarūp transcends the established boundary, from the physical realm - as distinct from just being the actor as defined by the western concept of an actor in a theatrical event - to the metaphysical being, taking earthly form in this *Leela.* In this context, the word *Leela* or *līla* is a technical term of Hindu theology, meaning 'play', 'interaction' or 'sport', e.g. Lord Krishna's sportive dalliance or playful actions with the *gopis* or milkmaids of Brindaban in *Krishna Leela*, or the divine miracle play of Shri Rām (Ramleela). What separates us human beings from the divine is that while our human actions create Karma – the law of cause and effect or stimulus and response - and as such determine our future destiny, Kapur (1990) sums it up succinctly by reminding us mortals that Gods are already perfect. They are not controlled by the karmic repercussions of their earthly actions. Their actions create karmic actions for others, but not unto themselves. They are above Karma. They are divine. Their actions are separated from humans because of their inherent perfection. Hence, their actions are classified as 'playful deeds' or actions in this earthly sphere or 'Leela'.

In this Leela, the village adolescent or young man takes on the earthly guise of Lord Rām. As an actor he consciously recedes and makes way for the entry of the Icon, Rām, into his body.He is transformed. This is, however, not the trance-like action of other rituals such as the Kali worship in our local environment, where devotees enter the trance-like states of consciousness after which period there is no recollection of what took place during the trance. He is Lord Rām, in full consciousness of his being. Hence the term, he 'plays' Rām. He has 'become' Rām. Hence the word 'Leela' or divine play. In doing this, the *swarūp* allows the audience, the *rasikas* or appreciators of the flavour or emotion of the occasion, to fully 'see' Rām the icon, to receive the 'darshan' of Rām , to experience an auspicious fleeting 'sight' or behold an apparition of the divine Rām or Sita in physical form. The audience or at least many in the audience, in looking at the Leela are transported to that realm of awareness where they can identify with the fleeting, temporary form of the divine being.

Ārti, the sacred waving of the lighted deya in the tharia in front of the swarūp can be performed to him with the same devotion as when it is done to the murti, the sacred object in the temple. He is now Rām, the incarnation of God. This is equally true for the roles of Sita, Lakshman, Bharat or Shatrughan - those who have been imbued with divine status. The Leela is thus a divine play, worship. From this phenomenological approach the devotee easily accepts the idea of the presence of the divinity of god in the swarūps of the Felicity Ramleela, and performs arti to them (during that time) with the same auspicious devotion of worshiping the divine in another form.

Then there is the second category of actors or characters called the *pātra.* The word 'actor' is used because of want of a closer term to define the *pātra.* The *pātra* is the vessel, the container that pours out the flavour; the character of the script being enacted, yet does not become the character, but at the end of the drama is untouched or unaffected by the role that was performed. The *pātra* is thus the human body that takes on the garb or qualities of the character to be enacted or to be portrayed.In this regard the pātra or actor becomes plastercene, being able to be molded, fluid-like into a new object and convey this to the audience in the same way as a bottle of wine conveys its product to the drinker, with the bottle not being affected by the alcohol. Further, as the taste of the wine does not stay in the bottle or the keg, but disappears, so too, the actor does not acquire the qualities of the character he portrays after the play is finished. The *pātra* is mortal. He performs the role of Raja Dasarath, Rajah Janak, Raja Rāwan, Bāli and the various queens. This is more akin to the essence of the role of the actor of the western theatre. The Felicity Ramleela goes beyond physical village folk theatre into divine play. It is worship.

The evolving aesthetic 'look' of the Leela

The term 'aesthetics' here relates to 'a principle of taste or perception…' to the concepts of sensations and perceptions. It is influenced by the mind and emotions and how the mind deals with the concept of beauty and art. Stretching this concept further, aesthetics also deals with the relationship of art within a particular time and space. It explains how a group, a community or a culture weaves art into its value system relating to divinity. Aesthetics is closely tied to culture, where 'culture reflects a dynamic set of norms, values, attitudes, behavioural patterns, the traditions, art forms and heritage (both built and natural), which shape character, influence collective consciousness and enhance lifestyles in a holistic way.' [3]

The aesthetic quality of the Felicity Ramleela has grown out of a unique, characteristic image as an open-air, village performance, brought by East Indian immigrants and planted in the local landscape. It gradually adjusted to the landscape with successive generations of those early migrants, creating its own niche that is today a mixture of secular folk drama and religious faith, enacted. Nobel Laureate Derek Walcott identified this aspect of the Felicity Ramleela in his acceptance speech for the Nobel Prize for literature in 1992. He describes his impressions of his chance viewing of this Ramleela, and his ignorance of the annual enactment of this Indian epic, just a couple of miles from where he lived in north Trinidad. Walcott spoke:

> *Felicity is a village in Trinidad on the edge of the Caroni plain, … and on the afternoon that I visited it …all the faces along the road were Indian, which, as I hope to show, was a moving, beautiful thing, because this Saturday afternoon Ramleela, the dramatization of the Hindu epic the Rāmayāna, was going to be performed, and the costumed actors from the village were assembling on a field strung with different coloured flags, like a new gas station, and beautiful Indian boys in red and black were aiming arrows haphazardly into the afternoon light ...*

Even though this Ramleela had been performed annually in Felicity for more than 80 years when Walcott saw it, he admitted to his prior ignorance of the performance of the Leela. Walcott continues his interpretation of the aesthetic 'look' of the Leela:

> *Deities were entering the field…Costumed actors were arriving, princes and gods, I suppose. What an unfortunate confession! 'Gods, I suppose' is the shrug that embodies our African and Asian Diasporas….*
>
> *I had often thought of but never seen Ramleela, and had never seen this theatre, an open field with village children as warriors, princes and gods. While nobody in Trinidad knew any more than I did about Ram, Kali, Shiva, Vishnu, apart from the Indians, a phrase I use pervertedly because that is the kind of remark you can still hear in Trinidad: 'apart from the Indians'. It was as if, on the edge of the Central plain, there was another plateau, a raft on which the Rāmayāna would be poorly performed in this ocean of cane, but that was my writer's view of things, and it is wrong. I was seeing the Ramleela at Felicity as theatre when it was faith…. One of the greatest epics of the world was seasonally performed, not with the desperate resignation of preserving a culture, but with an openness of belief that was as steady as the wind bending the cane lances of the Caroni plain.*[4]
>
> He confessed that he: "…*had no idea what the epic story was, who its hero was, what enemies he fought,…*" yet, he noted that he had, "…*recently adapted the Odyssey for a theatre in England, presuming that the audience knew the trials of Odysseus, hero of another Asia Minor epic…*"

The selection process for the various roles to be performed in the Leela in the early days was carefully undertaken, in keeping with the aesthetic traditions of the culture. The selections of the Swarūps were done in accordance with strict caste considerations. The swarūps of Rām, Lakshman, Bharat, Shatrughan and Sita were chosen from the youthful group of boys. They must first be of the highest caste or Brahmin. In the absence of Brahmin the second socio-economic caste, a Kshatriya (the warrior caste) was considered, but nobody lower in their social status. No Shudra or persons of the lowest caste - usually referred to as chamār (leather worker), or further still those outside of the caste system (the kujāt[s]) - were remotely considered for selection to perform these roles of swarūps. The swarūps must also be physically healthy, handsome, of good height and mostly of light complexion. Voice was not a consideration in the selection process since they did not deliver lines. The casting was thus influenced by caste considerations, with Brahmins at the top and the lesser castes receiving roles of lesser importance. The pageant was performed in a village type, pantomime format.

The difference between the secular drama and the Leela is that the main actors selected, the swarūps in the Leela, could be of pre-puberty age but were usually adolescents. The Pātras are the second level or category of performers in the Ramleela. There were initially no females allowed in the production, so all roles were done by males - boys and men. The fighting warriors of the armies of Rām, Hanuman and Rāwan and extras for minor roles or for crowd scenes were however selected without caste distinction. Aesthetic considerations often merged with personal 'discretion'. This method of casting was borne out by Sahabir's recollection. He remembers that even up to the decades of 1960-1970s: "Latchman Maharaj performed as Rāwan. His elder son, Khedar Maharaj, played Rām. Harry played Lakshman. Satoo played Bharat. Latchman's younger son Kesho played the role of Sita..."[5]

Training of cast

With regard to training for the performers, the history of the Ramleela - whether documented or oral - does not show evidence of any prior systematic or sustained formal training undertaken for the cast and crew, save for when they lived as a commune in the Shiv Shankar ashram in the 1950s and received instructions and guidance during the Ramleela period itself. There were also no rehearsals for this village drama, whether for the *Kathakars* or the *swarūps*. The performers - many being new entrants - simply donned the garb of the particular character of the section, whether from Shri Rām's side (Ayodhya) or Rāwan's side (Lanka), or whosoever's role he was performing. Dressed in the garb of, or as close as possible to the understudy, he came onto the 'grong', imitating the actions of the performer whose character he was to eventually play. No previous training was required. He received 'on the job' training.

There was, therefore, the need to engage the same Pundit or narrator on an ongoing, annual basis to maintain the comfort level of new players while keeping the story line. This was also necessary since the performers had to be familiar with the actual chanting or narration and dialogue on a moment by moment basis, a day to day basis, so as to be able to have that measure of comfort to dramatize, in pantomime format, the scene being unfolded. This also resulted in many of the major roles and characters being played by the same persons for years. These included the major roles of Rām and his three brothers, Lakshman, Bharat and Shatrughan; Hanuman the son of the God of Wind (Pawan); Sita, the wife of Rām; Rāwan, the King of Lanka and abductor of Sita; and Narad, the interplanetary messenger. This casting of the same persons in the same character roles on an annual basis, for a number of years, significantly reduced the need to train new persons to perform the roles of these various characters.

Role of the chanter cum narrator: The Pundit

There are many terms used to describe the person who chants the various verses, interprets, narrates and links the unfolding story of the Rāmayāna. The person who simply sings the verses is referred to as the *Ramayani,* the chanter of the verse. Then there is the one who chants the verses of an epic, interprets them and carries the narrative of the story. This person is called a *Sutradhār*, one who reads from the *sutra* or sacred text and delivers the explanation. There is also the *Vyas*, the one who performs the combined roles of chanter or singer, interpreter of the verses in a dramatic way and then narrator of the story to musical accompaniment.

The Pundit literally means a learned man, a wise man, a sage (*El sabio*), a maestro (if a musician) or one who delivers a sermon, a lecture or is the chief advisor. By this explanation, the one who performs the rites and rituals for worship or puja in the temple or at home is the *purohit* who may or may not be a Pundit. While the Pundit may, from time to time, take on the function of the purohit, the purohit - the equivalent of altar boy/man/woman of the Christian faith - usually does not possess the intellectual knowledge and experience and so cannot perform the function of the Pundit. In our local Ramleela environment, the Pundit tells the story and the actors or players; the swarūps and pātras, elaborate on the story using body movements, gestures of the limbs and hands, accompanied by music, rhythm and other appropriate support. These include V*achit* (sound, words) A*ngik* (limbs) and *Aharya* (costumes, makeup, arms and armament that are in the possession and use of the player). There are also the external props and sets which form part of the dance drama, the *Nritya Nataka.* In this regard the person we loosely term the pundit performs part of the role of the Vyas, the story teller, the other part being his extensions, the actors. In the context of the Trinidad Ramleela, the Pundit performs the combined roles of the *Ramayani (*the chanter of the verses*),* the *Sutradhār* and the *Vyas,* all wrapped into one. The performers in the Ramleela are also, technically speaking, village Kathaks telling their story of the wonderful deeds of Rām as contained in the Rāmayāna. From the *singhasana* (the fearless seat of the lion), the Pundit also performs the role of the technical director of the production.

In the Felicity setting, however, the person who has traditionally sung the verses, interprets these and then narrates the unfolding episodes of the story is the Pundit. But the Pundit carries a much more composite role. He or she is also the *Vyas*, the director of the epic on the village greens. In some Ramleelas in Trinidad there has been more than one chanter cum narrator. Some are just *Ramayanis,* singing the verses in chorus with a main *Vyas*. In Felicity's Ramleelas recent history it has had the distinction of having both a *Ramayani* and a *Vyas* functioning in concert with each other, albeit for a short time. This role was performed by Mayawatie Maharaj and Gita Ramsingh.[6]

In current times the Pundit takes on the role of stage manager, chastising the artistes when they are not miming and dramatizing his explanations to the audience. He hurries them up to complete some scenes. In normal theatrical productions the director and stage managers are always behind the scene, hidden from the audience's view. In the Felicity Ramleela and many other Ramleelas the *Vyas* or Pundit cum director stage manager is in full view of the audience, stationed high up, literally and figuratively, on his platform, controlling each evening's performance.

At the beginning and end of the performance the pundit takes on another role. He is guru to the performers; they bow and touch his feet, receive his advice and blessings. He thus combines many functions, directing the Felicity Ramleela, delicately balancing its presentation as religion and faith, as worship, as secular pageant or *mela* and as folk theatre, all at the same time. What a unique concept! This folk theatre presents a totally different perspective from normal theatrical productions. It is not new but rather a perspective that has survived over 100 years in Trinidad. It is woven into the fabric of this folk tradition and now can be considered indigenous, having been performed continuously for over five generations on Trinbago's soil and 100 years in Felicity alone.

Presentational aspects of the Leela

The story of the Rāmcharitmānas is presented through the Felicity Ramleela by a combination of theatrical formats utilizing music, dance, pantomime, props and décor to capture the scenario and convey the intent of the story. The emotional rendition of the lyrics delivered by the Pundit is interpreted sometimes through the *nritya,* a wordless dramatic presentation by the performers in a tableaux format, either still or moving procession. In India this is referred to as *Jhaki* theatre.[7] On the last day, the return of Rām from his victory in Lanka back to Ayodhya, the processional cum tableau format or *Jhanki* assumes a greater impact. Rām's entourage proceeds out of the maidān on the village roadways, around the village and back into the maidān for the rituals and festivities associated with the royal coronation. The distance travelled on the night is approximately 2-3 kilometres, covered in approximately one to two hours at dancing speed viz. the speed of the Ramleela procession as they dance their return journey to Ayodhya to musical accompaniment.

This processional array of artistes - the swarūps and pātras of the Ayodhya's camp - were originally referred to, (and continue even at present) as the 'Red side' and the pātras of the Lanka side, the 'black side'. The colours represent their camp allegiances during the earlier days of performance. Today all wear red costume, thus increasing the number of warriors and followers of triumphant Rām, Sita and Hanuman. No dialogues are spoken by either the pundit or performers throughout the period of the procession. It is a combination of processional theatre, pantomime and pageantry.

Selection of music for the production

As the audience for the evening's performance arrives at the maidān of Green Park they are usually greeted with amplified, 'Indian' music. It gives the mood of a festive atmosphere. This offering represents a whole range of music; from bhajans, light classics and instrumentals, to filmy Bollywood songs. These songs range from the older Bollywood classics to spicy, upbeat versions of contemporary film fare. There is, however, the overriding delivery of devotional music, especially those songs speaking of the religious heroes from the Rāmayāna.

Just prior to the commencement of the evening's play, this music changes to more devotional music. At the appointed time for the actual commencement of the Leela, it shifts again to appropriate bhajans, more in keeping with the mood of the occasion. The Pundit takes over with his live broadcast to begin the evening's performance. It commences with the evening ārti. This involves the chanting of a selection of mantras or sacred verses in the Sanskrit language, an invocatory prayer or Vandana ending with a bhajan or song of praise to God. The bhajans are usually popular ones from Bollywood films. The Pundit accompanies himself with his harmonium. Other musicians sitting flat on the ground next to him accompany him with dholak (a double mouthed drum), a 'dandataal' or dhantāl and a pair of majeera (a miniature cymbal). The pundit may also have another harmonium player cum vocalist who lends vocal support for the ārti and during the chanting of some of the verses for dramatization of the actual evening's performance. During the dramatization of the selected texts from the Rāmcharitmānas, the music is both recorded and live. The live accompaniment comprises harmonium, dholak, dhantaal, majeera and the tassa ensemble which comprises a dhol or bass, a tassa or kettle drum and a jhanj or medium sized, brass cymbal. The closing ceremony at the end of the performance of the evening's episode of the story is similar to the commencement.

Components woven into the Performance: Dance, moods, humour and satire

Dance

During the period 1950s to 1980s, the Ramleelas in Trinidad included separate and distinct dance items, done as interludes in their daily performances[8] rather than as integral parts of the story line itself. These dance items were announced separately and were generally performed by village girls and sometimes by both males and females in the middle of the performing space in the maidān. They were popular insertions into the evening's episode of the story.

Traditionally the organisers and managers of the First Felicity Ramleela have not normally included dance as a separate form of entertainment or interlude within their annual eleven-day performance of the Leela. Whatever dance items are included in the production are selected on the basis of their relevance to the script. For instance, dance is performed for the birth of Rām and for the celebrations associated with his coronation. Here items are performed with lighted deyas in open tharias to capture the celebratory mood of both Rām's return to Ayodhya and his coronation.

However since the production is a dance drama or *nritya natika*, the entire performance begins daily with the distinct set of movements and dance sequences around the maidān to the accompaniment of the live tassa ensemble. This is called the 'Ramleela dance'. Performing a lively 1-2-3, hop-skip-skip sequence, the entire cast comprising the two opposing sides - Rām and his followers and Rāwan with his troupe of performers - circumambulate the outer periphery of the maidān, but within the bamboo barrier. Each group begins from its respective end of the savannah - Ayodhya to the north and Lanka to the south - and moves in synchronicity in an anti-clockwise direction, then returns to its respective starting point. The dance movements also include the performers wielding their respective weapons in their hands, all flowing into flawless traditional, choreographed sequences. From then onwards, all the scenes are enacted with the same theme steps of dance or with minor variations of these steps. When not executing this theme step the actors walked with stylized movements.

Nobel Laureate, Sir Vidya Naipaul recalled his childhood memory of the epic which was performed. Even though he was seeing it for the first time, he was still familiar with the story, giving credence that one can never read the Rām story for the first time. It simply pervades the consciousness of every person of Indian influenced culture, from childhood, in some form or another, not only in India but in Trinidad. Naipaul recalled that as a child, he saw it being performed:

> "...*in an open field in the middle of sugarcane, on the edge of our small country town...The male performers were bare backed and some carried long bows; they walked in a slow, stylized, rhythmic way, on their toes, and with high quivering steps; when they made an exit...*"9

This is most likely the *Ramleela* which Sir Vidya must have seen as a young lad; the Ramleela was then performed a stone's throw from his ancestral home, the 'Lion House' in Chaguanas. It had earlier moved, though temporarily, to Felicity where it spawned the present incarnation of The First Felicity Ramleela and returned to Chaguanas West. The performers have continued to maintain their steps and stylized movements and never go out of character. This characteristic method of movement is referred to as the 'Ramleela dance'. It opens each evening's episode and then brings to an end the evening's episode of the story. The closing 'Ramleela Dance' is immediately followed by the closing ārti.

Moods and emotions: Bhava and Rasa

The Rām story or Ramleela is a heroic romance which makes use of a judicious mix of human moods and emotions. As theatre - whether it is classified as religious or secular folk theatre - it comprises a whole range of moods or emotions, all falling into the technical terminology of *Bhava* and *Rasa* within performance. There are many texts that devote countless pages to the explanation of these terms. Performers of theatre, whether of folk, contemporary or classical theatre - including expressive dancing or *nritya* and dance drama or *nritya natika* - are required to study these moods and emotions and practise them so that they can convincingly undertake the emoting during the Leela. While there is no history of this aspect of this folk theatre being formally studied, it is nonetheless judiciously applied during the performance of the Leela. But what are *bhava* and *rasa*? For our purposes, a short explanation of the terminologies, *bhava* and *rasa* are given.

Bhava: A simple definition of *Bhava* is that it is an expression reflected through the face and other related body parts. However a more in-depth definition of bhava is that which contains *'Vak'* (*vachit*-sound, word), *Ang* (a*ngika [angikam]* or hand gesture [mudra{s}] using the limbs), and *Satva* (essence). Bhava are of two types; *Vibhav* (motivation) and *anubhava* (consequence of motivation). For instance, the fear of cockroaches or a scorpion in a room is *Vibhav*; the panic that ensues when one is actually confronted with it, is the *anubhava*. There are three types of states in the Bhava viz the dominant state such as love, energy or disgust. This is the *Sthayi* state; the second state is the transitory state, such as anxiety, shame, and joy. This state is referred to as the *Sanchari bhava*. The third state of the bhava is the temperamental state. The dancer or actor temporarily reflects a state of paralysis, starts weeping or perspiring. There may also be a temporary change of voice. This is the *Satvika bhava*.

Rasa: *Rasa* on the other hand constitutes 'that which is tasted (*Āswādayet*)'. It comprises a sort of distillation of an emotion or flavour, a human emotion. Such emotions are not usually long lasting but on the stage the artist can materialise them, carefully cultivate and further develop them so as to deliver them with convincing authority.

Rasa and its use in the Ramleela

There are nine major types of moods, flavours or *rasa*. Within these main emotions there are sub-divisions. The Ramleela makes judicious use of the different *rasas,* for it is said that: "The tasting of Rasa – the vision of beauty - is enjoyed only by those who are competent there to."

The names of these rasas and examples of their uses or applications are identified hereunder:

Names of Rasa		Application
Sringara (love, erotica)	-	Rām and Sita's feelings for each other; Sita's love for the Golden deer, Shurpanakha's initial response on seeing Rām.
Hasya (laughter)	-	Rām's reaction to Rāwan's sister, Shurpanakha, on their first encounter.
Karuna (compassion)	-	Rām's feelings for the dying bird, Jatayu.
Vir (valour)	-	The warrior's moods of Rām, Lakshman and Hanuman, Khar, Dushan and Rāwan in battle.
Rudra (anger)	-	Parasurama's reaction on learning that Shiva's bow was broken. The periodic moods of Lakshman, Shurpanakha, Khar, Dushan and Rāwan.
Bhayanak (bhaianak) (terror or fear)	-	Shurpanakha, Khar, Dushan, Rāwan, Jatayu, Mārīcha in meditation, Sita on being captured by Rāwan.
Bibhatsa (disgust, odium/odious)	-	Lakshman's reaction to Shurpanakha's aggressive display of love/ lust towards him.
Adbhuta (marvel or wonderment)	-	Sita on seeing the Golden deer; Rām and Lakshman in exploring Mithila on their arrival, before the bow ceremony.
Bhakti (devotion)	-	Hanuman's and Lakshman's feelings for Rām.

Even within some of the *rasas* there are sub-classifications or slight variations of that flavour. For instance, within the *Sringara* or love mood, there is *viraha* or love in separation. Within the Rāmayāna and the Felicity Ramleela, this mood or rasa is very prevalent. *Viraha*, or love in separation, is experienced by Rajah Dasarath when Rām goes into exile; then individually by Rām, the hero of the epic for Sita the heroine. The characteristics of *viraha* includes Rām pining away for his wife; the low ebb of his general enthusiasm, his faltering courage and his world suddenly becoming devoid of happiness. He cries "Sita, Sita!" Sita, Oh Sita! when she becomes separated from him, she having been kidnapped by King Rāwan of Lanka. In this classical context the whole of nature is sympathetic to Rām. In our local folk context in Trinbago, at the secular level, this state of mind and resultant behaviour (the *rasa*) is referred to as a cross between the words 'tabanca' and 'tutulbay'. It is also experienced by Sita for him when she is abducted by Rāwan and collectively, during the period of their separation.Three of the most popular moods or *rasa* in the Rām story and the Felicity Ramleela are that of *Vir* or valour, *Karuna* or compassion, and V*iraha* or love in separation; grief and longing for the return of the loved one.[10]

Just as people eat a sumptuous meal with a lot of flavours and taste these flavours (r*asa*), so in experiencing or tasting the various *rasas*, the audience becomes satiated, experiencing many moods within short periods of time, and in quick succession. They leave the performance, full of joy, romance, mixed emotions and satisfaction, having been bathed in its many moods and experienced the rush of the feel-good hormones or endorphins that are secreted by the body during the performance. The use of *bhava* and *rasa,* with r*asa* being born out of *bhava*, or expressive performance, is thus critical to a successful performance and a lasting experience, both for the performers as well as the audience.

The role of humour

Even though the Felicity Ramleela script is closely aligned to the Rāmcharitmānas, there is adequate room for improvisation of the story within the local environment. The humour that is introduced into the drama is sometimes as subtle as it is patently bawdy, yet just short of that which would be termed vulgar. Here the humour borrows as much from, as it lends to, the carnivalesque culture of Trinidad. For instance, one may find that parallel with the narration and enactment of a serious part of the story when the audience is consumed in the scene, a totally unrelated character enters the maidān wearing a ridiculous mask and carnival- type 'old mas costume' with a thick head of red hair. In order to appreciate the humour, sometimes one has to read between the lines to detect the message that may be applicable to our local political culture, past or current. This clowning and the interpretation of local and national contemporary issues are presented with satire and burlesque, using the carnival and the carnivalesque to cross cultures while delivering messages. The application of the use of both verbal and nonverbal language, of music, of facial and other body language and expressions is rich. The usage of all of the above distils the essence of rasa as is portrayed in the epic.

Masked characters add local humour to the Felicity Ramleela pageantry

ENDNOTES

1. Kelvin Saith, a member of the Executive Committee of the First Felicity Ramleela and Cultural Organisation. P.I. over a 9 year period, 2008-2017.
2. Geeta Ramsingh. P. I. in 2012.
3. Satnarine Balkaransingh, *Ramleela: Community Identity and Aesthetic Experience, The First Felicity Ramleela of Trinbago.* Research paper delivered at the 2nd World Conference on Ramleela, Nov 22-27, 2015 at the Indira Gandhi National Centre for the Arts, Delhi, India.
4. Derek Walcott, "Fragments of an Epic Memory", Nobel Prize Acceptance Speech 7 Dec, 1992.
5. Sahabir 2012.
6. Geeta Ramsingh and Mayawatie Maharaj together performed this function during the years 1993-94. P.I with Geeta Ramsingh in 2014. Currently, this is an integral

feature of the Bal Ramdilla of The Hindu Prachar Kendra in Enterprise Village, Chaguanas which Geeta, now Geeta Vahini, leads and where Mayawatie is a key person.

7. In Old Delhi there used to be a Ramleela during the period 1960-1980s, performed in the grounds outside of the Red Fort (Lal Quila). When the characters donned their attire they walked daily, in tableau format, to the performance ground. The residents of the area came out to see them, referring to this format of presentation as *Jhaki* Ramleela. P.I. interview with Ashwini Parashar May 2016. He was then a resident of that area. This is the same format undertaken by the First Felicity Ramleela on the last day of the performance when they return to Ayodhya via the streets of Felicity.
8. Personal observations between 1956-61 in the Sangre Chiquito Ramleela, Sangre Grande, Trinidad. This was possibly the first Ramleela in the Eastern Counties of Trinidad that ran annually for 5 years.
9. V.S. Naipaul, *Between Father and Son: Family Letters* (New York: Vintage, 2001) 7.
10. Sattar is of the view that *viraha* or 'love in separation' is the most popular one. See A. Sattar, The *Rāmayāna-Valmik* (Delhi: Penguin Books, 1996).

Chapter Seven

PREPARATIONS FOR THE OPEN-AIR PRODUCTION

The Preparations

The annual preparation for the production of the First Felicity Ramleela is very complex and time consuming. It involves a cadre of planners, technicians and workers from the village and its surroundings. When the various activities associated with the planning, implementation and management of the production are listed it amounts to over 30 headings with each heading subdivided into its own sub-heads and further sub-activities. Activities include negotiations for the use of the ground, rental of tents, sound system and tassa groups; the preparation and assemblage of costumes and attire, masks, weapons, props, effigies, ground preparation and stage settings; financing, marketing and then the sanctification of the performance 'space'. It is a combined effort of the village artisans and other helpers who give of their time, expertise and experience, many free of charge, to ensure that the Leela is ready for the opening night. Some of these activities are elaborated hereunder.

Costumes and attire

In the performing arts, and especially the dramatic arts, the costuming of the performers has become a very technical and exacting aspect of stagecraft, almost a science. This includes selection of fabric with the appropriate texture, weight, weft, colour, sheen, design and fabrication. All are intended to create the suitable mood and give the feel of the character which is to be portrayed. The artistes of the Felicity Ramleela have been perfecting this aspect of their stagecraft by trial and error over the last four generations. They have developed a degree of intuition, expertise and experience to know which fabric, the texture of the fabric, the colour combinations and their tonal quality will evoke the appropriate mood and emotive flavour to capture the dramatic essence of this timeless story.

In this regard significant attention is placed on the selection of costuming and general attire for their annual Ramleela celebrations. This attention to detail has been so since the early days of the Leela when the performers stayed together as a group in the Shiv Shankar Mandir for the duration of the 'play'. During those earlier times the Ramleela management committee selected and purchased suitable fabric for the costumes for the entire cast of players. There was bulk buying and stitching. The village tailors also undertook the preparation of much of the costume jewelry for the main cast of players - stitching, tacking, and gluing - assisted by the performers who stayed in the ashram.

After the middle of the 1930s, the costume designs and fabric colours would have, no doubt, been influenced by the new wave of movies coming out of the rapidly expanding Indian film industry. This trend continues even today, especially with the large number of religious films, documentaries and 'soaps' made especially for television audiences and which reach our TV and movie screens. These continue to influence the evolving changes in the 'look' of the Felicity Ramleela production.

The performers are now responsible for the purchase of their own costumes, the selection of the fabric, costume jewelry, face and body make-up, plus the stitching charges of the costumes. Both Rām and Lakshman do their own shopping - as do many others - choosing fabric which can withstand the rigours of open-air weather (rain, wind and mud) and hardy enough to engage in battle scenes involving tumbling, rolling and physical contact. The fabric is selected not only for it durability, but its capability of reflecting light, and its ease and comfort in wearing. When draped on the body as a costume it must enhance the tonal quality of the body, the character role being portrayed, and the wearer must feel comfortable in it. This ease of wearing is necessary since each night the performance time is two and one half hours, running into three hours, requiring rough use. The fabric selected is usually a soft satin in two shades of yellow, orange, white and red.[1] Other performers select different types of cloth, depending on their preferences and their budgets. They must also choose appropriate colours of fabric and the costume jewelry to supplement what they already have.

For instance, in 2012 Lakshman wore seven full costumes over the

11 day period depicting various aspects of his evolving roles and changing scenes in the epic: youth, student in the ashram, marriage, exile, forest dweller, warrior in battle and then for the coronation. Five of these pieces of fabric were stitched and two were full saris draped as dhotis.[2] The costumes, each of five yards of cloth, consisted of four pieces: a pant (dhoti); shoulder piece (an *Angwastram*); waist band (*kamarband*) and a sleeveless, tight fitting waistcoat, covering the chest. The dhoti alone consisted of three yards of fabric with two additional yards used for the other pieces that form the total costume.

The stitching of the costumes, both for Vikash (as Lakshman) and for Shivaram Ramoutar (as Rām) are undertaken by their aunt, Savitri Rambharose.[3] She has been the seamstress for the family for a number of years, having received training at the Carapichaima Senior Comprehensive School and at St. Martin's Fashion Institute in Chaguanas, apprenticeship at two institutions and having gained considerable experience in this field. The fabric for the costumes and imitation jewelry are purchased at several fabric and costume stores including the Indian fairs held periodically around the country.

While the fabric for five costumes cost just over TT$700.00 (Trinidad and Tobago currency)[4], the two saris cost TT$2,500.00 each. Stitching charges were TT$160.00 each, and that too after a 15% discount. Total stitching charges amounted to TT$1,600.00. Two sets of costume jewelry (totaling TT$5,000.00), rudrāksha malas and footwear (TT$760.00), crowns, breastplate & armbands (approx. TT$680.00) were added to the wardrobe. The total cost of outfitting 'Rām' and 'Lakshman' for the eleven-day period of the Leela amounted to roughly TT$15,000.00 per person. Their face and body make-up cost TT$1,083.00, This did not include the expenses involved in paying for body exercise routines at the local gym (3-6 months before the actual production begins) and food supplements to prepare their bodies for the rigours of the 11 day Leela, all of which can amount to a tidy sum, say close to twenty thousand dollars.[5]

Other cutters and stitchers engaged for the Ramleela include Larry Maharaj of 'Larry Tailor shop' and Mala Daley, both residents of Felicity. The total wardrobe for this production of between 40-50 ' players' consists of approx. 130-150 costumes: 5 sets each for Rām, Lakshman and Rāwan and 3 sets for each of the other performers.

Over the years many changes have become apparent. From the 1980s, the cast of performers shifted their 'dressing' to other venues. Commencing from the 1990s the performers started using the available spaces at the Shiva Seva Sangha and the Shree Shri Gopal Krishna Ashram, on Nolan Street. This temple was formerly known as Bhasaraj Temple. Other performers dressed at the residence of the Ramoutars (from whose house emerged Rāwan and Lakshman) at 32 Nolan Street. As at 2015, this arrangement was still in effect.

Crowns made by the performers for the Felicity Ramleela

Facial and body makeup

Each player purchases his or her own supply of face and body make-up; these include foundation base, eyebrow pencils, eyeliners, mascara, blushes, lipstick and powder. This does not mean that they do not share some items when they are dressing as a group or when in need. However there are personal items which are usually not shared for hygienic reasons such as sponges, powder puffs and lipsticks.

During the 2014 Leela, there were four makeup artistes, all female from the community itself. Each day the make-up artistes assisted the performers - Rām, Sita, Lakshman, Bharat, Shatrughan, Narad muni and the legion of young actors and warriors - to undertake their face make up. They applied

Neela Indar applies base on the face of Lakshman (Deon Daly)

base fixative with a wet sponge, translucent powder, eye liner, and lipstick - mostly red and varying shades of red - to the face. The arms, backs and chest make up, putting on the garlands or malas, earrings, necklaces, arm and wrist bands and tying of their waist bands (*kamarband*) over the dhotis were done by the artistes themselves or with assistance from other performers.[6]

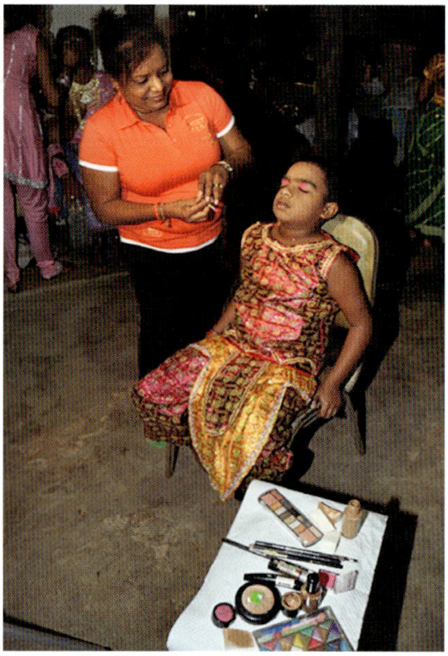

A helper assisting in applying makeup to a young performer

The females and the young performers - Kaikeyi, Severi etc. – also receive assistance in having their facial make-up applied. This allows for a uniform type of stage make-up that is presented to the audience during performance. Many performers, however, undertake to do their individual dressing and make-up at home and go to the maidān ready for the evening's performance.

The preferred brand of cosmetics used is the local *Sacha* products. Felicity Ramleela, performers have recognised its proven suitability for their type of skin colour, shades of colour, texture and physical environment and performing in the open air in a hot and humid tropical climate. This cosmetic brand was supplemented by other brands.

Weapons

There are innumerable instances of battle within the 84 kathas of the Rām story. There are battles between mortals and rākshas or demonic beings and great wars between armies. Naturally, these lend themselves to much thought-provoking concepts on the types and designs of the weapons used in these battles. Three different bows or 'dhanush' are currently used by each of the main characters from the 'Ayodhya' side during the eleven consecutive days of performance i.e. gold, silver and purple. Some bows are simple and medium sized; others are large, multi-coloured and incorporate technology within their design and fabrication. The superstructure of the bows are constructed from the wood of the *Jamun* tree and covered with PVC, tinsel, vinyl and iridescent foil. The raw materials for the construction of the weapons are purchased

A colourful array of battle attire and weapons

but their fabrication by the performers themselves commence a few months before the Ramleela begins. The arrows are incendiary sticks purchased from the 'Carnival' store in Port of Spain.

This is the same case with the designs and fabrication of the swords and shields used by the 'demons' in their early battles with Rām and Lakshman, and then with the 'warriors' of King Rāwan of Lanka. The swords and the bows are fashioned with interesting designs and embellished with luminous fabric. This allows for unique interpretations of futuristic inventions of this old military arsenal, or is it ancient designs brought back to present time with innovative reproductions.

The mukdars or battle weapons of the army of King Sugrīv and Hanuman were made by the 'warriors' who wielded these armaments. Much of the costs incurred is borne by the players themselves with very little or no sponsorship. It is a labour of love.

Effigies

Effigies have been an integral component of the Ramleela since its inception. The effigy has enhanced the theatrical aspect of the village drama. This is the view of at least three generations of players and audiences. They are usually crude constructions and artistically poor representations of the actual images that they imitate. Anuradha Kapur (1990) in her interpretation of effigies of another Ramleela in India (the famous Ramleela of Ramnagar of Banaras) sums it up rather cogently: "It is the spectator that gives them roles that far exceed their often artless structures."[7] These objects are endowed with specific roles and the audiences 'read' these roles, shifting them from being just symbolic representations to actual living roles. The interpretations of the effigies in the Ramleelas in Trinidad, and indeed those of Felicity, are very similar. They become representations of the mortal beings, and in this case, representations of those legendary characters which open up the minds of the audience to 'seeing' them from an inner perspective, interchangeably.

Recognising the multiple dimensions of these observations, the production team of the Felicity Ramleela constructs many effigies during the annual run of the Leela. These include the golden deer which Sita desired while she lived in Panchavati; Rāwan's horse which he 'rode' to meet Mārīcha, the magician; Kumbhkaran, the brother of Rāwan, and Rāwan himself.

Kumbhkaran is portrayed as a giant who sleeps for six months of the year, then awakens with a humungous and ravenous appetite. His effigy towers above the audience making them, and his opponents, Rām and Lakshman, look like dwarves in front of him. Kumbhakaran's body is 14 feet tall. His crown is 5 feet high, making him 19 feet tall. Kumbhakaran is painted green and pink, the artist's impression of his skin colour. This gives a level of symbolic proportion of the person with whom the brothers must do battle.

Rāwan too has an enormous size. The skeleton is fabricated with a bamboo and wood superstructure and held together with wire. The various limbs, torso and head are built separately, covered over with paper and paste (papier maché) and then assembled. Both effigies are then hoisted in their upright position on the tenth day, just before their mortal representations are 'vanquished' in battle (*Vijay Dashami*) and then burnt. The hoisting is usually done in the afternoon and used to be undertaken with the help of ladders and rope pulleys. Within recent times it is undertaken with the assistance of a mechanical crane, mounted on a truck. The effigies are then staked securely to the ground by ropes emanating from various parts of their bodies. The effigies tower above the audience, Rāwan's being higher than that of Kumbhkaran and reflective of the sheer magnitude of the task that Rām, Lakshman, Hanuman and Sugrīv's army have to perform to succeed in this epic war. In the year 2010, Rāwan's effigy measured 44 feet (32 feet of body, with a head height of 7-8 ft and a crown of 4ft). The skeleton was covered with old newspapers and a mixture of flour and other adhesive paste, and painted black and red. The effigy, armed with a miniature sword and a shield relative to its body size, had ten heads, representing the capability

Effigy of Rāwan in Green Park Savannah, Felicity with laser light in his eyes

of this formidable opponent. The eyes of both brothers were inset with laser lights so that they 'glowed with anger' on the battlefield – in the dark night – just before their final demise.

In the history of the Felicity Ramleela, the Rāwan effigies have been constructed by Moonasar and Sitipal (from beginning to 1962), then by Sarran Kanhai, Sitipal and Chabilal Orie (1962-1995). For the last 20 years the effigies of Kumbkaran and Rāwan have been fabricated by the village artisan Mr. Chabilal Orie, a deaf–mute. The builder begins the planning and construction of the effigies about two months before the commencement of the Leela.[8] Some years both effigies are constructed while in others only one is built, depending on the existing financial status and the level of local sponsorship received by the organisation.

Spiritual, mental and physical preparations for performing in the Leela

The swarūps - Rām, Lakshman, Bharat and Shatrughan - must look like, or close to, incarnations or avatars of God. They must look young, handsome and in the prime of their lives, reflecting the timelessness of God, both in earthly time and sphere, yet simultaneously being present as divine entities in the same guise in other spheres and worlds. To achieve this image, the youths physically work out in the local gym many months before, building and improving muscle mass and tone, body curvatures with appropriate proportions of body mass to muscle. Their bodies become compact and lithe as they work at becoming the necessary role models of Felicity and its Ramleela, indeed of this Trinidad and Tobago annual performative epic.

Much attention is also placed on their eating and drinking habits. There is abstinence from meat and alcohol of any kind. They eat a balanced diet of vegetables, fruits, nuts, grains and dairy products. The vegetables are all local: baigan, ochro, bodi, bhaji, callaloo soup (a soup made of dasheen [taro] leaves), caraille (the fruit of the bitter gourd), saijan (the fruit of Moringa Oleiflera, commonly known as drumsticks), soya and pumpkin. They get adequate carbohydrates from boiled ripe, plantains, sweet potatoes and imported potatoes (aloo), all prepared in a variety of ways, some with much seasoning. Adequate cereals are also consumed. They eat lentils (daal), rice and roti (flat bread made of whole wheat and white flour), plus a variety of salads comprising lettuce, tomatoes, cucumber, apples, grapes, dried cranberries, and finely sliced cabbage. Chutneys, made from roasted coconuts, golden apple (pommecythere) mango and other condiments and mixed with pepper, provide spiciness and satisfaction to the taste buds and stomach.

They drink lots of water, juices, tea, coffee, channa punch, milk and milk products. While in the gym, Lakshman drinks water and 'sea moss' - a local, high protein, high iodine concoction derived from dried sea weed or kelp[9] – or barbadine punch (giant granadilla of the passion fruit family), made by his aunt (Phua) Janke Ramoutar[10] who lives in the same house as part of their extended family. 'Lakshman' advises that he: "maintains his body weight as needed for his role, and can add or lose weight whenever it becomes necessary for his performance." In this regard his diet is also enhanced by protein and other vitamin supplements to ensure he does not fall sick during the rigorous eleven consecutive days of the performance of the Leela, even as they perform their normal daily work schedules.

The physical preparation is accompanied by daily prayers and abstinence from meat and alcoholic beverages for many days preceding the commencement and during the period of the performance. While these interviews on the preparations for the Leela were conducted over several sessions from 2008 to 2014, this format for the spiritual, mental and physical preparation for participation in the Leela remains the norm among the 'players'.

Engagement of Community

There are no fixed methods or time frames for the engagement of the community in the preparatory process. Artisans are engaged by both the players to make costumes and individual props - swords, shields, bows etc. - and by the Management Committee of the Ramleela for the preparation of the main effigies and other related activities. The helpers either present themselves or are requested to assist in cutting bamboo, fabrication of barriers, food preparation, wardrobe and makeup. Individual members of the community or families negotiate the rental of tents for sale of finger foods during the period of the Leela. Sponsorship and other financial matters are handled by the Management Committee.

The Performance venue: Location and preparation

The Green Park recreation ground has been the traditional venue for the annual First Felicity Maidān Ramleela since its inception. The space has a very interesting history, with many name changes over the years; the 'Coconut' (it was initially a coconut field and even after the coconuts where cleared it was still called the 'Coconut'), then as the 'Ramleela Ground', the 'Felicity Sports and Recreation Ground' and finally 'Green Park Recreation Ground.'[11] The park is now maintained by the Chaguanas Borough Corporation.

The Park is rectangular in shape, comprising approximately two acres of grassed surface. It is bounded on the north by a short street, Mc Millan Street which borders the northern periphery of the ground, terminating on the ground itself. On the south are the Felicity Community centre and another building, both facing Boundary Street, running East to West. On the eastern edge of the savannah is Nolan Street with its row of dwelling houses, all facing the savannah. On the west the savannah is bounded by Clarke Street. Up to 2012, all of these streets were in varying stages of disrepair. Today they are all paved with asphalt, a result of the work of the political representatives and administrators of the constituency and the Borough of Chaguanas under whose administration Felicity falls.

The savannah serves as the venue for a diverse range of sporting activities, depending on the season and based on weather conditions: There is football in the rainy season, cricket and kite flying during the dry season, and a pasture for the cows and other grazing animals owned by the villagers. These animals are tethered there, throughout the day. On weekends, they are tethered on the periphery of the ground to allow for the sporting activities. It is a familiar pastoral scene throughout the year. Within recent times the Borough Corporation upgraded the field and its physical infrastructure, installing flood lights for night-time, village sporting activities. The Ramleela festival has benefitted tremendously from this upgrade.

Preparation of the maidān or the ground for the enactment of the Leela

The central performance space of the Ramleela celebrations is a clearly demarcated area in the middle of the Green Park Recreation ground. The utilised space, however, encompasses an area much larger than the prepared area. This includes part of the village of Felicity which is traversed by a procession which accompanies the entourage of Rām returning from his battle with Rāwan in Lanka. The procession, on the last day of this village theatre, travels from the central performance area around the village and back, a distance of approximately three kilometres.

Every year this park is transformed into a multi-dimensional venue for the unfolding of the drama. For the eleven-day period it is a beehive of socio-economic activity, theatre and mela (bazaar) - temporary constructed stalls and vendors' booths, selling a variety of snacks, Indo -Trinidadian street foods, confectionaries or methai and soft drinks.

The annual conversion of the two-acre Green Park Recreation ground into the maidān for the Ramleela celebrations is an exercise in event planning and management. The whole ground is designed and laid out into distinct parts. There is an inner sanctified area where the drama will be performed and an outer periphery that is allocated for audience accommodation - both standing around the periphery and seated in a temporary pavilion. Behind the audience are the food and other stalls and the public entertainment areas, with the 4th section identified for vehicular parking. When fully operational, the entire space is transformed into concentric, elliptical shapes. Some years the configuration changes slightly, to either oval-shaped or rectangular shape.

Prior to the commencement of the Leela, members of the Planning Committee perform the ritual of 'cutting bamboo' for erection of the physical infrastructure. An auspicious time of the month is identified when the bamboo stalks are to be selected and freshly cut by the villagers. Earlier, the bamboo was cut directly from bamboo patches along the water courses in Felicity. Today bamboo must be fetched from further afield and transported by open-tray vehicles to the ground. Some of the bamboo are stripped while others are cut in varying sizes and lengths; the thin ones are for flag poles. Short, thick ones are for posts, and medium sized ones are for erecting the barriers to separate performers from the audience.

In the early years, the barrier was fabricated entirely from bamboo. The bamboo rods were large, about 4"-6" in diameter. These were cut into varying lengths. Some were 4ft in length, others 12-16 ft., while a third category of thinner rods were 16-20 ft. long. The 4ft lengths were used as posts for the barrier; one foot buried in the dirt and the other 3ft above the ground. They were securely planted at 8-10 ft. intervals to be able to withstand the pressure of the audience's weight against the barrier for 10 consecutive days, and especially during the last few days when thousands came to strain against the barrier to witness battle scenes, especially Rām in battle with Rāwan and Rāwan's demise and final immolation.

The 12 ft. lengths of bamboo were securely lashed, horizontally to the posts by rope. The 20 ft. thinner rods were used as flag posts on which the triangular *patakas* or fabric pennants were inserted. When consecrated, these various, coloured flags - red, yellow, black and white - on their flag posts became jhandis. They were buried in the earth next to the short, bamboo posts and were also lashed to these, at about 15 feet intervals or at alternate barrier posts. The inner performance area was then measured, staked and cordoned off by a low barrier approximately 3 ft. high. The inside of the barrier measured approximately 150 feet long by 110 feet wide. When fully constructed, this inner performance area reflected either oval shaped or elliptical or rectangular design.

From 2007 to 2009 the performance space appeared more oval than rectangular, the oval shape allowing the audience easier line-of–sight viewing of the pageant. The low barrier separated the performers from the audiences[12] by an arm's length. In 2007 the cordon also temporarily changed, from bamboo to steel barrier; the steel rods were ½"- ¾", 'tacked' together. This change reflected the changing socio-economic circumstances and the improved status of the Leela within the community. By 2015, with deteriorating economic fortunes at the national scale, the barrier had returned to a combination of bamboo and steel barriers. This method of barrier construction and jhandi erection continues to be an integral part of the aesthetic of the Ramleela ground.

Consecration of the performance space

The consecration of the performance space is generally held on the day before the actual commencement of the drama. While this consecration is an event held in a public space, the maidān (this space as 'Ramleela ground'- locally referred to as the Ramleela 'grong') is not fully open to the public as yet. In 2015, as in previous years, the consecration was performed by the Pundit; with the Organising Committee, the actors, other technical directors and workers preparing the props, décor, wardrobe and make-up personnel and their close associates participating.

It is a dry, cool Thursday evening, nearing the hour of 7.00 pm. The Green Park recreation ground reflects the air of anticipation. There are heaps of canvas and steel lying on the ground, waiting to be assembled into tents. Plastic tables and chairs are lined up. Bamboo cuttings, multicolored cloth, bamboo rods with pennants or patakas are neatly placed to one side, to be attached to the top of the rods and planted as jhandis or flagpoles. There is also a very long bamboo pole, washed and stripped of bramble, save for a few bits of bristles or 'jhakhi' at the very top. Steel barricades are lying in another area, and will be attached to short bamboo posts to function as the barrier between audience and performers.

About two dozen people - key performers, the executive committee and some parents and well-wishers of the Ramleela - have arrived at the savannah to participate in the performance of the *Bhoomi Pūja* and the ritual planting of the main prayer flag, or the *mool jhanda staphna.* This is an integral part of the sanctification of the performance area within the ground or maidān, in preparation for the commencement of the annual celebrations of the Ramleela. The word *bhoomi* refers to the earth as in *bhoomi mata* or Mother Earth. The earth is the symbolic mother, since it brings forth produce. This pūja is an invocation to Mother Earth, seeking her blessing and permission for yet another successful village, theatrical production. This puja has been performed in an annual unbroken chain for the last 99 years in keeping with the injunction that the stage - on which all theatrical presentations are to be undertaken - must be first consecrated in accordance with established guidelines of religious conduct and spiritual development.

This consecration includes the 'invitation' to the various forms of divinity; their installation by offering each of them gifts in the form of *vastra* or clothing; incense such as googol or lohbān; food; rice, etc.; fresh flowers (*pushpanjali*); water or *jal*; the waving of a lighted flame or ārti to purify the area; amrit (the nectar of immortality) and finally, prasad or consecrated food. This food, comprising both cooked (*halva*) and fresh fruits, is usually sweet in taste. It is intended that way so that it may sweeten the mouths of both the performers and audiences alike, for the duration of the performance. Both the performers and audience will figuratively experience pleasure, in the performance of and in the enjoyment of the drama. Today is therefore of particular importance since the recreation ground is being converted into the stage for the commencement of the Leela. This is also a particularly auspicious day since it is supposed to mark the 100th year of this Ramleela.

The congregation comprising Ramleela performers, assistants, executive members of the group and the Pundit are assembled under a rented, white canvas-covered tent in the middle of the ground. An upraised rectangular shallow box, approx. 2 ft. long, 2 ft. wide and 9 inches high, filled and smoothened over with dirt, is positioned at the eastern end of the tent. Flour has been used to draw or demarcate sacred, geometric symbols or *yantras* and designs at the top of the leveled dirt. A small banana tree is planted on the eastern side of the rectangular box. This is the *bedi*, an area on which all the objects of worship will be placed and worshipped. It will be consecrated by the sacrificial symbolic offerings to all of these energy forms, with emphasis placed on Hanuman[13] and will function as the nucleus or, in religious parlance, the sanctum of the performance area.

The performers are positioned directly in front of the bedi, facing an easterly direction. The Pundit takes his sitting position to the south of the bedi, facing north, to perform the puja which, according to Hindu astrology, is supposed to exert influences on all life-form on planet earth. The *bedi* or sanctum of the puja is then slowly and meticulously decorated with the ingredients and images of worship. These objects include photos and miniature statues of Shri Rām and Sita; Hanuman, Ganesha the remover of obstacles; the *nav graha* jhandis - miniature flags of nine planets. The dimensions of this bedi are relatively large and high, so as to allow the audience a view of the daily ārti by the performers, prior to each evening's performance.

A triangular-shaped hole, about six to nine inches deep, has been dug in the earth a few inches north of the bedi. This is going to be the *hawan kund* for the puja, a burning open-pit flame, fed by mango and pitch pine woodenchips, camphor, incense and other ingredients. Into this flame the offerings are placed, invoking the blessings of the various divinities for yet another successful production.

A conical hole, 4ft deep, has also been dug a few inches away at the eastern end of the bedi. A 65ft. bamboo pole which was previously cut from a bamboo patch and cleaned of bristles - some of the *jhaki* or bramble at the top of the pole were retained - is brought to the ground and washed.

With all of the performers assembled under the tent, the pūja begins. The Pundit recites various incantations, simultaneously taking water from a lōtā with the aid of a mango leaf that has been fashioned into a spout, and sprinkling it sequentially; it is first done on the bedi, in the four geographical directions, and then onto the performers. The conch shell or *shankh* is blown; its vibrations purifying the surrounding areas. A small hand-held bell is rung. A thick, hand-held, brass gong or *ghanta* is struck with a wooden mallet three consecutive times and allowed to reverberate for the length of its vibratory capacity. Various ingredients are placed on the bedi; mango leaves, cotton wool, rice, sugar, flowers, camphor, supāri seeds, dūb (locally referred to as nut-grass or Bermuda grass) and money (coins in denominations of silver and copper).

The fire is then lighted in a specially indented steel vessel, a *hawan kund*. It is ignited using sticks of pitch pine wood, camphor and ghee or clarified butter. More invocatory verses are chanted. In this format the name of the various presiding deities of the Hindu pantheon are all symbolically 'invited' to 'take a seat' on the *bedi* and witness the prayer performed in their names and for the specific purpose or *Sankalph*. The *Sankalph* is the affirmative resolution to successfully undertake this project. In this case it is the request for the successful performance of the Leela of Shri Rām. All of the performers actively participate in this sacred worship, each following the instructions of the Pundit and making the necessary offerings at the various geographic positions on the bedi, to the representations of the nine divinities or *Nav graha*.

More chanting is done, more bell ringing; *ghanta* knocking and *shankh* blowing are performed. Then the prepared offering, both cooked and uncooked - all vegetarian - is brought to be 'offered' to the fire. It is then gradually 'fed' to the flame, small portions at a time, by the main person (the *Shrota*) performing the ritual while the Pundit chants the appropriate verses. As the 'offerings' burn, a white smoke curls upwards from the *hawan kund*. The smoke encircles the devotees, enveloping them with its sweet-smelling fragrance. They are being blessed.

The long bamboo pole is then brought by two helpers. A tri-colour rectangular pennant or *patak*a is attached to its top, just under the bramble or *jhaki*. It is a pennant of solid colours: white, red and yellow. No one has been able to ascertain just when the shape of this pennant changed from the normal triangular design to a rectangular one. This was explained away as 'tradition'. The presence of the bristles at the top of the flag pole is also explained as 'more of a tradition than as a religious injunction.' It has also been accorded meaning, signifying continuity. The positioning of the three colors of the pennant are also given symbolic meanings i.e. "white to the top, representing protection; red in the middle, for energy and devotion as represented by Hanuman; and yellow at the bottom, symbolizing the Devi, the female energy principle."[14]

Several ingredients are then placed into the open hole: water, milk, ghee, flowers and copper coins. This offering sanctifies the hole or foundation. With the help of five able-bodied men, the 65 ft jhandi is planted in the 4 ft hole, leaving 61 ft above ground. It is flying the tri-colour flag with the bramble at the top. This main Jhandi is planted in the middle of the performance area of the maidān. It will become the central flag pole, the root or *Mool Jhanda*, the *axis mundi*, the symbolic, mystic pillar that connects the three worlds, the three regions of the universe - the heavenly, earthly and nether regions.

The term *"axis mundi"* is symbolically the "hub" or "navel" of the universe as it is conceived in the world view of a particular culture, and in this particular case, Sanatan Dharma, the eternal way of life. At the metaphysical level the *axis mundi* is also called the *skambha (*meaning both "pillar" and "support"), and is referred to in the *Atharva Veda* [*10. 7. 35*). It stands at the centre of the cosmos, supporting the entire universe. It is thus the locus or point where cosmic regions (the heavenly, earthly and nether regions) intersect and are accessible to the spiritual seeker - the bhakta or devotee - in any one of these cosmic regions. It can also be interpreted as the intersection of planes from where different states or levels of consciousness may be attained. This point of intersection is the "navel" of the world.[15]

This 'navel' is referred to in the *Taittirīya Upanishad* (III.x.5-6) explaining the omnipotence and omniscience of the *Brahman* or Godhead: "I am the *navel* (italics mine) of immortality. …" As a result, the "navel" of the world is considered to be a place sacred above all others. The offerings made in the consecration of the jhandi are figuratively "the food to the Gods." The narrative in the *Taittirīya Upanishad* [III.x.5-6]) continues: "He who offers me thus (as food), protects me just as I am. I, food as I am, eat him up who eats food without offering…"[16]

This *mool jhanda* is thus the navel or centre-point from where the spiritual energy for the Ramleela resides and radiates outwards. It represents both festivity and sacrality. This *mool jhanda*, flying in the wind for the entire period of the event will be the locus of not only the physical but the spiritual attention, the *axis mundi,* for the entire performance period of the Ramleela. The community and other visitors will use this 'pointer' flag to locate the venue of the Ramleela for the next 11 days.

A second, short, ten-joint bamboo with a separate solid red triangular pennant or *pataka* is erected next to the long one. At the 6th joint above ground, on the long jhanda, a solid, yellow cotton fabric, a *langot*, is tied around the joint. This thin, long piece of cotton cloth also connects and secures itself to the smaller jhandi. At the third joint from the base of the smaller jhandi, another piece of solid red cotton fabric, another *langot*, is tied. Both jhandis are fastened together. The jhandi planting is now complete but the rituals continue. Sandal wood paste is then applied to the middle of the forehead of the main persons, the main characters who 'listened', and all the others who participated in the pūja. Essence is similarly applied to their respective heads or wrists. The final bhajans are sung and ārti – the waving of a light in clockwise formation around the 'installed' images of the various aspects of divinity - is performed. During the singing of the bhajans by the entire congregation, to accompany the ārti, the *shankh* or conch shell is again blown and the ghanta struck with its sturdy wooden mallet, producing complementary harmonic sounds.

By 8.45 pm., the puja is complete and the *amrit*, the symbolic ambrosia or nectar of immortality, is given to those who participated in the puja. A few drops of this specially prepared liquid - milk, honey, ghee, yogurt and sugar - are poured in the outstretched cupped palm of the right hand of each puja participant, and sipped. The hand is wiped clean on the hair of the head; this wiping itself being a local folk tradition. Simultaneously with the passing of the amrit, the ārti plate - a lighted deya on a brass plate or tharia, containing some fresh flowers - is brought to each devotee. Gifts of varying amounts of currency are given by the devotees to the person carrying the light. They then proceed to fan both their hands across the flame unto their heads and faces, in the act of bathing themselves in its smoke and thus receiving purification. This ārti procedure will be repeated nightly by the audiences in the maidān. Small parcels of the consecrated food or *prasad* (parsad) that was prepared for the occasion are then shared to the congregation. From this day, to the end of the Leela, the Ramleela space is made pure and holy, and no alcoholic beverages or meat dishes are permitted to be either sold, or consumed on its premises.

The gift of money 'offered' by the audience during this and each of the night's ārti will be tallied up as the public's contribution to the performance.

Finally, Pundit Budharat Yankatessu is presented with his *cēdhā*, or gift. It is a tradition that pundits serve their community and are not supposed to charge a fee for their services. So a gift is always given for services rendered by them to the community. The gift usually comprises raw, uncooked food; the equivalent of a full meal for the pundit and his family, some clothes and money depending on the financial means of the host offering the gift. The *cēdhā* is presented in a large, brown paper bag, accompanied by either the touching of the feet of the Pundit or the clasping of the hands and bowing of the gift-giver to the Pundit. This is a continuing, traditional way of making such offerings to Pundits. The Pundit then blesses the giver. It is now 9.15 pm. and the ground, now fully consecrated, will be prepared for the Friday opening night of the First Felicity Ramleela celebrations.[17]

The tall jhanda and the miniature jhandis on the bedi will remain in place for the entire performance period of the Ramleela and, with the other 'decorations' on the bedi, will be the subject of adoration for the entire period of the performance. The adoration will take the form of performing worship, offering lights (ārti) and receiving the blessings from the installed devatas at the bedi, both at the beginning and end of each day's performance for the next eleven days. This sanctified spot will figuratively become the hub of the universe. It will witness both the *rang manch ka puja (*the worship of the stage), as performed by the invocatory ārti commencing each day's performance, and the *mangalam or visharjan,* the benediction by all of the performers at the end of each day's play in the First Felicity maidān Ramleela.

As the days progress in the telling of the epic story, the Ramleela 'grong' will be decorated and redecorated, constantly transformed with appropriate props and other paraphernalia to represent the scenes and reflect the ambience of the environment of each episode of the unfolding story that will be both narrated and dramatized.

ENDNOTES

1. Vikash Ramoutar, P.I. 18th November 2012.
2. Interview of 'Lakshman' at Nolan Street Felicity, 18th Nov 2012, by researcher Jassie Singh
3. Interview of Savitri Rambharose at Nolan Street, Felicity on 18th Nov 2012.

4. This is calculated at the exchange rate in 2014 when the estimates were being finalised.
5. Shivaram and Sirju Ramoutar P.I. in 2014, 2015 and on 24th Nov 2016.
6. Author's personal observations and interviews with both performers and the make-up artists during 'the dressing' period in Nolan Street, during Ramleela 2014.
7. Anuradha Kapur, *Actors, Pilgrims, Kings and Gods: The Ramleela at Ramnagar* (Calcutta: Seagull, 1990)16-18.
8. Messers Saith and Nanak, both members of the management team of the First Felicity Ramleela production. P.I. by author over the years 2008-2015.
9. The stock for the drink is derived from dried seaweed which has been soaked in water for a few hours, then boiled till very soft. Sugar and milk (fresh or condensed), with a dash of vanilla essence, are added. The mixture is then blended to a rich consistency. This local popular drink is claimed to add "prowess" to the muscles.
10. Personal interview of Vikash Ramoutar with researcher Jassie Singh in 2012-2013, and again with the author on 24 Nov 2016.
11. Jasodra Ramoutar, P.I. with author on 24 Nov 2016. Jasodra's uncle, Ramdass Daharrie, then lived in the middle of the 'coconut field' which is today's Green Park Savannah.
12. Satnarine Balkaransingh, *Trinidad Space Speaking through Indo-Trinidadian Rituals and Festivals: 1990-2009*, Ph.D. Dissertation. University of Trinidad and Tobago, 2010.
13. In some Ramleela venues a puja is also performed to the village deity or *gram devta.* In Trinidad this energy form is referred to as *Dee Baba.* See Primnath Gooptar, *The Ramleela of Sangre Grande: Celebrating 25 years of the Sangre Grande Ramleela Committee, 1990-2015* (Trinidad: Caribbean Print Technologies Ltd., 2015) 26-27.
14. P.I. with Pundit Yankatessu, 16thSept 2014.
15. *'Axis Mundi'*, *Encyclopedia of Religion.* Macmillan Reference, USA (2005) 712-713. This is also referred to in Satnarine Balkaransingh's *The Shaping of a Culture,Rituals and Festivals in Trinidad compared with selected counterparts on India, 1990-2014* (Great Britain: Hansib Publications Ltd., 2016) 294-297.
16. Swami Gambhirananda, *Eight Upanishads Vol. One: With the Commentary of Śankarācārya* (Calcutta: Advaita Ashram, 1972) 392-3.
17. These recorded observations were personally made in 2014, the supposedly 99th year of the First Felicity Ramleela production.

PART : III

Fire & Mud: Pageantry on an Epic Scale

Chapter Eight

DAILY PERFORMANCES: DAYS 1-2

Presentational Dynamics

The Leela or story is enacted on an epic scale in 11 consecutive days. It begins with the birth of Rām, the hero of the epic, moving through the various phases of his life; his youth, marriage banishment, his travails during years of exile, the defeat of Raja Rāwan of Lanka, and his return to Ayodhya and coronation as its King. In some earlier years, attempts were made to extend the production to 12 days. The 12th day involved the continuing saga, the story of the banishment of Sita, the birth of Rām's and her sons (Lava and Kush), and their return to Ayodhya to 'sing' the story of Rām to their father, the King. This episode however has not survived in the current production and the Leela has returned to its 11-day, presentation format.

Day 1: Introduction of the Ramleela and Bala Kanda

It has been a long tradition in Felicity for the performance of the Leela to commence on a Friday during or close to the nine nights or *nawrātam* (or *navarātri)* of the bright half of the moon of the month of Ăshwin, so that the burning of the effigy of Rāwan is undertaken on the tenth day (*Vijay Dashami*).This is usually on the following Sunday when a maximum number of spectators can attend.

Today, the first day, the maidān has a spartan look, containing rudimentary props and settings.The performance area, referred to in local parlance as the 'grong', has been measured out in the middle of this Green Park Recreation ground and is 150 feet long by 110 feet wide. This area is staked with fresh bamboo posts, buried 1 foot in the dirt with 3 feet above ground, and cordoned off by an oval-shaped bamboo barrier lashed tightly to the posts separating players from audience.It also conformed to a safety requirement i.e. the need for the barrier to withstand the pressure from the growing daily audiences, especially during the concluding phases of the Leela. In 2007 this barrier became a mixture of bamboo and steel, reflecting local socio-economic changes. In 2016, tall bamboo flag-posts, buried and lashed to the barrier at regular intervals, are flying triangular pennants in solid colours of red, yellow, black and white. They form an aerial, oval-shaped, multicoloured design around this 'playing' area.

The barrier is punctuated by four covered enclosures; three are raised wooden platforms and the fourth is erected flat on the ground. The three elevated platforms are situated on the north, north-east and south of the performance area. Each platform measures 16 feet x 8 feet. Each is of equal height, approximately 5 feet above ground and accessed by wooden steps. The northern, wooden platform has traditionally represented the palace of the kingdom of Ayodhya, the birth place of Sri Rām. This platform is covered by a coloured tarpaulin and sparsely decorated with some small potted plants, colourful fabric and multicoloured light bulbs. Its backdrop carries a painted scene and icons of the royal court of Ayodhya. Ayodhya, the legendary kingdom of the Raghu royal race of the solar dynasty and ruled by Raja Dasarath, is decorated in yellow and gold, and trimmed with braids and sequins, with a colourful palanquin hanging directly over the 'throne' chairs. The throne is actually a short wooden bench positioned in the middle of the platform, covered by a coloured bed sheet. It stands in front of a large, painted backdrop that is the back wall of the 'throne' room. Four red flags, 25-30 feet tall, fly on each corner of the stage representing the royal colours of the kingdom. This structure will be used as the 'set' for several scenes, converted and enhanced accordingly, during the course of the drama.

The southern platform, directly facing 'Ayodhya' represents the palace of the kingdom of Lanka and home of King Rāwan. A palanquin also hangs over the 'throne' of the King, with a similar wooden bench covered with a bed sheet being his throne. Behind the throne stands a brightly painted backdrop of a local artist's impression of a chariot on which is mounted Rāwan in royal attire. Lanka's palace is decorated in bright shiny green, black and dark blue fabric with tinsel. Four black flags, the same height as those of Ayodhya, flutter in the four corners around Lanka's palace.

The staircases, of 5 steps each in both of these 'palaces', are placed in front of the platforms, and are mounted directly from the performance 'grong' on to the throne. The structure, of minimal décor and representative of the story, will also be used for enacting various episodes of the story as it unfolds in Lanka. An area of at least 10-15 feet in diameter, extending to the front and two sides of both palaces, is delineated as the outer reaches of the kingdoms of Ayodhya and Lanka respectively. Jhandis are erected and lashed to the bamboo barrier, symbolically demarcating the kingdoms' geographical control. The decors of these physical structures will change to depict other scenes and locations in the environment associated with the winding narrative and changing scenario of the story.

The barrier at the north-eastern periphery of the performance space merges into another covered tent housing a raised, wooden platform, approximately 20 feet square and about 4'-4½ feet high. Except for the floor or platform in this tent which is covered with a rug, the rest of the tent is not decorated. There is a small table at its south-western edge. On the table are a harmonium, the script of the Leela and an open copy of the Tulsidas Rāmcharitmānas on a wooden book stand or *rehal.*[1] This is actually the *singhasana*, the metaphorical 'seat of the lion' where the Pundit stands, chants and delivers his *katha* or story. In this case it is the recitation of the verses, their interpretation and dialogues from the scenes so that the performers can enact them in a pantomime or dance drama (n*rityanatika*) format.

Immediately behind the *singhasana*, in the same tent, is an empty area into which a 3 ton, flat-bed truck had earlier in the evening driven and parked. On its open tray is the equipment for the entire sound system of the Leela - amplifiers, sound mixers, microphones and speaker boxes.The sound technician, Natty Ramjass who accompanies the truck will perform the same function daily; driving into this secured, covered enclosure and providing the sound system for the entire period of the Ramleela. This enclosure functionally will be the engine room of the production, the 'command centre' and 'seat' of narration cum direction of the Leela.

Lower down the field, to the south and left of the command centre, is a smaller tent about 10 feet square. It juts out a few feet into the performance area, providing a line of sight to the entire maidān. It is floored with a low wooden ramp approx. 8'x4½'x4" high. The tassa ensemble of drummers and other percussionists perform from this vantage point for the entire period of the Ramleela. Eighteen jhandis are lashed to the barrier, around the 'grong', nine in the vicinity of Lanka (all fluttering black flags), and nine of red, yellow and white nearer to Ayodhya. Shrubs are planted at various spots in the consecrated, performance area.

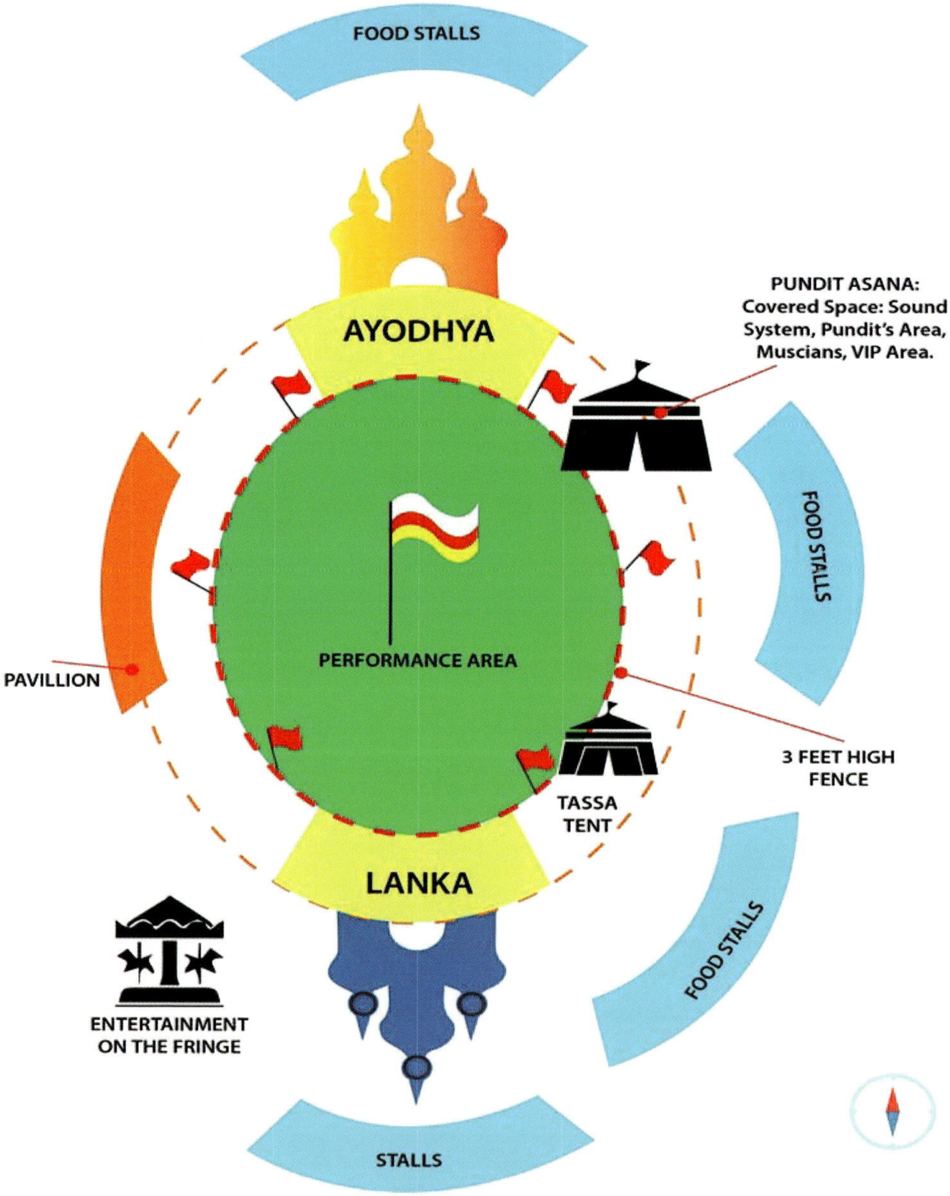

Diagramatic representation of the performance space: the 'grong'

This is the basic design format for the performance space and will continue to be so, save for additions and subtractions of props, sets and décor to suit the changing scenario. Areas within this open-air performing stage will be demarcated for various important sites and events as the story progresses. These will include hermitages or ashrams of the various rishis or sages; gardens, temporary dwelling locations for Rām and his wife Sita; Pushpavātika, the flower garden where Rām and Sita first set eyes on each other; and Ashok Vātika, the grove of Ashoka trees, in Lanka where Sita was held captive by Rāwan.

Behind the barrier and around the entire play area is the audience enclosure. This space also contains an uncovered, steel fabricated pavilion at the western end. About 25-30 ft. behind the audience, at the northern, eastern and southern sides of the 'play area' is an area identified for the sale of street foods and other village knick-knacks: confectionaries, local beverages, plastic toys and fabrics. These activities will be undertaken in the temporarily erected tents stretching in a line; the centre of village commerce and much animation for the next 11 days. At the south western corner of the Park a refurbished chair-plane and merry-go-round are being assembled. This will also attract the young and young at heart to snatch quick rides between scenes in the Leela. This Ramleela ground is anticipated to be a hive of intense activity, attracting thousands of people of all ages, races, creeds and socio-economic status.

At 6.45 pm., the performers begin arriving at the 'grong'. The main characters of the Leela-Rām and his three brothers; Lakshman, Bharat and Shatrughan - arrive. They are dressed in fabrics of yellow, white, green and blue, with heavy facial make-up and are adorned with crowns and jewelry. Each one carries his respective bow and arrows. There are five members of the opposing side, led by an imposing character wearing a full-body costume. He wears a white face mask and a striped cape of shiny cloth falling from shoulder to heels. He carries a sword and shield. This masked character is Rāwan, the main antagonist in the story. His entourage all wear elaborately decorated costumes, jewelry and crowns and carry weapons. There is Nārad muni, the interplanetary messenger, and his understudy. All wear ghungroos or ankle bells strapped to their bare feet. The ensemble of tassa drummers, four grounds men, the Pundit and children are all suitably attired depending on whose side (Rām's or Rāwan's) they are performing. There are also two life-size birds in unfinished costumes.

The cast of the First Felicity Ramleela performing Ārti at the foot of the Mool Jhanda

The performers enter the maidān and head directly for the evening benediction where they line up, facing east, under the tall jhanda, in the middle of the performance area, in front of the bedi. There are now 20 performers standing left of the Pundit's singhasana.These comprise the complement of the first day's performers.

Pundit Yankatessu chants from the Ramcharitmanas and delivers his narrative from the Singhasana

Instead of the Pundit taking the usual, traditional seat on the singhasana to read the text from the Rāmcharitmānas, he stands behind a microphone and his harmonium, with the copy of the Rāmcharitmānas now resting on the harmonium. Next to this is his written script as his guide, placed on the low book stand (rehal*)*, in front of him. On his immediate right are the live musicians sitting on the ground, on a rug. Behind them are chairs for important visitors. Pundit Budharat Yankatessu chants the opening verses from the text, translates it into *Trinhinglish (*the mixed dialect of Trinidad English, mixed with Sanskrit, Hindi, and Bhojpuri languages), and conducts the Ramleela proceedings. In this standing posture, he will conduct each evening's programme.

The opening verses are chanted to commence the ārti. Ārti is a significant part of the Leela. It begins and terminates the evening's performances. It is really an important ritual in which a devotee pays respect to the divine, represented in several forms, both male and female. A lighted deya or incense is rotated in front of a person, the image or the visage of the deity being propitiated in an act of homage. Ārti can be done at any time of the day but there are usually six auspicious times - based on energy levels in the atmosphere - for its performance; at 3.00 am. 6.00 am or dawn, 9.00 am, noon, at *sandhya* or twilight, and at 9.00 pm.

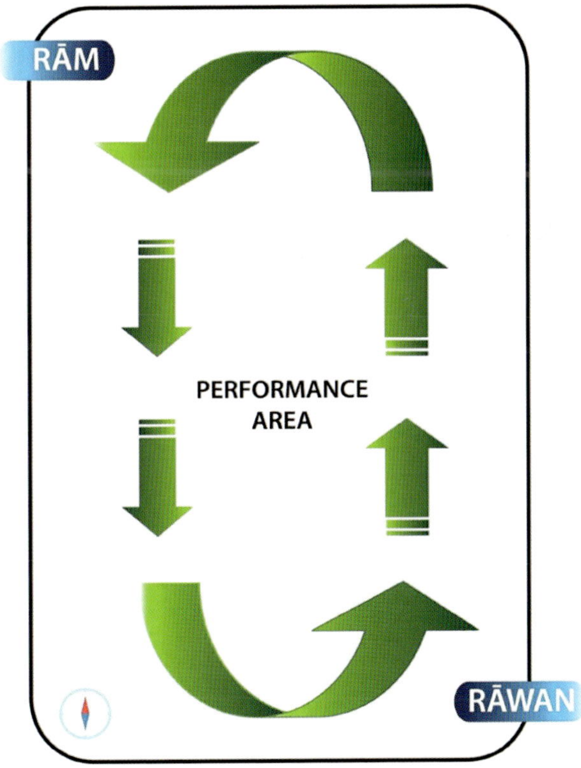

The processional movements of the warriors of Rām and Rāwan which begin and end each day of the Ramleela performance

As the ārti begins, each individual performer takes a brass plate or tharia containing a lighted deya - small clay pot with oil and wick - and some flowers, approaches the bedi and proceeds to wave the light in a clockwise direction bathing the several images that were installed there yesterday, with light and sanctified smoke. The live music continues until the entire row of performers have done the ārti. At the end of the benediction some of the main actors, the *swarūps* and *pātras* proceed to the Pundit's *singhasana*, performing the respectful gesture of individually touching his feet, seeking his blessing for success in this their first day's play.

A national election campaign is currently in progress, hence the small audience. Today (2007) the UNC Alliance political party is having a well-advertised, public meeting at Montrose Junction, a few kilometres away from the maidān. This is a traditional opposition territory (read Indo-Trinidadian area), and the campaign is in full heat, as they present their battery of platform speakers. The Pundit explains to the sparse audience of approximately one hundred people that they are witnessing the beginning of the first day of the Ramleela which is actually a Rāmayāna Yagna that has had an unbroken history of over nine decades.

At 7.20 pm., the two main groups, beginning from the opposite ends of the maidān and moving anti-clockwise, proceed to circumambulate the 'grong'. One is headed by Rām, his brothers and Narad muni. Armed with their respective weapons Rām's group, beginning from Ayodhya, travels west in double file. They travel around and then across the 'grong', with their bows and arrows moving in synchronized characteristic choreographed movements. Simultaneously Rāwan and his troupe of performers, the *pātras* from the opposing encampment travel around the periphery of the savannah, wielding their shields and swords in another loosely choreographed formation. Both 'sides' or groups are constantly executing their characteristic Ramleela dance steps, a hop-skip-skip (1- 2-3) action.They then return to their respective bases.

After this 10-minute parade in synchronized movements to the accompaniment of tassa drum rhythms, the story begins. The Pundit, standing behind his table, gives the genesis of the Ramleela in Trinidad. As he narrates, a long line of performers assembles. They are dressed in traditional village Indian attire; females are in long skirts and bodices with orhni or head veil, males in dhoti and kurta, all looking haggard and lost .A young boy, clad in a white shirt and dhoti at the top of the line, carries a copy of the Rāmayāna on his head. He leads the procession in the circumambulation of the maidān in a clock-wise direction to the singing of the popular bhajan, '*Siya Rām, Jai Jai Rām, Jai Jai Ram.*' The rhythm is supplied by both dholak and tassa drum ensemble. A *chowpai (*a four line verse from the Rāmcharitmānas) is then sung above the tassa drumming as the Pundit narrates the struggle of the indentured immigrants to keep the story of the Rāmayāna alive, while crossing the 'kala pani' the black waters of the ocean. He sings the *chowpai,* narrates in English and sings again while playing his harmonium. As he narrates in the Trinidad English dialect: "They pray, they don't know where they are going." The performers dramatize the journey at sea, the swaying of the ship."Then they see a land mass. It is Trinidad." They enact the disembarkation, bowing to the sacred soil, touching it with their foreheads. The performers enact the story on the greens of the maidān. The Pundit continues: "They have arrived in beautiful Trinidad… and then commence to introduce their religious beliefs, creative and dramatic arts."

Following this prologue, the story of Valmiki's *Rāmayāna* is introduced by the Pundit Yankatessu.It is taken from the first of the seven books that comprise the Rāmcharitmānas, Bala Kanda. He introduces this Rāmayāna, starting with the legend of the sage Nārad, speaking to the former highway robber, Ratnakar, who was in the act of robbing him of his meagre belongings. He asks Ratnakar why it was necessary to perform this act. Ratnakar replied that it was to meet his family obligation. He was then asked whether his family was aware of his method of sustaining them. The sage suggested that Ratnakar return to his home and enquire from his wife about her reaction to his method for supporting her. He did. She replied that she was not concerned with how he earned his livelihood, only that he supported her. Ratnakar was shocked. He had received a revelation. His family did not care how he provided for their livelihood, so he left home and gave up his brigandry to become a holy man, chanting the name of God. But as he chants, Rāma, the words sound like 'maara, maara' (kill, kill) until the words finally emerge as 'Rām, Rām'. After much chanting Ratnakar achieves enlightenment and is named Valmiki, meaning the one around whom an ant hill grew.

The tassa ensemble performs as sage Nārad enters the ashram of the meditating Ratnakar, now sage Valmiki. They embrace warmly as Valmiki welcomes Nārad and offers him a seat. A white plastic chair is rushed to the ashram and Nārad is seated. The Pundit narrates and mimetic action takes place on the 'grong'. Valmiki asks: "Oh knowing Nārad, tell me, who among the heroes of this world is the highest of virtue and wisdom?" Knowing, through his supernatural powers why Valmiki has put the question, Nārad answers, "Rām is the hero you asked for." Sage Nārad then briefly narrates to

Valmiki the story of Rām. So impressed is Valmiki when he hears the story that long after Nārad has departed, his mind is fully immersed in it, and he is pondering on it as he goes to the Tamaso River for his morning ablutions. Valmiki walks to a piece of blue fabric spread on the ground. This fabric represents the river.

As he walks on the riverbank his attention is caught by two love birds on a nearby tree, 'Ramajaying', or sporting and singing on their joys of life and love. The male bird suddenly falls, hit by a hunter's arrow. The female bird seeing her lover rolling on the ground, laments in piteous fashion. Miming continues with the archer, the birds and Valmiki. Valmiki shouts out a curse, "Oh hunter, as you have killed one of those love-intoxicated birds you will wander homeless all of your long years." In a moment the sage recovers himself and wonders why he had lost himself in anger. He soliloquises: "What right had I to curse the hunter? Why was I so deceived by emotion?" Recalling the words of his curse, the Rishi marvels at the rhythm of the words. He discovers that his pity has taken shape in a beautiful *sloka,* a poetic stanza. He thinks that all this is part of the mysterious Leela of God and goes into meditation.

Lord Brahma, the Creator, appears to him saying; "Be not afraid, these things happen to start you on the story of Rām. From sorrow (*soka* - mourning) springs verse (*sloka*) and in this metre and rhythm the story should be told. I shall give you the boon of vision, narrated in a metric style, of what has happened, and even how the characters thought and looked, as clearly as one sees the things lying on the palm of one's hand. You shall sing it for the benefit of the world. My blessings go with you". Valmiki fixed the pattern of the verses firmly in his mind and then composed the *Rāmayāna* in that metre and rhythm.

The scene changes. Gods, rishis or learned men, and other holy men are being troubled by evil demonic forces stalking the land. This is being dramatized with the assistance of the tassa rhythm. The holy men pray to Lord Vishnu, the protector of the universe, and to Mother Earth, Pritvi Mā, for help to rid them of this evil. Lord Vishnu and Pritvi promise to take birth on earth, as deities, and wipe out all evil.

The narration of the story takes place through the singing of various types of verses: *dohas, chaupais and chhands,* sung from Tulsidas' Rāmcharitmānas. This is the Gobind Bhavan Karyalaya, Gita Press Gorakhpur, Fourth Edition, 1986. In this regard the text taken from the Rāmcharitmānas is delivered with many variations. There is the variation of seeing that part of it chanted and simultaneously enacted in mimetic, pantomime format. Then there is the other part of the text that is only read by the pundit and heard by the audience without the performers' dramatization. This is equally important to establish continuity of the story and the linking of important aspects of it.

At 8.20 pm., the performance is interrupted by a member of the Organising Committee of the Felicity Ramleela as he welcomes the audience. Then the tassa music plays as the performers of both sides 'dance' down the middle of the field, parallel with each other but dancing in opposite directions. The audience has now grown to approximately two hundred. The political meeting is in progress a short distance away. It has pulled the usually large audience on day 1. General elections are due on 5th November, 2007.

As the Pundit continues the narration, the swarūps sit on the wet grass. Rain had fallen during the day and the audience area behind the barrier is soggy. The second part of the evening's story begins. The Pundit reads from the book: "There was great enmity in the land. Hate, violence and crookedness reigned. Mother Earth, in the guise of a cow, goes to Brahma's abode to plead the case for a peaceful earth." A player climbs inside a papier maché form of a cow, hangs the straps - that support the costume of the cow - on his shoulder and 'dances' (in Ramleela rhythm) towards Brahma Loka, the abode of Lord Brahma. Brahma Loka has become the stage where 'Ayodhya' is located. Pritvi Ma, the earth, bows to Brahma pleading for its cleansing of all negativity.

Brahma consoles her. Then Shiva, the lord of annihilation who stands nearby, advises. The Pundit gives Shiva's advice: "Oh Brahma, that bond you are speaking about is one, and is equally present everywhere… It is revealed by love, as fire is manifested by friction... It resides in the heart where there is love". Tassa stops. Brahma, with tears in his eyes, begins to pray. The Pundit advises that it is that prayer of Brahma that resulted in the coming of Shri Rām. Prithvi Ma listens. The cow actually shakes its head in the act of listening. He also informs the audience that the narration of the episode of "Brahma's prayer is for tomorrow", Day 2. The evening's episode of the Leela comes to an end. The tassa drumming begins and two groups of players perform their closing dance, moving parallel with each other but on opposite sides of the maidān.

At 8.50 pm., the performers assemble for the closing prayer under the *Mool Jhanda*. They perform ārti to live musical accompaniment of dholak, dhantāl and harmonium. They sing: "*Ārti Shree Rām ayana Je Ke jai...*" Closing prayers are chanted by the Pundit. This ends with the entire cast of players and the audience singing the verse: "*Twamewa mata cha pita twamewa...*" ending with "*Prem se bolo ... Hara Hara Mahadev...*"

While the ārti is not a part of the text of the Ramleela, it is part of the tradition of the reading of the Rāmcharitmānas, and hence in which the folk Leela is performed. The evening's episode ends at 9.00 pm. Even as audience departs, tents are still being erected for the sale of foods and other items of village commerce.

Day 2: Bala Kanda

Rām's birth, youth, training and first test of ability

The second day's play is also taken from the first of the seven books that comprise the Rāmcharitmānas, *Bala Kanda.* It describes the kingdom of Kosala and its capital city, Ayodhya where King Dasarath ruled. It explains the circumstances surrounding the conception and the birth of Shri Rām and his brothers, and their early years. As adolescents, their education and training in the *gurukul* or hermitage of the Guru Vashishta in preparation for their later life is explained; and finally the brothers return to the palace. They are then sent to destroy the demons who were molesting the meditations of the holy men.

It is 6.45 pm., the performers are assembling in a line in front of the temporary sanctum for the evening's ārti. A few minutes later, the Pundit commences to chant verses in Sanskrit and then sings a popular bhajan, accompanying himself with his harmonium. His other musical accompanists sitting next to him on the floor play the dholak, the double mouthed hand drum; the dandataal, the iron percussive rod, struck by another horse-shoe shaped iron; and majeera or small hand-held cymbal. Today, the Pundit dons a white t-shirt and white pants with his musicians wearing orange t-shirts and pants.

Some members of the small, early audience of about 100 sing along and gently clap their hands. Older ladies, with their heads covered by orhnis, or light, fabric head scarves (a common sight of yester year), bow their heads, and close their eyes in pious supplication; they gently clap along as they sway to the rhythm, completely absorbed in the music and the moment. As the music continues, the performers, singly and in groups, take turns to perform ārti on the bedi, and then with open palms fan the smoke on to their bodies in symbolic purification. A long blast of the *shankh* is sounded, energizing the surrounding atmosphere and sanctifying the maidān. The main performers proceed to the pundit's singhasana, touch his feet and receive his blessing for yet another successful day's play.

At 7.00 pm., with the ārti rituals complete, the performers proceed directly to their respective areas of Ayodhya and Lanka. Tassa drummers commence their drumming in a uniquely Trinidad style of *Kaharwa taal*, the time cycle of eight beats, and the groups begin their circumambulation of the 'grong' in characteristic Ramleela 'dancing' movements. Rām's entourage is immaculately and regally dressed in yellow, saffron, green and red dhotis, garlands around their necks, and is bare-chested. Their waists are tied with *kamarbands*, fan-shaped sashes dropping in front of their dhotis. Each one wears a sash draped across the chest from the shoulder, bright golden crowns atop their heads, elaborate facial make-up and jewelry. They proceed in double file, wielding white, crepe paper–covered bows and arrows wrapped in parts by bright tinsel foil. They move down and then across the stage, bows and arrows swinging in unison to the rhythm of the drums.

Lanka's entourage is also impeccably attired in long sleeved, shiny green, mauve, purple, yellow and golden lamé tops and dhotis, fabric face-masks and sparkling, jeweled crowns. Brandishing intricately designed, shining, vicious-looking swords and shields, they begin the circumambulation of the field in anti-clockwise direction, commencing from the south.

Both adversarial groups performing the hop and skip theme step, move parallel to each other as in day one. When they complete their movements to the length of the field they wheel around in rhythm, never out of character and approach their opponents, circling one another in mock combat. Arrows are shot in the air. The opponents raise their shields over their heads in protection against the falling arrows and with upraised flashing swords they engage and disengage. Disengagements are made through quick pirouettes (*chakkars*) and each group returns to its respective camp.

Tonight, the advertising poster which had been initially planted on the wrought iron barrier - three feet high around the ground, advertising brand name soft drinks and water - is almost removed. Two pavilions constructed out of two-inch angle-iron rods and steel have been erected. They are fabricated seven stair cases high, each row seating approximately 10 persons. They were installed courtesy the National Carnival Commission of the Ministry of Community Development, Culture and Gender Affairs.

At about 7.20 pm. Pundit Yankatessu commences his narration of the evening's script. He tells his growing audience of about 300 persons - as time passes the audience will grow larger - of the need for the appropriate environment necessary for this incarnation of God on earth. He explains that: "Each incarnation requires different sets of circumstances and environments for God to manifest in a particular form on earth to undertake the specific duty for which he or she has come. Shri Rām is to be conceived and be born in the royal household of Raja Dasarath in the city of Ayodhya in the kingdom of Kosala." Reading from his text he elaborates on the description of Ayodhya, on the King and his ministers, and on the wise sages who are part of the royal advisers viz Guru Vashishta and Vaanadev.This ancient kingdom of Kosala is situated in North India. In this case, the incarnation of God (also referred to as Vishnu), will be renamed Rām.

The scene changes. Raja Dasarath is depicted forlorn and dejected. He paces the ground, hands folded behind his back. The Pundit narrates that the Raja acknowledges that he has been adequately blessed materially, pointing out his worldly possessions. He has three wives but is sad that he has no progeny. He considers undertaking a sacrificial ritual so as to beget children. Sage Shringa is invited to perform this ritual.

On the field the sage (a young boy, hardly a teenager, wearing a rope-like beard) comes and sits on a low platform - about six inches high. He faces north. In front of him a small fire is kindled in a make-shift *hawan-kund*. Raja Dasarath, clad in a *pitambar* or yellow dhoti, an *angwastram* or stole around his shoulders and a crown, and sage Shringa (suitably attired), perform the sacrificial ritual to the fire.Cooked, sweetened rice or 'paisan' is being blessed as the Vyas chants a few appropriate chaupais or sacred verses over the microphone and describes the nature of the puja. He is reading from page 160 of the Rāmcharitmānas. With the ritual completed on the wet grass, Dasarath goes to his three wives, the queens, all played by women: Kaushalya, the eldest; Kaikeyi and Sumintra. They are sitting on the Ayodhya raised stage. Blessed 'paisan' is distributed to each wife, to eat.

The Pundit instructs the musicians to "play some drums to herald the birth of Rām." He reads: "The sky is filled with the sound of the kettle drums. The *shankh* (conch shell) and the *ghantas (*gongs) are sounded." A festive hand of tassa begins. Shortly thereafter four babies are born to the wives. The Pundit raises his voice to a crescendo: "...Rām is born... *Hara Mahadev*." Four large dolls are produced for the audience to see. "Lord Vishnu, the protector of the world, incarnates as Rām, the son of queen Kaushilya. Bharat is born to Kaikeyi, the second queen and Lakshman and Shatrughan are born to Sumitra. Another *chaupai* is chanted (p162). Lord Vishnu standing in heaven - symbolically represented by an upraised pedestal in the 'grong' - raises his right hand in the direction of Ayodhya, and gives blessing. There is rejoicing in the palace and the kingdom. There is music and dancing to celebrate the births. The tassa drums accompany the dancing of the people of Ayodhya. They dance in the 'grong'. A little boy child is produced from the palace (the raised stage), and brought down to the rest of the performers - courtiers and servants of the palace- on the 'grong'. Nārad, the interplanetary messenger in traditional head gear (he wears his thick, black, long hair tied in a top-knot), and his understudy (wearing a crown

Nārad muni and his understudy with their veena on their shoulders perform their parikrama around the 'grong'

'because it looked pretty and the audience liked the costume') make their way around the field, each strumming his veena (an ancient string instrument) and clashing his *kartaal* (a wooden, tambourine–like instrument), spreading the good news through mime. There is overall happiness at the birth of Rām. The tassa drum rhythm enhances the festive mood of the occasion.

There is a quick scene change, fast forward. Four young swarūps with bows and arrows make a circumambulation or *parikrama* of the ground. Nārad muni joins them. The rhythm of the tassa accompanies them. Fast forward the scene again. King Dasarath is happy at seeing his children growing up before him. The Pundit informs his audience: "Rām is an ocean of felicity, a bundle of joy to his parents and the citizens of the kingdom." Raja Dasarath walks with four little boys on the ground, in front of the kingdom of Ayodhya, to the accompaniment of the tassa drums.

The *Vyas* continues his narration, reading from the Rāmcharitmānas. Guru Vashishta visits the palace and informs the King that the time has arrived for the boys to commence their education and training. After much hugging and blessings, the swarūps take leave of their parents and with graceful, stylized movement, depart with the guru to his *gurukul*, the school and hermitage where they will reside during the period of their studies. At the *gurukul* these future leaders of Kosala receive education in a number of subject areas. The Pundit elaborates: "These include statesmanship, diplomacy, leadership and jurisprudence, civil administration plus instructions in military warfare; the use of arms and ammunition for the protection of the kingdom. All of this is in preparation for their later life. …" Some of this training is demonstrated on the field as Pundit-ji speaks.

The audience has grown to about 400 by 7.25 pm. Meanwhile, the merry-go-round and chair planes, now fully assembled at the southwestern end of the savannah, are in operation. The young members of the audience have gravitated to this area. The two engines of the machines which have seen better days chug along with a characteristic, muffled sound.

Notwithstanding the on-going drama inside the barriers, the village vendors continue to erect stalls around the periphery of the play area, behind the audiences in pre-identified locations. At least five stalls have been fully constructed and are doing a brisk trade. Audiences are split between viewing the performance and visiting the stalls with their mouth-watering aromas, enticing customers to patronize.

After their training the swarūps return to the palace, much to the delight of their parents. It is 9.00 pm. The Pundit introduces Sat Balkaransingh, 'a national cultural icon' and asks him to briefly address the audience. He complies, wishing them well and asks them to continue to attend and bring others to the Ramleela. He wishes success to the performers "for the next nine days" and ends with the salutation: "*Shri Rām Chandra ki... .*" The audience finishes the salutations with him, collectively responding, "Jai". Another member of the executive committee of the Ramleela speaks to the audience, reading out the list of sponsors, acknowledging their assistance for contributing to this year's festival.

The final "dance" of the twenty four performers is done, the Ayodhya group wielding their bows and arrows, the Lanka group their swords and shields. They circumambulate the inner periphery of the barrier to the live tassa drumming, in the same format as when they began earlier that evening. This is immediately followed by the closing prayer and arti, led by Pundit Yankatessu, in his standing position, playing his harmonium and singing into the microphone with his live musical accompanists sitting on the floor at his side. The evening's episode ends at 9.15 pm.

ENDNOTES

1. The *rehal* is a short wooden book-stand. In Trinidad holy books are placed on it, and from which the verses are chanted, or the narrative is read, without the reader having to keep the book in the hand.

Chapter Nine

DAILY PERFORMANCES: DAYS 3-4

Day 3: Bala Kanda

Rām and Lakshman clear the Danadaka forest of rakshasa and Sita is discovered

This is the third day of the annual Felicity Ramleela folk drama. More flags have been erected around the inner periphery of the maidān. Additional buntings have also been strung across the ground and above the heads of the performers. This evening's episode begins at 7.05 pm. with an invocatory prayer, sung in praise of the supreme God in the forms of Ganesha, Saraswati and Rām. Ārti is performed to Pritvi Mata or Mother Earth, to the Rāmayāna, and the other sacred books, including the Puranas. This is followed by prayer to Devi Durga as Shakti, the female principle, mother of the earth.

The initial processional group 'dance' is announced by Pundit Yankatessu. The entire entourage of Rām 'dances' down the performance 'grong' on their right side, north to south, moving in an anti-clockwise direction. Those of Rāwan's group 'dance' up, south to north also in anticlockwise direction. They cross in mid field, briefly engage in mock combat and retreat to their respective groupings.

The Pundit chants from the book and commences the narration of the evening's episode. He explains that Sage Vishwamitra is seeking from Raja Dasarath the assistance of Rām and Lakshman to help him rid the area around his hermitage of demonic beings, Mārīcha and Subaahu. As he talks, the destructive actions of the two demons are demonstrated through pantomime in the maidān. Rain begins to fall. Umbrellas go up, but play continues.

Sage Vishwamitra unexpectedly arrives in Ayodhya. He is dressed in yellow garments, dhoti and kurta with a large beaded garland. He is welcomed by King Dasarath in a joyous mood. Dasarath descends from his throne on to the 'grong' and performs the usual salutatory welcome accorded to Gurus. A white plastic chair is fetched from the main tent. Plastic bottles of water are brought and handed to Dasarath. He pours the water on the guru's feet and washes them.

Raja Dasarath washes the feet of Sage Vishwamitra

The rain is now falling heavily. A few members of the audience continue to sit in the uncovered western pavilion. The rain comes in torrents, pushed by a steady north-south breeze. It pelts unto the pavilion as the audience now scrambles for cover. Open umbrellas, large and small and plastic sheets are visible everywhere. There is a profusion of coloured coverings. People also dart for shelter under the food stalls. Despite the rain, the food vending stalls are doing a brisk trade.

Back on the 'grong', the king is unaware of the purpose of Vishwamitra's visit. Pundit Yankatessu chants the verses from the text and explains in English to the audience what is happening to the holy men of the Dandaka forest. There are two ferocious demons or *rākshas*, Mārīcha and Subaahu who are disturbing the peace and well-being of the generally peaceful atmosphere of that area. They are showering blood and raw meat on the rituals and worship as sage Vishwamitra and the other ascetics perform their prayers and make the sacrificial offerings to the sacred fire.

The chaos that reigns in the forest is being portrayed on the field. Tassa drummers are beating a battle rhythm as the two demons, dressed in black, appear on the 'grong'. The demons continue to shower 'blood, raw flesh and other unclean things' into the sacrificial offerings of the sages, contaminating their rituals. They are creating fear and havoc, uprooting trees. The trees are really shrubs that were planted earlier that day as part of the props for the evening's drama. These symbolic tree props are uprooted and flung about, destroying the hermitages of the holy men. The jungle folks (performers dressed in simple attire) are terrorized by the demons. They run helter-skelter as the demons, wielding huge bows, covered by pink crepe paper, chase after them.

The scene shifts back to Ayodhya. Raja Dasarath and Sage Vishwamitra engage in dialogue. Dasarath enquires from Vishwamitra the purpose of his visit so that he can fulfill it. Then Vishwamitra, miming the dialogue of the *Vyas*, gets up from his seat, walks away, turns, faces Dasarath and asks for Rām and Lakshman to accompany him to his hermitage to destroy the two demons so that peace and order can be restored. Dasarath is stunned and bewildered at the request. He hesitates to accede to this request to send his young sons to battle *rākshas*.The Pundit narrates: "He pleads that the princes are too young to face such ferocious enemies." Sage Vashishta enters and reminds Dasarath: "*Raghu Kula riti...prana jaye...vachan na jaye...*" The Pundit interprets: "A king who gives his word cannot take it back. His life may go but his word is his bond".[1] Dasarath relents and summons Rām and Lakshman to the Royal Court. Both princes receive their instructions and the blessing of Rani Kaushilya before leaving with Sage Vishwamitra.

As they leave the palace, the Pundit reminds the audience of the injunctions and discipline of the cultural traditions. One is that they must think carefully about making a pledge, for a pledge must be kept. The second is that in the household, the children must always receive the blessings of the parents and immediate elders before embarking on any journey or major endeavour. It is an injunction prescribed in the scriptures for Hindus and all peoples to follow. The audience listens attentively. The refurbished engine of the chair plane, with its full payload of riders, keeps up its chugging sound as the chairs whirl, fanning out into the rain. The food stalls continue their thriving trade. The tassa plays on as the Pundit speaks above the drumming.

The tassa accompanies the departure of Rām, his brother and the guru as they depart westwards, towards the hermitage. As this is happening a new scenario, a side scene that is local in origin, unfolds on the 'grong'.

A masked male character, wearing an old pair of ragged khaki pants and tattered white shirt, head covered with a tight skull cap, walks the 'grong' inside the barrier with a brown dog (a village mongrel) on a leash. An old pair of green binoculars hangs from his neck. Neither man nor dog is bothered by the heavy rainfall. Occasionally he stops, his dog also stopping at his side, and peers at the audience through his binoculars. Concurrent with this hilarious side show, Rām and Lakshman are "jumping" away in their "hop skip" step, searching for the demons while the guru shelters. Synchronizing their movements with the tassa rhythm, covering the entire 'grong', they are oblivious to the dramatic irony of the transposed scenario of the estate 'overseer' of bygone days. It is a satirical, playful protest, possibly a bitter comment - using this subversive metaphor of the estate overseer supervising his workers in a different village setting - to express dissent with a political socio-economic situation of earlier times. Performance art has blended with performative tradition. The rain is falling but nothing stops the unfolding scene. Yet even as this scenario plays itself on the periphery of the barrier, the action of the main story continues in mid-field.

The warrior clan crosses the Ganges River and enters the dense forest of Dandaka. A rākshas, a terrible demon named Tādakā is lurking in the bushes. Tādakā sees the two brothers and thinks that their destruction will be easy. They

Rām and Lakshman battle Tādakā in the Dandaka Forrest.

engage in battle, encircling one another. Other demons are looking on from the sidelines, doing their hop, skip movements in anticipation of the battle. The tassa is drumming in battle tempo.

Rām, whose bow is already strung, shoots at Tādakā. The Pundit announces the demise of the demon. But the bow's string is not carrying. The arrow falls lamely to the ground. The Pundit again announces: "Tādakā is shot by Rām's arrow". The audience waits with bated breath. The arrow again does not reach its mark. The demon has dodged it. The tassa rhythm is running. The Pundit announces for the third time "Tādakā is shot by Rām". Rām dances closer, takes aim and shoots. The arrow now finds its mark. Tādakā falls to the ground on his back. A cheer rises from the audience which has grown to about five hundred.

The high frequency sound of the tassa has disturbed the alarm on the Pundit's car. It goes off in a siren wail. He calmly stops his narration, takes out the car keys from his pocket, deactivates the alarm and returns to the singing of his chaupai, accompanied by his live musicians, chanting the mantras over the microphone as the sages at the ashram of Vishwamitra prepare for worship and for making offerings to the sacred fire. A fire is kindled. A few male characters in sage attire make offerings to a burning sacrificial fire. Meanwhile, Nārad muni, the interplanetary messenger, continuing on his cosmic rounds, dances pass the sacred fire. "Nārāyana, Nārāyana", chants Nārad muni. Nārad, with his characteristic top-knot hair style and a large veena resting on his shoulder - travels around the cosmos. His travel is represented by his constant circumambulation, moving in his unique 'dance movements' at the periphery of the maidān, just inside its barrier.

The rākshas (as) Mārīcha and Subaahu, who have been sent by Rāwan to disturb the sacrifices of the holy men, are alerted by the fire and make their appearance. The havan fire continues to be guarded by Rām and Lakshman with their bows strung with arrows in readiness for a battle. Mārīcha and Subaahu, after their movements in the nearby bushes, now appear and begin to shower unclean things on the sacrificial fire, defiling the purity of the worship. They approach the two young brothers, circling them in midfield. The tassa drums provide the rhythm for the battle. The young warriors cross the demons with bows drawn. The demons wield their swords and shields. Rām and Lakshman continue to encircle, shooting with their bows and arrows. The narrator informs his audience that: "The first arrow, a blunt one, is released. It is blunt, just a warning to Mārīcha, the uncle of Rāwan…"

Then other arrows are released. Waves of attack and repulsion take place between the young princes and their opponents. Pundit narrates: "Then Rām releases the weapon, *Maanavaastra*, which wraps Mārīcha and flings him a hundred yojanas,[2] near the sea" Mārīcha actually falls on the ground, flat on his back. He then takes aim at Subaahu and releases the *Aagneyaastra,* a fire projectile, from his bow. A lighted, arrow-like, fire cracker is actually released from his bow into the night sky. The princes' weapons figuratively find their target, utterly destroying the entire rākshas' army. The sages are overjoyed. Flowers are showered on the brothers. By this time, the performers are wet to the bones but they continue as if there is no rain. They remain in character, not missing a step, in rhythm and tempo to the tassa.

The Pundit shifts his narration to another scene. In the kingdom of Mithila ruled by Raja Janak the Pundit narrates: "Janak is plowing the soil." Both Janak and his plough are yellow; yellow costumes (dhoti, sash, waist band and crown). The tassa drummers have changed their drum 'hand' into a more festive rhythm to accompany the ploughing of Raja Janak. His plough approaches a jar. The jar is represented by a little mound fabricated out of cloth, and placed in the middle of the field. The plough accidentally breaks the jar and the young beautiful damsel, Sita, emerges. Sita was crouched low behind the mound under an umbrella, sheltering from the heavy rains. She now rises and is embraced by Janak. Nārad muni hop-skips down the 'grong', approaches and advises Janak that he is blessed and as such must take care of Sita as his daughter. There is a brief dialogue, in pantomime.

Raja Janak breaks a jar while ploughing his fields and discovers child Sita

It is 8.20 pm., the rain continues its downpour. The ground is muddy, the mud being particularly heavy in front of the vendors' stalls. In an effort to keep the presentation going, the Pundit tells the swarūps and the audience: "The Ramleela is the play of God…there is no rain". The performers, now soaking wet, young and old, continue their circumambulations around the 'grong'. Their costumes are sticking to their bodies. The chanting from the Rāmcharitmānas continues. Some of the young performers, merely children, are valiantly keeping up with the action of the adults.

Pundit-ji narrates to his now dwindling audience the circumstances of Sita's growing up in the palace of Raja Janak, indicating that: "The time has come for Sita to be married. She will marry the person who lifts the great Bow of Lord Shiva which is kept in the palace of Janak." Guru Vishwamitra has been invited by Janak to his kingdom of Mithila to witness the 'Bow Ceremony,' the *Dhanush Jag* (in Hindi it is pronounced as *Yagna)* that will result in the marriage of Sita to the person who lifts the great Bow of Shiva. Rām and Lakshman, having conquered the demons Mārīcha and Subaahu, now accompany Guru Vishwamitra to this anticipated spectacular event.

The drama temporarily stops. Another member of the Ramleela executive addresses the audience, reading the list of sponsors who have contributed to the production of this year's First Felicity Ramleela celebrations. The torrent relentlessly continues in its heavy downpour. The audience has been reduced to just about one hundred. Pundit Yankatessu ends the evening's performance with the closing 'dance' of the full cast, (twenty-four performers) to live music, followed by ārti at 9.15 pm. As the ārti begins, the sparse audience, many of whom are completely wet, trudges through the mud and grass on its way out. Within minutes, the 'grong' is empty, save for the sheets of rain pelting down on the maidān as the muddy water slowly rises above the cropped grass.

Day 4: *Bala Kanda*

Mithila: Sita Swyamvar and marriage

In preparation for this evening's episode the soggy maidān has been reconfigured to reflect three different scenes. The entire 'grong' is redecorated to depict the kingdom of Janakpuri with flags, buntings and other festive symbols and tents. In one small section to the northeast of the 'grong', some shrubs and small plastic trees are 'planted' in the soft dirt. This represents the royal flower gardens, *Pushpavātika.*

The midfield now looks like a royal court, reflecting a combination of village aesthetics and its folk theatre. The *Swyamva*r Ceremony, prior to the marriage ceremony, will give princess Sita the opportunity to choose her husband from amongst the kings and princes who will gather to test their strength, prowess and luck in lifting Shiva's mighty Bow.

For this event some chairs, roughly constructed benches, and a crude version of a large bow (Shiva's Bow) is mounted on a low platform in the middle of the seating arrangements for the royal invitees. A decorated marriage pandal *(māroh)* is erected on the western corner where the marriage ceremony will take place later that evening.

At 6.45 pm., the Ramleela players are all assembled in front of the bedi, under the Mool Jhanda. The Vyas commences the chanting of the invocatory mantras. The performers, some individually and others in groups - their right hands stretched out and touching the shoulder of the one in front, up to the lead worshipper - wave the lighted deya in the tharia in front of the images of the gods positioned on the central altar. After all have performed the ārti, the main performers take the blessings of the Vyas and return to their respective areas for commencement of the evening's episode of the unfolding epic story.

With the thematic 'dance' by the entire cast of performers around the field completed, the *Vyas* commences the day's narration of the text. He tells his audience that: "In the royal court of Janak, in the city of Mithila, young princess Sita was cleaning the area where King Janak kept the Bow of Lord Shiva, Shiva's *Dhanush.* Sita effortlessly moved the Bow, swept the area and carefully replaced it in its original spot, a feat which no ordinary mortal could do." Raja Janak later notices that the Bow has been moved and realises that Sita had moved it. He then decides that Sita should marry only the person who can lift Shiva's Bow.

Messengers are dispatched by the palace to make royal proclamations in all kingdoms, near and far, extending invitations to suitable suitors for the ceremony (the S*wyamvar)* in which Sita will choose her husband. Sita will marry the one who can lift Shiva's Bow. Janak wants no one omitted. To the accompaniment of drums, messengers fan out in the four directions to make the proclamations. This scene is being dramatically enacted in the 'grong'.

The scene shifts. Sage Vishwamitra with his royal charges, Princes Rām and Lakshman are on their way to Mithila in Janakpur. Vishwamitra has been invited by Raja Janak to Sita's *Swyamvar* and the princes are accompanying him. They travel on foot, in synchronised movements and steps, to the accompaniment of the tassa drums. On the way they enter a deserted hermitage which has a life size, stone statue of a woman. The Pundit explains to the audience the circumstances of the deserted place and the presence of the statue. He sings a verse from the text and narrates in English: "Once a beautiful woman, Ahalya lived there with her saintly husband Gautama. One morning as her husband went for his bath; Lord Indra of the heavenly abode assumed the image of her husband and visited her in her bed. Ahalya, at first mistaking Indra for her husband, begins an amorous tryst with him. In the course of the lovemaking she realised that the man was not her husband but was Indra whom she secretly admired. She continued the unfaithful escapade. Her husband returned to the hermitage and caught the couple in each other's arms. He pronounced curses on them with the result that Ahalya was immediately turned to stone and Lord Indra was rendered impotent. Ahalya had remained in this form since then". Rām on hearing of the story touches the stone statue of Ahalya, with his foot. The curse is immediately lifted and Ahalya is redeemed, returning to human form in all her beauty. The Princes continue on their trip to Mithila, crossing the grassy Ramleela 'grong' of Felicity. The Pundit then narrates to his audience another Katha, that of the legend of the River Goddess Ganga, as the travelling princes cross the Ganga River on their way to Mithila.

They are approaching the kingdom of Janakpur. Guru Vashishta enters the gates of the kingdom and the entourage approaches the palace of Raja Janak. The same covered platform, with a bench for a throne, which was originally the Ayodhya palace, is now used as the palace of Janak. Raja Janak descends from his throne and with much fanfare, to the accompaniment of tassa drumming, he bows to the feet of guru Vishwamitra. With upraised hands, his right one in a gesture of blessing, the left hand with a mala or garland hanging from it, Vishwamitra blesses King Janak. They are welcomed into the palace by Raja Janak.

Rām and Lakshman now take leave to explore the city and visit its various sights. With much curiosity they accidentally stumble upon and enter into the royal gardens. The Pundit's narrative now transports the audience to the scene of *Pushpavātika*, the flower garden. The setting for this scene is within the 'grong' itself. Its interpretation is novel. *Pushpavātika* is the place where Rām and Sita have their chance meeting for the first time. The garden setting is actually a small space in a barricaded area where a few shrubs had been planted earlier in the day. The space is constructed or actually 'miniaturised', as the other venues in which action has taken and will take place. The sets and props are minimal, comprising some shrubs and a miniature garden hut, set on the green lawn of the maidān. It is intended to capture the symbolic effect of a flower garden. The audience imagines the rest and lives in the moment.

Sita and her friends enter *Pushpavātika* to pluck flowers for their evening prayer ritual. While collecting flowers, Sita accidentally glances in Rām's direction. Her eyes fleetingly sparkle with a shy admiration for this handsome young man. He casually returns the look. It is more of restrained inquisitiveness. Lakshman notices the exchanges. The audience just embraces the moment, enjoying the spark of budding romance in front of their eyes. Within this short interlude images are stored in each other's hearts.

The Pundit continues his singing of the appropriate *chaupai, sortha, doha* and *chand* from the katha taken from Baal Kand, (pages 181 - 209) of the Rāmcharitmānas, Gītā Press publication, Gorakhpur. By 8.00 pm., the audience has grown to approximately 1,500 people. There is constant movement from the performance area to the periphery, behind the audience, to the chair plane and food court and back to the performance. The tassa strikes up and is beating a festive rhythm. The audience hurries back to witness the scene that is about to unfold.

Shiva's Bow is resting flat, on a low stand. It ought to have been placed on a bow stand with the dignity befitting its status but this is rural, rustic aesthetics. Suitors dressed in various types of attire and demonstrating different gaits and attitudes are entering the palace. Rām enters, dances around in the hop/skip movement, looks at the audience, greets them appropriately and sits. Lakshman accompanies him in similar fashion except that he stands protectively next to his brother. With the royal court full of princes, kings and other dignitaries, the suitors are invited to lift and string the Bow. Many try to lift it singly and fail. King Rāwan is also present, dressed in attractive, golden attire, with a royal blue cape and a white mask. He also tries and fails. Then many suitors come together to collectively attempt the lift. They also fail. There is much drama and humour associated with the process of trying the lift and straining or falling down, humiliated. The tassa drummers switch their rhythmic pattern to a lilting 'hand', adding to the excitement of the occasion.

Nārad, the inter-planetary messenger is omni-present, circumambulating the 'grong' in his characteristic movements, a silent witness to the unfolding chain of events. Younger performers are also making the *parikrama* in rhythm, emulating the older ones; this is their on-the-job training. Two neighbourhood dogs, village mongrels, wander into the royal court, near the bow. They are shooed away, much to the entertainment of the audience. Meanwhile, Guru Vishwamitra is also moving around the chamber, behind the seated royal guests, quietly observing the unfolding situation.

Raja Janak, on observing the pitiable sight of the failed and embarrassed suitors, now stands and addresses his august guests. He spurns them, asking whether there is none among them who is suitable and competent enough to win his daughter's hand in marriage. He wonders aloud if she will have to remain a virgin.

Lakshman, incensed with Janak's taunting, comes forward. He informs Janak that he belongs to the royal race of Raghu, of the solar dynasty of Ayodhya. He continues, saying that now his entire lineage has been insulted by the statements of their host, Raja Janak. Rām looks on. Lakshman announces that he can lift the bow and in the process angrily makes a lurch to perform the feat. He is quietly but firmly stopped by Vishwamitra who suggests that Rām should perform that duty. Rām stands, bows to the guru, his host, the assembled competitors and the audience and hop-skips up to the weapon, clasps his hands together, faces the bow, and says a silent prayer. This is all dramatically enacted. The tassa drums have whipped up much anticipation. Calmly, Rām grasps the bow and with a slight jerking action, lifts it and attempts to string it, breaking it in the process. The other Kings, who should have been astonished by the action, demonstrate no such emotion. They are embarrassed.

Parasuram then makes his dramatic entry in the scene. He has long, yellow rope-like hair, a beard falling at his waist, and wears a face mask. He carries an axe in one hand and a bow in the other. With exaggerated gestures and wielding his axe with anger, Parasuram, the protector of Shiva's Bow, demands to know who has broken the sacred weapon. He threatens the breaker of the bow. Lakshman, with some taunting language, asks Parasuram what concern is it of his as to who has performed the act. The Pundit speaking sometimes in

Rām lifts Shiva's Bow. In the background Nārad muni observes

an angry voice, other times in a calming demeanour, delivers the lines for the actors to imitate. There is an exchange of heated dialogue between Parasuram and Lakshman and feigned attempts to attack each other.

Rām intervenes and pacifies the antagonists. He then addresses Parasuram, advising him that it is he, Rām, who has performed the feat. However, Parasuram must be satisfied beyond a shadow of a doubt. With exaggerated movements he hands Rām the bow of Lord Vishnu and asks him to string it, which Rām dramatically accomplishes. Parasuram is now convinced of the divinity of Rām. He bows in reverence to Rām and exits.

Invitations are then dispatched from the palace including to Raja Dasarath in Ayodhya, for Rām's royal wedding to Sita. The invitees, with a large entourage, arrive from Ayodhya into Janakpur and the grand wedding of the 4 princes – Rām, Lakshman, Bharat and Shatrughan - takes place with much fanfare in the specially constructed marriage pandal in the 'grong'.

Following the short wedding ceremony the ārti is performed to the newlyweds, Rām and Sita. The gods, now on the earthly plane and having received the sanctions and blessings from many elevated souls, are married. Those of the heavenly abode have enacted the Leela or 'play' in the earthly sphere, within the precincts of the Green Park savannah. Sacred, spiritual place has merged with physical, temporal place and space. Sacred time has also coincided with present time; in this case it is Trinidad local time. Astrological charts have also concurred and synchronized into the present time. The ārti is thus equally as sacred as it is festive on this occasion. Rām, Sita, Lakshman, and their other two brothers walk around the periphery of the 'grong', acknowledging the presence of the wedding guests – who, in this case, are the audience. Many in the audience are overjoyed - and receive the blessings of the newlyweds. The gods are walking the earth of Mithila, but in Felicity, thus making the ground of Felicity sacred ground. The Ramleela actors have been transformed into heavenly beings and in keeping with the description of Anuradha Kapur (1990), 'without being totally crushed or submerged by the weight of the spiritual presence in their bodies', having much room to maneuver as physical, human beings, as actors. Within this drama there is icon worship. The other two brothers having also married in Janakpur, the wedding party (including the newlyweds) returns to Ayodhya. There is an all-round happy mood at this juncture in the epic. Thus ends the narrative of the first book, *Bala Kanda.*

This evening's episode ends at 9.00 pm., with the entire cast from both sides, Lanka and Ayodhya, taking the final 'dance' around the ground, criss-crossing with full, festive attire and weaponry and then assembling and performing the closing ārti. Whatever the episodes or sub stories being narrated on a particular day, the beginning and ending of each day's play remain the same.

ENDNOTES

1. The Pundit has used poetic licence to transpose this quotation from another part of the text to this part.
2. A 'yojana' equates roughly to nine miles.100 yojanas are 900 miles.

Chapter Ten

DAILY PERFORMANCES: DAY 5

Day 5: Ayodhya Kanda

Proposal for Rām's coronation and his exile (Rām Banbas)

Today is the 5th day of the Felicity Ramleela. The story moves into *Ayodhya Kanda*, the second of the seven books of the epic of Tulsidas' Rāmcharitmānas. Today, 18 jhandis flutter over the 'grong' as part of its decor. Pink and red pennants are flying atop the flagpoles over Ayodhya. Black pennants are atop those in Lanka. Between these, there are white and yellow pennants atop other flagpoles. The grass in the maidān has been freshly cut, low and green. It glistens in the night light. Red, white and yellow triangular-shaped, crepe-paper buntings are flying above the central altar. They radiate from the central or *mandap jhanda* to those flagpoles on the outer barrier. A miniature hut representing the ashram of Vishwamitra stands on the eastern periphery, inside the barrier. Trees and forests (actually shrubs) have been planted to represent the forest or *banbas*.[1] The entire maidān is lit by bulbs from four tall pillars planted on the periphery of the grounds. Each pillar carries six powerful high intensity, white lights mounted at its top.

The open-tray, pick-up truck of "Natty Sound System", filled with the sound boxes and (4) mixers, arrived since 5.00 pm. It had driven under the main tent, the 'command centre' and parked on the eastern side of the stage. Its equipment has been set up, ready to begin the amplification of the evening's programme.

It is 6.45 pm., already 15 minutes later than the advertised time for commencement of the evening's performance. Artistes are still converging on the ground from all directions. Some of the stalls on the outer periphery of the performing area are completing their minor finishing touches, to reflect the festive atmosphere. As of tonight, there are 17 food stalls: 12 covered and

5 open-air ones, each doing a brisk trade. Village dogs are on the eastern side of the ground, playing among themselves and running among the audience who are now busy patronizing the food court.

At 7.00 pm., the players converge at the foot of the *mool jhanda*. The Pundit chants the salutary hymns and sings invocatory prayers from his *singhasana*. The players stand and pray, and then individually they perform ārti to the images on the consecrated area. The ārti ends with Rām, Lakshman and Sita going to the *singhasana* of the Pundit garlanding him, touching his feet, receiving his blessings and returning for the beginning of the performance. The entire cast commences its standard opening Ramleela 'dance' around the maidān doing their stylised 1-2-3, 1-2-3 step in their *Kaharwa* taal (a time cycle of eight beats) drumming. They swing their weapons and instruments in choreographed synchronicity.

Following this prelude the *Vyas* welcomes the audience and announces that: "Raja Dasarath and his four sons are returning with their wives to Ayodhya." He exhorts them saying: "Devotees look at Raja Dasarath with his four sons and their wives." But there is actually only three females in the entourage. The audience is not troubled. They mentally blot this obvious error

The married couples return from Mithila to Ayodhya

out of their senses. The four brothers, each with an arrow, with Sita (a little girl of about ten - twelve years old), dressed in yellow or *pitambar* sari, are lined up in one row at the head of the returning entourage. The swarūps now dance around the 'grong'. Sita and the other brides walk with them with village elegance, their hands hanging loosely at their side. The brides do not dance. But that stylized walk itself is dance. This is the procession returning from Mithila.

Nārad muni and his understudy dance down the track. With a gliding gait they are performing their 1-2-3-brush-4 movement with grace and masculine elegance. They are dressed and look like twins, with ghungroos on their feet, each having a musical instrument resting on his shoulder and supported by his palm at the other end. They blissfully dance along the inner periphery of the oval-shaped barriers, symbolically surveying the cosmic regions, appearing almost unconcerned with the animation on the physical plane. Mythology is merging with physical reality in a seamless enactment of village theatre, recollected from the experiential memory of the Indo-Trinidadian village folks of Felicity, living on the edge of the Caroni swamp.

At 7.30 pm., the wedding party from Mithila arrives in Ayodhya, the grooms with their brides. All of their mothers, (Dasarath's wives) emerge from the palace, descend the 5 steps of the raised Ayodhya stage and embrace them. The meeting or *milan* of this returning *barāt*, is performed to throbbing tassa rhythms in keeping with the celebratory atmosphere of the returning wedding party of a typical Trinbago's Hindu or rather, 'Indian' wedding. Local religious ritual and cultural practices in all its hues and symbolism have merged into the Felicity Ramleela.

The story has been fast forwarded. Years have passed. The Pundit announces in his elaborate narrative that: "Bharat and Shatrughan are on their way to their in-laws for a vacation". The two princes accompanied by their wives perform the Ramleela hop-skip dance movement around the ground on their way to Mithila. The wives, however, are not doing their husbands' stylized movements but are simply walking next to them. They then exit as the scene shifts.

Pundit-ji continues his narrative from the text as the action is mimed with dramatic flair: Dasarath now looks at himself in the mirror, considers his old age and decides to pass on the reins of power to his chosen next of kin, Rām, to crown him as King of Ayodhya. The narrator's chanting from the text and its translation brings an atmosphere of excitement to the scene. Dasarath announces his plans. The subjects of Ayodhya are pleased with the announcement and are looking forward to the grand coronation. As the palace announcement is being made the 'grong' is simultaneously being reconfigured. Many of the props are repositioned. The greenery is uprooted and replanted in different areas in preparation for the anticipated coronation of Rām. The performers are themselves the stagehands, rapidly repositioning and redecorating the set. The narrator's chanting from the text and the drums lend an atmosphere of excitement to the unfolding scene.

Manthara, a congenitally lame hunch-back chamber maid of Queen Kaikeyi notices the festive preparations and atmosphere of excitement and enquires from the other palace servants as to the purpose of the intending festivity. Manthara's role is performed by a full-bodied, mature, busty, dark-skinned village woman, dressed in a lemon coloured sari. She is informed accordingly and hobbles to Kaikeyi's chamber and gives her the news; but she also offers advice, whispering in her Queen's ear. Manthara suggests that the queen should not allow this coronation to take place, for she and her son would suffer dire consequences. Manthara advises that Kaikeyi should recall the two

Manthara hobbles away after poisoning the mind of Queen Kaikeyi with her advice

boons or promises made to her by Dasarath for favours she had previously rendered to him. These requests should include Dasarath banishing Rām from Ayodhya for 14 years and installing her son Bharat, as the King of Ayodhya. With the advice given, Manthara is satisfied with herself and hobbles away hastily, hunched over her walking stick.

According to the Vyas, after Manthara's 'poisoning' of the mind of her Queen with the suggestions, Kaikeyi is at first confused at the advice, but later, with ambitions for dynastic rule; that of her lineage and of her son, she reconsiders the advice and then decides to act upon it.

Kaikeyi gets up, leaving the plastic chair on which she was sitting, and walks to the *Kōpa Bhavan*, the sulking chamber. This chamber is represented by a 4 foot long, 4 inch thick sponge mattress – a bed - covered with a yellow and white bed sheet. It lies flat on the bare grass; now glistening in the night light. The audience imagines the rest.

Dasarath goes to speak to Kaikeyi, to give her the good news. Not finding her anywhere he proceeds to the *Kōpa Bhavan* in search of her. She is sprawled on the bed in a foul mood. Dialogue follows between both parties. She makes her demands of him and stands her ground.

King Dasarath begs Queen Kaikeyi to withdraw her demands

Dasarath recognises the weight of these demands and the implications for the future of the kingdom. In anguish and agony, he begs her - the Pundit narrates, he mimes the actions - to withdraw her wishes but to no avail. After much pleading, he tells her that instead of a coronation she may as well see his funeral.

Queen Kaikeyi makes her demands to King Dasarath

Kaikeyi takes no heed of his plea, angrily turning her back to him and walking away. He falls unconscious, unto the sponge mattress on the grass. Sumantra, the minister, arrives at the chamber to inform the king that all the preparations for the coronation have being completed. He sees the king unconscious on the ground. Kaikeyi, on being questioned as to his condition, replies that he is tired and asleep and asks Sumantra to fetch Rām.

Dasarath falls unconscious while Kaikeyi's back is turned to him

He is summoned and Kaikeyi informs him of her demands of the king. With total equanimity, Rām agrees. But when Lakshman hears of them he is outraged and advises Rām not to accede to her demands. A lengthy dialogue follows between Rām and Lakshman as Rām explains why he must honour his father's promises. Meanwhile, Dasarath remains unconscious on the sponge mattress in the maidān. Kaikeyi remains there, nonchalant. The whole of Ayodhya is now in distress. The performers, now playing the roles of the citizens of Ayodhya, enact various states of sorrow and despair.

As Rām prepares for his departure into exile, Lakshman and Sita decide to accompany him on this journey for the period of his banishment. They take leave of their parents; then Lakshman takes leave of his wife, while Shri Rām goes to get his father's blessings. King Dasarath is distraught. Sumantra prepares a chariot for the trio's departure. Amid the Pundit's chanting from the text, the tassa drums are beating a 'sad hand', evoking the painful emotions arising from Keikeyi's instructions, the sadness of exile and the overall distress in Ayodhya.

It is 8.00 pm. The audience has grown to about five hundred on the barriers and about another one hundred around the food stalls. Approximately another fifty, mostly children and adolescents, are concentrated around the chair plane and merry-go-round. There are about 50-60 vehicles, some parked in the muddy savannah while others are along the shoulders of the roads bordering the grounds. At this point in the drama many spectators are making a beeline for the food area. These food stalls, varying in size from eight by ten feet rectangles to approximately sixteen feet square, are covered with old galvanised iron sheets. They are about eight feet high and enclosed with a combination of stripped bamboo, plywood, old wooden laths and other old boards. There are tables and glass cases mounted on the top of tables advertising and selling a variety of finger foods: Bara and channa (chole- bature or the local version referred to as 'doubles'), pakora, saheena, kachouri, phulouri and chutney, achār, sweet mangoes, paime, barfi, ladoo, pera, kurma, jelabi, soft drinks, bottled water, cotton candy, popcorn, ground nuts and coconut 'sugar' cakes. The finger foods and popcorn are being constantly replenished with fresh, hot supplies from the back of the tents where the cooking is being done. The rice cake and tulum - a confectionery prepared from molasses - of the previous years are missing. So, too, is the itinerant vendor of the previous year, walking around the maidān, among the audience selling his paper windmills stacked to a straw-covered rod.

The key person in each stall is identified and we talk between their servicing of their customers; they are all family businesses which have been part of the Ramleela for several years, some as long as twenty years. Almost all the stalls, i.e. the entire line framing the northern and eastern periphery of the 'grong' are mostly managed by women. They all have male helpers but the women are in charge of the daily operations. This was very evident from their behavioural style and body language - giving instructions, organising the human traffic flow behind the makeshift counters; supervising the preparation and servicing of the customers even while they were performing their respective share of the duties. They mix flour, knead dough and help to fry the baiganees, aloo pies and other foods. There are no gender or age preferences. All members of the family, and sometimes extended family, have come to help; they comprise young boys, girls, brothers and their wives, sisters and their husbands.

At 8.20 pm. Rām, Lakshman and Sita prepare to leave for Banbas. The Pundit sings a bhajan that evokes the necessary pathos in his rendition: *Dharti aur Akāsha Prabhu Rām Chale Banbas…* (The earth and sky are sad that God Rām is going into exile).

While the singing is in progress, a stray dog runs through the field in front of Ayodhya. "Look devotees, even the dog is disheartened, even the dog is sad, Shri Rām is going into exile," wails the Pundit. The audience smiles their approval. Young kids point to the dog and tug at their mothers' dresses and fathers' pants to draw their attention to it.

The audience is informed that the trio has departed Ayodhya in the chariot provided by Sumantra, with its grief stricken citizens trailing behind. Tassa accompanies their departure from Ayodhya. In the Felicity enactment, however, they depart on foot, moving from one part of the 'grong' to another, with no accompanying entourage. The audience is behind the barrier which prevents spectators from physically interacting with the performers. The departing trio does not walk but maintain the tassa tempo constantly, dancing their 1-2-3; 1-2-3 steps.

Accepting his banishment Rām departs Ayodhya into exile with Sita and Lutchman

At 8.32 pm. Felicity time, the 'chariot' arrives at the banks of the Tamasa River where they decide to spend the night. The procession camps on the banks of the river. Shri Rām meets Guha, the head of Nishad clan, who live alongside the river bank. At dawn the following morning, Guha arranges for the exiles to leave before their followers awake. Guha approaches a ferry man, a Kewat, at the bank of the river to arrange a boat for the crossing of the River Ganga.

The ferryman comes with his boat. The boat meanders through half of the field until it is finally anchored. It now stands between the Pundit's tent and Ajodhya's platform. It is framed out of bamboo with the sides covered with black and red satin cloth and a short red flag on its bow. The 2012 version

Guha, the bearded tribal leader, summons a Kewat, a boatman

of the boat reflected many innovations to the basic bamboo shell, viz a steering wheel borrowed from an old automobile; it was covered with red satin cloth and named "SS Minnow - 50th Anniversary of TT Independence." It has no hull. The flimsy contraption is suspended from the shoulders of two boatmen.

The boatmen (Guha and his Kewat) are dressed in garments representing a cross between a clown and a folk character of Trinidad Carnival. They are wearing yellow, white and red outfits, face masks and gloves. (In previous years they wore black outfits.) They leap out of the boat, diving unto the ground at the feet of Shri Rām, as if the dirt was the river itself. The crowd is elated. They clap in delight. The ferryman or Kewat, now standing next to his boat, declines to take the trio across the river. Guha is in the boat. This scene lends itself to much burlesque, satire and humour. The Pundit tells the story and the dialogue is mimed between Rām and the Kewat. His refusal to accommodate them in the boat is based on Rām's miracle, performed earlier, when he returned Ahalya to human form. The Kewat reminds Rām that since he "changes stone to woman, by just touching it with his toes," referring to the Ahalya story, "then what would you do with my boat which is made of wood?" He asks Rām: "I can't take a woman home. My wife will kill me." The audience witnesses the scene with glee. There is much dialogue between the two, in a typical Trinidadian banter.

The Kewat finally agrees to take them across, only if Rām allows him to wash his lotus feet with his own hands, prior to the crossing. Rām concedes. The washing is a hilarious scene, a humorous ritual. A brass plate and a plastic, 2-litre soft drink container filled with water, are brought. Rām's feet are placed in the tharia and the water is poured on his feet. In the process, water is deliberately sprinkled on everyone nearby, including the audience. On his knees, the Kewat begins washing Rām's feet, scrubbing them with his hands. It is an elaborate display of burlesque. The feet are then completely washed. The water from the tharia is drunk by the Kewat. Rām's feet are extended a second time. Water is poured on his knees, and on his saffron coloured dhoti. More washing is done. With exaggerated, comic, miming actions, the Kewat and his helper drink the remaining portion of the water, sprinkling some on the people around them including the royal entourage. The crowd is absolutely delighted.

Then with elaborate movements and village humour, the Kewat invites the trio, beckoning with his gloved hand, to enter into the boat. He and his fellow boatmen try to lift each of their passengers bodily, each time falling on their backs with Rām and Lakshman on top of them. The tassa drums are providing the background rhythmic accompaniment. When the Kewat realizes that they are too heavy, he and Guha lift up Lakshman - one holding his head the other his feet - and toss him, like a sack of rice, into the boat.

The Kewat carries Rām, while Guha lifts Lakshman, into the boat

The boat has no bottom. The passengers' feet are the keel, the rudder and the oars. With minimum protocols, the other two passengers scramble inside. It is a hilarious scene of village humour and jest but physically dangerous. The Pundit sings the appropriate chaupais from the Rāmcharitmānas and interprets, sticking to the text, the happenings on the river bank. The fine line between narrative and actual action blurs and even disappears. The amused audience laughs throughout the scene.

All three guests are finally in the boat but actually standing on the ground. The five occupants shove off into 'open water'. With the tassa drums now beating a fast tempo, they actually take off at running speed. The entire maidān has now become the river. They navigate the boat throughout the field, running aground; directly on the "command centre", then again at the southern end into Lanka's stage. Sita disembarks and Rām, Lakshman and the boatmen accelerate at double speed, navigating through and around the floating debris in the river; freshly planted trees, some small shrubs and branches.

The Kewat and his passengers cross the river

At double speed around the maidān

They collide head-on with huge debris in the water; a (banana) tree. It stops them dead in their stride. It is a river collision. Extracting themselves from it they sway the boat from left to right and side to side as they run, indicating a dangerous turbulence in the swiftly moving current. There is a major spill. The boat has capsized. All passengers are on the wet grass glistening in the night light. They quickly hoist themselves up and continue running, in rhythm with the throbbing tassa drums. The boat zigzags around plants, spins around, reverses - as if fighting the swirling waters of the river - and moves again. The audience is laughing and clapping. The kids in the audience are screaming with delight. It has turned out to be a dangerous boat ride. The flood lights reflect the beads of sweat streaming from the bodies of the ferrymen and his passengers.

Meanwhile another costumed character goes around to the audience on the inner periphery of the barricade with a brass thali in his right hand. It contains fresh flowers and a lighted deya. He is giving 'ārti' to and collecting the evening's *dakshina* (offerings) from the spectators cum devotees. The audience, some with coins, others with notes, circles the currency around the flame in clockwise formation. These are then dropped into a plastic bag hanging from the other hand of the 'collector'. Then with open palms of both hands and much reverence, the devotees scoop the flame and its perfumed smoke from the lighted deya on to their heads and faces, literally and figuratively bathing in it.

The boatmen's antics continue while the Pundit narrates his story and the collector passes 'ārti', around the 'grong'. It is 9.00 pm. and the boatmen are exhausted. The boat and its passengers reach the other side of the river, completing a full ten to fifteen minutes ride with the music of the tassa. They are dripping with sweat. The boatmen are still wearing their gloves and white masks. One of them pours water on his foot. He has injured himself and is washing off the blood in front of the 'command centre'.

The Pundit continues the story with the help of the appropriate chants, reading from the text. After crossing the Ganga, Shri Rām, Sita and Lakshman leave for Chitrakoot while Guha returns to his home, as instructed by Shri Rām. The exiles arrive at sage Bharadwaj's ashram, and then proceed to Chitrakoot hill, where they are welcomed at the ashram of Atri muni. On his invitation, they erect a hut as a temporary shelter while they enjoy the hospitality of Chitrakoot. Meanwhile, Sumant has returned to Ayodhya.

Back at the palace, Raja Dasarath is full of remorse; having been separated from his son. As he pines away in grief, he recalls an incident that had happened to him a long time ago. The Pundit narrates the episode. Dasarath recalled that once while hunting on the banks of the Sarāyu River, he had accidentally killed a boy, Sarwan Kumar who was filling his pitcher with water at the river to take to his blind parents. The parents, on hearing of their son's death, had uttered a 'curse' or *sarāp* on Raja Dasarath, saying that 'one day he too will also be painfully parted from his son' in unfortunate circumstances. The memory of the 'curse' of the blind couple takes its toll on King Dasarath. His life slowly ebbs; he breathes his last breath.

At this point there is a break in the narrative of the story. An executive member of the Ramleela, Mr. Seenath, speaking on the microphone, publicly acknowledges the various sponsors and workers and all those who have contributed to "the success of the Ramleela" for the current year. A long list is read out. These include Bachew's Fabric and Bridal Store, Roti Masters of Freeport, Central Sporting Initiative (ASI), Hudson Mahabir, Sitaram Balroop and family, The Junction Bar of Pierre Road, SM Jaleel & Company, Chaguanas Borough Corporation, and the audio sound engineering crew.

The Pundit returns to the microphone and probably with reference to the boat scene, informs the audience that he chants and explains the scriptures but he "refrains from interpreting the scriptures for fear of misinterpretation. The audience must interpret it itself to suit their own circumstances. ..." He only provides an "analogy to the local condition when he feels comfortable with the interpretation." He also announces the parts of the text which will be narrated and dramatised the following day. The evening's episode ends shortly after 9.00 pm. The closing thematic dance and group ārti are performed following which the Pundit blesses the performers.

Later, as the Pundit is packing up to leave, I enquire of him: "Pundit why do you not make use of local examples within a local context to bring home the moral of the story of that respective episode?" I point out that other narrators do it during their explanations in their Ramleela presentations, including the *Vyas-jis* of the Baal Ramdilla presentation in Bala Kanda, as I had seen earlier in that Ramleela. Pundit Yankatessu responds: "Raviji is my Guru; he is qualified to do that. I am still not competent to do that..."[2]

ENDNOTES

1. The word 'ban' means ' wild' or 'forested' and 'bas' is literally translated from Hindi or Bhojpuri language to mean 'bamboo'.
2. Rabindranath Maharaj (Raviji) is the spiritual head of the Hindu Prachar Kendra, the organisation which produces and presents the annual Bal Ramdilla of Raghunanan Road, Enterprise, Chaguanas in Trinidad.

Chapter Eleven

DAILY PERFORMANCES: DAY 6

Day 6: *Ayodhya Kanda and Aranya Kanda*

Cremation of Dasarath; Bharat goes to Chitrakoot; Rām moves to Panchavati

This evening the Ramleela grounds have again been partially reconfigured and redecorated in keeping with the evolution of the story. The main sets have remained in place. Smaller ones have been added. Shrubs and trees have been replanted in different locations, forming a natural setting for the evening's narrative. The flags and buntings remain positioned, flying in the evening breeze and enhancing the festive mood that pervades the maidān.

There are 35 performers including, for the first time, one of the main characters of the epic, Hanuman of the banar or monkey-looking tribe. With a long tail, from coccyx to neckline and curling like an 'S'; Hanuman is portrayed by a well-built, male villager who has been playing this role for over three decades. He wears a wrist band, a waistband and a red short pant bordered with yellow fringe falling at his knees. With a shawl draping from Mr. Jookoo's shoulders, a mala from his neck, he carries the familiar battle weapon, the *mukdar*. Pundit-ji commences the evening's benediction promptly at 7.00 pm. Standing on his singhasana, playing his harmonium and chanting from the text, he sports a white jersey and pants - for the second consecutive day - instead of the regular kurta-pajama that is his normal *Vyas's* attire. The entire cast performs the ārti. Following the invocatory hymns the narrative of the story progresses.

Pundit-ji continues, chanting and translating in his unique *Trinhinglish* dialect: "King Dasarath of Ayodhya dies while his 2 sons, Bharat and his younger brother, Shatrughan, are vacationing at the home of their maternal grandparents. Queen Kaikeyi dispatches a messenger: 'Go and bring Bharat back to Ayodhya, and tell him it is the request of Guru Vashishta. But do not say a word of their father's death' to Bharat." The message is delivered. As the brothers enter the kingdom of Ayodhya, they notice a general mood of sadness of its citizenry. No one talks to them. People are casting sympathetic glances in their direction. They are baffled.

Bharat arrives at the palace. He is dressed in a saffron dhoti, waist sash (*kamarband)* and shawl (a*ngwastram)* hung around his neck with a crepe paper mala (red and saffron) falling at his solar plexus. He wears a crown or *mukut* of gold, decorated with tinsel and foil of different colours. It glitters in the glare of the double spot lights, now located above the western barrier and directed at the performance area.

Kaikeyi descends the palace steps. She is holding a tharia in the middle of which is a lighted deya to perform the traditional welcome-home ritual. Her white sari shimmers in the light. Facing him and waving the light in a circular action, she performs ārti. Then miming the Pundit's prompting, Kaikeyi enquires about the health of her family. Then she conveys the sad news of his father's death and its relevance to him. She offers the kingdom to him, to be its ruler.

Kaikeyi welcomes Bharat home after the death of Raja Dasarath

Bharat appears thunderstruck at the sad news. He then refuses to accept her proposal for him to be the successor king of Ayodhya. He reacts angrily telling her how wicked she is, as a woman and a mother, to replace Rām, as heir to the throne, with him. She responds that: "It is done only for you, on the advice of Manthara".

Manthara the maid servant now emerges into the spotlight. She is wearing a black mask and walking, crouched over, with a hump on her back. A full bag, stuffed under her clothes at her back, amplifies her hump. She is happy, saying 'everything is now in place.' The miming is intense; emotions are high in front of Ayodhya's palace. Shatrughan reacts more aggressively. He goes into a rage at the news and begins to physically beat Manthara. Her character rapidly switches. She is now played by a man. The beating continues mercilessly: dropkick, running and leaping on her chest, pitching her many feet away. She tries to deflect the blows and physically protect herself. With the drums beating a battle rhythm, the fight progresses. It covers almost half of the 'grong'. The audience stares in stupefaction. Manthara's clothes are being ripped apart. She rolls on the ground. Every time she tries to get up, Shatrughan jumps on her. The action moves from pantomime to actual blows, physical violence. The audience which has grown to over five hundred is leaning heavily on the steel and bamboo barriers, absorbed in the theatrics, caught in the mood of the moment.

Small shrubs and palm fronds are ripped out and used as whips on her body. The sound of the physical beating is heard around the ground. The audience winces. Religious, village theatre has crossed the thin line of realistic acting into irreverent and crude violence. Bharat intervenes and with great force, he restrains Shatrughan. The Ministers of the kingdom then come to implore Bharat to accept the position of King. At least ten persons are facing him, begging him with extended arms and imploring faces to accept the regency of the kingdom. Bharat shakes his head. He declines, gesticulating "no" with his hands. The Vyas 'sings' and explains that Bharat has decided to go and implore Shri Rām to return to Ayodhya to rule the kingdom.

But Bharat has many things to do in Ayodhya before he can visit Shri Rām. The scene shifts to the cremation ceremony of Raja Dasarath. The royal corpse, draped in white fabric, and borne on a hand bier or

Bharat and Shatrughan bear the corpse of their father to the cremation ground. Manthara, Rani Kaikeyi and others follow

khatia, is lifted above the heads of the four pall bearers (including Bharat and Shatrughan). The cortege of over fifteen mourners - men, women and children, as well as Guru Vashishta (played by a very young, clean-faced boy, unlike the previous bearded character who performed the role), sets out for the cremation site on the banks of the River Sarāyu. As the procession moves, the Pundit sings the bhajan. *"Ek din hame bhi jaana hai…"* made popular by the late Sookdeo Sookraj of Diego Martin. The lyrics inform us that one day I too will take my leave of this earthly existence. The pathos of the lyrics and its accompanying music send the entire audience in a somber mood, of sadness and mourning. Some old folks weep silently, overcome by the occasion, dabbing at their eyes with their orhnis. The audience has become mourners.

From Ayodhya the cortege travels south, down the 'grong' in front of the Lanka pavilion. Although the corpse passes within 2-3 ft. of Lanka with its imposing palanquin over the stage, neither the audience nor the mourners in the cortege see Lanka with its entourage of warriors sitting there. The Lanka warriors are all elaborately attired in blue, green and black costumes; tops and dhoti (or pajamas), with long shoulder capes, crowns, and each wearing a white face mask. This scene is blanked out from their minds' eye, almost as if that part of the stage has been blacked out of view. It is a way of 'seeing' the action, viewing only that which is relevant to the immediate narrative of the moment, omitting everything else. Both audience and performers are accustomed to changing their approach to 'seeing' as the scenario changes. Even the warriors of Lanka do not 'see' the procession.

Accompanied by his harmonium, the Pundit chants: '*Shri Rām, Jai Rām, Sri Rām, Jai Rām*' to the funerary march. The funeral procession makes a full circumambulation or *parikrama* of the 'grong' and terminates at the banks of the River Sarāyu for the cremation, in keeping with rituals befitting that of royalty. While this ritual symbolically takes place on the banks of the river, physically it is being performed on the western side of the inner barrier of the maidān, in front of the fabricated, temporary pavilion. The Pundit continues his chanting '*Rām Nam Sat Hai, Rām Nam Sat Hai,* (The name of Rām is eternal. God is eternal). He informs the audience that: "Fire is placed inside the mouth of the deceased".

The pyre is piled with old newspapers and lit at one end. As the fire rises the 'corpse' rolls away on the grass, away from the flames. As the flames shoot up in the night sky the audience with the ring-side view is forced to move further afield because of the intense smoke and heat.

Bharat performs the final rites for his father, Raja Dasarath

The 'grong' functions as a split screen. While Bharat and his entourage are at one end returning from the funeral, the exiles - Rām, Sita and Lakshman - "jump" dance on the other end. They are moving around Chitrakoot, their temporary residence. The tassa provides common melody and rhythm to both parties, even though they are metaphorically great distances apart. The exiles meet Sage Agastya who advises Rām to leave Chitrakoot and go to live in Panchavati. The Pundit sings intermittently from the Ramayan, the harmonium, dholak and dhantāl accompanying him. A synthesizer provides background harmony, melody, sound effects and thematic music to evoke the relevant rasa.

Bharat decides to go in search of the exiles, resolving to bring Rām back to Ayodhya to install him on the throne as its rightful king. With a full entourage, he sets out in search of Rām in his forest abode. They arrive at sage Bharadwaja's ashram and receive directions to Chitrakoot where Shri Rām, Sita and Lakshman are still encamped.

The temporary ashram residence is located on the eastern side of the 'grong', amidst a leafy orchard of trees and branches planted for the day's performance. Latchman is on watch. Pundit Budharat informs his audience that: "Lakshman notices a cloud of dust in the distance, rising to the sky. He is suspicious and agitated and voices his opinion to Rām that it is an army led by Bharat, coming to kill them. Lakshman promises not to spare the life of Bharat but Shri Rām pacifies his younger brother, telling him that it will disgrace the integrity of their noble father to do such a thing." Bharat and his entourage are, however, not bearing arms; neither bows and arrows nor swords and shields.

Bharat arrives and affectionately greets Shri Rām, Sita and Lakshman. There is much embracing. Then, Bharat sadly informs the brothers of their father's death and pleads with Shri Rām to return as King, in keeping with their father's last wish. Shri Rām is grieved but he refuses to fulfill his father's desire, or Bharat's entreaties. Instead, Shri Rām gives Bharat his wooden sandals, his *Kharaw,* and a lecture on leadership, instructing him to govern the city of Ayodhya in his absence. The sandals are to provide the symbolic rule of Rām.

As all of this is being enacted Nārad muni glides in and out of the scene, his *veena* – a fiberglass fabricated instrument made in Felicity itself - in the left hand and resting on his shoulder. He is dancing, swaying and clacking his *kartaal* in his right hand as his ankle-belled feet beat out the standard Ramleela dance step; 1-2-3-brush, 1-2-3-brush steps (flat foot, toes, flat, brush heel and repeated on the other side) to the accompaniment of the tassa rhythm. This movement sways the body from side to side in a natural, lilting movement. Nārad is the legendary 'witness' to all that happens in the three spheres.

Bharat returns to Ayodhya but decides to stay in Nandigram until Rām returns to Ayodhya. As his entourage returns to Ayodhya through the circuitous route on the periphery of the Felicity maidān, he holds up Rām's *Kharaw* for the people - the audience has become the citizens of Ayodhya - to see. A large audience, now packed 2 rows deep around the barrier, surges forward to get a glimpse of the sacred sandals.

Bharat returns to Ayodhya with Rām's Kharaw (sandals). Shatrughan accompanies him

The Pundit narrates an episode in the life of the exiles in Chitrakoot. Jayant, a bird, comes to visit them on a rock on the banks of the Mandakini River. Jayant pecks Sita's foot. The three-some pay a visit to Sage Atri who is living in Chitrakoot. He blesses them, gives the young men divine weapons and advises them to spend the rest of their exile at the beautiful location of Panchavati.

The scene changes. The story progresses, shifting to the third book of the Rāmcharitmānas, *Aranya Kanda*. On their way to *Panchavati,* the princes meet the vulture Jatayu, brother of the old vulture, Sampati, son of Aruna, who's the brother of Garuda. Jatayu informs them that he is a friend of their father. He promises to protect Sita in their absence. It is 8.10 pm., and the audience is now tightly packed; in some places it is two or three people deep behind the barrier. They fill the areas around Lanka, Ayodhya, the pavilion on the western side and behind the Ashram on the eastern side of the 'grong'. The tassa drum ensemble is beating a lilting rhythm. The pundit chants, accompanied by his musicians. The entourage has now made three to four *parikrama* of the 'grong', performing their 1-2-3, 1-2-3 thematic steps, swaying in traditional, choreographed unison with the music. The food stalls are filled with customers; children, their parents and out-of-town visitors. The maidan is in a festive mood, one happy village bazaar, a great *mela.*

Back to the story; the exiles are now residing in Panchavati. Shurpanakha, the daughter of a *rākshasi* and sister of Rāwan, is introduced. Shurpanakha, a huge, black, buxom woman is dressed in a salmon coloured halter top blouse and long flared skirt, with a small salmon shoulder scarf or dupatta

Shurpanakha attempts to attract Rām and Lakshman

draped around her shoulders, falling in front, to her knees. Her long black hair cascades unto her shoulders. She wears a tiara and her face is masked with a black-cloth mask. She walks sensuously, inside the inner barrier of the ground, engaging in conversation with the audience. She has the capacity to change her appearances at will. (In the 2012 episode, Shurpanakha wore a shimmering pink dress, while in the year 2013, Shurpanakha was played by a teenage girl with long hair, wearing a blue Bharat Natyam classical dance costume.

Today, she does a crossover of a local 'Chutney' and Bollywood dance number to a recently released Bollywood tune. She wiggles her voluptuous breasts rapidly and shakes her buttocks in the same tempo; then bending her body at the front with her behind facing the audience, she wines, rhythmically. In the local parlance this body movement is referred to as 'pushing your bumper'. She stands upright, faces the audience on slightly bended knees, and wines her waist at them. The obscene vulgarity passes for village lasciviousness. It is a natural, joyous delight to the common rural folk. They lap it up, reveling in the mood of the moment with a passion. They press closer to the railings to get a more commanding view of the performance.

Meanwhile, the Pundit, unperturbed at Shurpanakha's actions, sings his verses from his platform. The filmy music continues. Shurpanakha cavorts; the Pundit describes her, saying; 'she has long fingers, and is big and black'. The actual performer in the maidān is big, a physically voluptuous woman with ample buttocks and breasts, with firm body parts on a huge frame. The audience claps, gleefully looking at her wiggling, wining and grinding pelvic movements, her shiny costume shimmering in the floodlights.

She now sees Rām and immediately becomes visibly, excitedly infatuated. She sensuously saunters up to engage his attention in an attempt at seducing him. He informs her that he is already committed to another. Rām points her to Lakshman who is standing guard a short distance away from his brother. His bow is hung around his shoulder. Shurpanakha redirects her attention to Lakshman who redirects her back to Rām, telling her that he is the 'slave of Rām' and is occupied with looking after his every need. Rām sends her back to Lakshman who is standing, sentry- like, in the middle of the ground. Shurpanakha goes from one to the other 'wining' both in front and back - carnival style - pushing her buttocks near to Rām and Sita. The tassa is drumming intoxicatingly. She shakes her breasts from side to side; she stoops down on all fours wiggling, wining and jerking her body in a mood, hopefully of attracting the baser, lusty instincts in her prospective admirers.

The older ladies in the audience partly cover their faces with their orhnis in embarrassment. The younger ones are in hysterics, enjoying the humour of the situation. It is a burlesque of our local carnival character, the "Dame Lorraine". Taped music ends and another tract begins immediately. Shurpanakha continues her seduction. Then the tassa commences. She shifts her attention to Lakshman. Tension mounts. Pundit talks about her enticing Lakshman. He has no time for her. Both brothers are jesting with her. She is again shunted to Rām and back to Lakshman, going back and forth between the two brothers. Rām tells her that he is already married and points out his wife to her.

Spurned by the two brothers, Shurpanakha becomes enraged at the disrespect being shown to her and assumes one of her demonic *(Rākshasi)* forms, a huge demon, and attempts to attack Sita. Rām physically rebuffs her. She is now enraged. Lakshman shoos her away. Meanwhile, at the command centre, two members of the executive are angrily discussing Lakshman's apparent lack of appropriate miming of his parts, remarking that: "He just holds on to his arrow string and his bow doing nothing."

In her demonic or rākshasi rage, Shurpanakha violently lounges at Lakshman. A battle ensues. Finally he grabs her, pulls out his sword and cuts off her nose. At this point, a balloon filled with red liquid is burst and splatters in the night light, the liquid catching the lights and looking like blood. Shurpanakha screams and flies- she actually runs - back to Lanka, flings herself down in front of Rāwan, crying loudly. The crying is done by another person on the mike. The audience is ecstatic. She rolls on the ground in front of Rāwan. The tassa is in full flight providing the appropriate mood for her actions.

Shurpanakha's brothers, Khar and Dūshan, who constantly roam the forest, agree to pay a visit to Panchavati. They have come to do battle with the ever-ready brothers. Sita is hidden safely inside the hut and both Rām and Lakshman enter into a major battle with the warriors of Lanka. The tassa ensemble is beating a battle rhythm. Arrows are released. Bow and sword fights take place. The entire performance space becomes the battleground. The entire 'grong' has become Panchavati. The audience is enthralled. The demons are finally killed.

While this battle continues, two performers are going around the inner periphery of the 'grong', one with the ārti plate, the other with a plastic bag in which to put the evening's monetary collections from the audience. At 8.45 pm. executive member Nanack makes the closing announcements, acknowledging all sponsors individually plus the presence of 'dancer- researcher Sat Balkaransingh and other foreign guests'. Then executive member, Kelvin Saith, announces to the audience over the mike that all those wishing to play on Friday (Day 9) must register immediately: "Put your names down tonight so that you would be a part of Friday's performance, otherwise you would not be able to come on Friday and play." The announcement is made with finality. Friday is the day that Lanka is burnt and many players are needed in the cast for that evening's performance. These will include those persons playing birds, horses, elephants and warriors.

At 9.15 pm. Pundit Yankatessu announces the culmination of the evening's performance and the final parade (in dance movements). This is undertaken by the entire cast following which they line up at the bedi mandap, centre stage. The Pundit sings the final benediction: *"Ārti Shri Rāmayāna Je Kee..."* to the accompaniment of dholak, dhantāl and harmonium. Each performer does ārti which is followed by the Mangalam or Shanti Path. The evening's programme ends with the collective chanting: *"Twamewa Mātā, Cha Pita Twamewa...* followed by *Asato ma sad gamaya ..."* The entire audience joins in the chanting. They have heard these chants so many times it is now common knowledge. The Pundit ends with the oft repeated *"Prem Se Bole Shri Rām Chandra Kee Jai"*. The crowd, now rapidly dispersing, responds in rhythm, "Jai". The merry-go-round which has seen better days is in full whirl, creaking away its last payload of customers for the night.

The performers are summoned to the command centre. Some are reprimanded 'for not remaining in character'. Pundit-ji explains that: "Each character in the Rāmayāna and hence in this Ramleela, exhibits specific attributes... Rāwan demonstrates all the negative attributes of man....so please stay in the character that is being portrayed... and mime as the Pundit narrates the dialogues," he cautions. It is already late and there is no time for arguments or questions. They all promise to 'improve tomorrow'.

Chapter Twelve

DAILY PERFORMANCES: DAYS 7-8

Day 7: Aranya Kanda

Sita Haran: The abduction of Sita by Rāwan

It rained the greater part of today, the seventh day of the Leela. The ground is saturated with water. The outfield behind the bamboo and steel barrier is muddy from yesterday's audience and from the vehicles parking in the outer perimeter of the savannah. There are new additions to today's edition. More flag poles and patakas have been added to those that were planted over the last six days. Seven strings of buntings cris-cross above the Ramleela performance area. Fourteen stalls are in full operation.

New, huge bows covered with white crepe paper are on display. The ashram (a hut) of Vishwamitra (and earlier of Bharadwaj of day 6), is now redecorated and identified as the abode of Rām in *Panchavati*. Three dozen trees have been planted to create the natural setting of the idyllic location of *Panchavati*. Props of miniature donkeys and deer are also introduced to enhance the area as a luxuriant, verdant forest with its flora and fauna.

A sound effects technician has joined the technical team. The technician will insert the sounds of nature appropriately - birds, wind, water, rustling leaves - to enhance this evening's dramatic sound effects. Nellie Britton, the wife of Jookoo, the current Hanuman, is armed with a script of the day's play and her laptop containing the sound effects which will be connected to the mixer board of the sound system. Nellie will follow the play closely and insert the relevant sounds as the Pundit chants his chosen *chaupais* and narrates the ongoing story. Trinidad village Ramleela is being enhanced with state-of-the art technology.

At 7.00 pm., all the performers have not yet arrived, the result of heavy traffic pileups on the nation's roadways. It is also affecting this performance. The spot lights are shining on the green and lush, short cropped grass on the 'grong'and the 'playing' area with its soft dirt, not yet muddy. Both the old, refurbished Ferris-wheel and the chair plane at the south western corner of the savannah are already chug-chug-chugging along. The operators collect the small fee directly from the 'passengers' after they sit, but before the engines are accelerated into motion to commence the 2-3 minute ride.

At 7.15 pm., the opening invocatory prayers are sung by Pundit Yankatessu as the cast and the Ramleela management teams perform the ārti. The Pundit then recaps some of the actions of the previous night's episode, including those discourses between Raja Rāwan and Shurpanakha. He explains the regal, peaceful countenance or 'shanta rasa' of 'Shri' Rām; the warrior's arrogance of Lakshman; the feminine grace or *lashya* and beauty of 'Mother' Sita versus the terrible or *bhayanak* countenance of Shurpanakha. The Pundit also informs the audience that the story has now changed direction, to one of deception: Mārīcha, the magician, has transformed himself into a golden deer. Sita's role is that of an illusion *or maya*, Rāwan as mendicant, a beggar of alms, and Rām as being deceived.

Shurpanakha has instigated her brothers - the demonic beings Khar, Dūsana and Trishira - to avenge her humiliation. With a battalion of *rākshas*, the brothers arrive at Panchavati and attack Rām and Lakshman. They are vanquished; Khar, Dūsana and Trishira escape and run for their lives. Shurpanakha then approaches Rāwan as he sits on his throne (the usual wooden bench on the 'Lanka' platform under a palanquin). Rāwan is dressed in regal attire: a green cape, falling from his shoulders to his ankles, golden crown, white fabric mask and full battle attire of breastplate with his sword and shield at his side.[1] A dialogue ensues between sister and brother. She vividly describes the beauty of Sita to Rāwan and begs him (in mime) to avenge her humiliation. He decides to kidnap Sita so as 'to teach Rām a lesson'. The Pundit narrates as Rāwan decides to solicit the help of the magician, Mārīcha, to execute his plan.

Rāwan descends from his throne on to the grassy 'grong'. He is intent on abducting Sita in retaliation for Rām's behaviour towards his sister. He mounts his 'horse'. It is a cardboard cut-out of a Burroquite or 'Sumerie masquerade' (Kat Ghora), supported by straps over his shoulder with his feet on the ground. This symbolic animal is the East Indian's insertion into the now world famous Trinidad Carnival. With his hands on the reins, Rāwan 'gallops' away, running on his feet. The 'horse' with its payload, enters the open 'grong' on its way to the residence of the super magician, Mārīcha. Mounted on the 'horse', in battle gear, Rāwan looks like a comic replica of *Don Quixote* on his horse, taken straight out of Cervantes' humorous, satirical, literary classic of the same name. It may be classified as caricature at the Felicity village level. But while this is satire at the secular level, it is symbolism in the interpretation of a serious matter of intrigue in Indian mythology that has merged at the 'religious' level. It is the makings of a battle between good and evil, the divine and the demonic, Rām and Rāwan.

Rāwan reaches the abode of Mārīcha, dismounts, tethers the horse and bows to Mārīcha. There is dialogue between Rāwan and Mārīcha. The Pundit speaks and the performers mime. They converse in the middle of the 'stage'. Mārīcha is wearing green satin and gold lamé top, green pants (a Jaipur-design pajama with gold lamé around the calves), a golden crown, green satin cape and tight fitting golden mask. Rāwan requests him to assist in his (Rāwan's) plan to kidnap Sita to teach Rām a lesson in chivalry and military protocol. You disfigure my sister, so I kidnap your wife.

Mārīcha first declines Rāwan's request for assistance, remembering that Rām in a previous encounter had flung him one hundred yojanas (900 km) away. The Vyas reads the text and explains to the audience. Mārīcha in an attempt at extracting himself from being a co-conspirator in this unfolding diabolical plot, tells Rāwan: "O King, I must not make enmity with the following kinds of people: Those who are skilled in weaponry; those who know your secret; a powerful master; a dunce; a doctor or healer; an expert cook or one skilled in witchcraft." Mārīcha, the supreme, quintessential sorcerer and magician, is aware that if he succeeds in creating the diversion for Rāwan to kidnap Sita, Rām will kill him. If he fails, Rāwan will kill him. Either way his fate is sealed. He is doomed. But Rāwan is insistent and Mārīcha reluctantly accedes to his 'wishes'.

The scene changes to the location in Panchavati. Lakshman, with a huge bow covered with white crepe paper and strung with an arrow, marches in front of Rām and Sita who are sitting on a blue wooden bench in front of the hut. He is on guard, ever vigilant of their security. Mārīcha magically transforms himself into a golden deer. Actually he jumps into the yellow costume of the 'golden deer', hoisting its supporting braces over his shoulders, in similar fashion as Rāwan had done with his 'horse'. The deer enters Panchavati, 'feeding' on the grass near the hermitage of Rām and Sita. It darts in and out, among the planted shrubs. Sita, played by a young performer - possibly a 10-12 year old girl - catches a glimpse of this enchanted animal and tries to lure it to her so as to touch it. The deer comes close to her several times then moves, just out of her reach. Unable to touch it, she begs Rām to capture it and bring it to her. With bow strung across his shoulder, Rām goes after the deer as it runs away from the hut.

Now, with an arrow in his bow, he chases the deer round and round the maidān to the accompaniment of a lilting tassa drum 'hand'. The Pundit narrates: "The deer hides behind a clump of trees" - The trees are a few shrubs planted on the ground - Rām climbs a hillock; (he actually stands on a wooden stump) looks for the deer, sees it, and the chase continues." Rām is in hot pursuit of the animal. The pursuer and the pursued are now far from the residence. Rām draws his arrow and shoots. The arrow finds its mark, piercing the deer and Mārīcha falls to the ground. A four or five year old child performer, dressed in the costume of Rām's entourage, runs to the fallen deer. The young lad is caught up in the emotion of the scene. He has actually begun his training early, having been dressed and brought by his mother earlier in the evening and deposited in the playing arena.

As Mārīcha falls, he shouts. Sita hears an imitation of Rām's voice, calling "Lakshman! Lakshman!" She instructs Lakshman to go to the aid of his brother. He, obeying his brother's previous orders not to leave Sita unprotected, declines to obey her. She becomes angry and chides him for not wanting to assist his brother. There is an exchange of dialogue between them. He reluctantly agrees to go, but before he leaves he draws a line around Sita, a *rekha*, telling her not to cross it. The line is a piece of rope, soaked in kerosene and formed into a circle on the ground around her. It is lit with a firecracker - a technological device - fired from his bow. As the flame of the firecracker hits the ground it ignites the soaked rope. With the fire sparkling in the night light, Lakshman departs at running speed in search of his brother.

Rāwan immediately appears in the maidān in the garb of a mendicant. Wearing a long kurta, pajamas with long, yellow, rope hair, an equally long beard up to the stomach, and a face mask, he approaches Sita stealthily, begging alms. "*Bhikshan Dihe, Bhikshan Dihe, Bhikshan Dihe, Bhikshan Dihe.*" The *Vyas* chants the words as Rāwan enacts the role of beggar. Sita fills a plate with grain and

Sita is surrounded by the line (ring of fire) drawn by Lakshman to protect her from harm

fruits and brings it to him. She stands on the inside of Lakshman's drawn line *(Rekha)* with Rāwan on the outside. Rāwan attempts to cross but jumps back in shock as the flames erupt.

Rāwan, in the guise of a mendicant abducts Sita and flees with her on his shoulders

Rāwan switches his image back to Rāwan the King as he escapes

With the rapid spread of the fire, the audience is also visibly startled by the pyrotechnic display. Rāwan cannot cross the line of protection of Sita. He begs her to cross it (the *Lakshman Rekha)* and give him the alms. A player, functioning as a stage hand, pulls out the piece of wick rope from the lighted bamboo in front of Sita, clearing an opening. She is at first hesitant but then crosses the fire through the opening to give Rāwan the food. The Pundit informs the audience that: "Sita has crossed the flaming line, creating the opportunity that Rāwan is waiting for ..." He grabs her, throws her over his shoulder and takes off in his *viman* 'a flying machine'. Actually she holds on to his shoulder as he executes his Ramleela dance steps as she follows behind.

Jatayu, a huge, yellow-feathered bird with a long black beak and wide wing span, enters the scene. A young actor imitating the bird-like movements of Jatayu, flying in the sky, notices Rāwan escaping with Sita. He swoops down to her rescue. With his wings (his hands) fully open, he blocks Rāwan's flight path. On the 'grong' Rāwan puts Sita down to fight Jatayu. The audience has to imagine this scene taking place in midair. Jatayu attacks Rāwan, a frontal blow with his wing. They physically lock fingers and begin spinning, and then Jatayu releases Rāwan, flinging him far away. He topples unto the ground.They engage each other again and again.

Jatayu is tired; his brother Sampati enters the battle. Sampati is dressed in a maroon bird costume with white chest. They battle. Jatayu re-enters and Rāwan cuts off one of his wings. Jatayu falls into a tail spin, out of the sky. He lands heavily to earth. Jatayu attacks with the other wing. Rāwan is flung to the ground, rolling over and over. Tassa drumming keeps up the rapid battle tempo. Nellie's sound effects of 'strong wind' and 'thunder' are heard over the amplified sound system. Jatayu again attacks Rāwan.

Each of the trio of actors - Rāwan, Jatayu and Sita - is exhibiting different emotions. Rāwan is terribly angry, Jatayu very brave and warlike, with Sita being very frightened. The battle rages on. Rāwan is physically tossed around on the ground, his body skidding 10-15 feet on the wet grass. Jatayu beats Rāwan about the body with his remaining wing, both performers now rolling on the ground. The fire at the front of Sita's hut is still burning, but the audience is only seeing the current battle, in a different setting. They have erased the flames from their sight. With one swipe of his wooden sword, Rāwan cuts off Jatayu's other wing but Jatayu still attacks, advancing frontally to Rāwan. Rāwan's sword pierces him and the bird screeches "Hey Rām", and tumbles to the ground, mortally wounded.

Jatayu attempts to prevent Rāwan from reaching Lanka with Sita

Meanwhile the brothers are separately searching the entire forest. While the battle between Rāwan and Jatayu is taking place in the mid-field, they are circumambulating the periphery of the inner barrier in rapid Ramleela dance steps; Rām searching for Sita while Lakshman is searching for Rām. They meet and realising that they have been tricked, Shri Rām and Lakshman return immediately to the hut, only to find her missing.

A quick switch in the roles is undertaken. Rāwan's understudy replaces him as the hypnotic sounds of the tassa drums thunder across the Felicity maidān. Rāwan resumes his journey to Lanka and Sita reluctantly follows behind him, holding on to his cape, as he executes his '1-2-3- brush' Ramleela step.

The Tassa drumming stops as Rām and Lakshman encounter the dying Jatayu, lying on the ground uttering the words, 'Rām, Rām, Rām.' Some parts of the bird's skeleton are now exposed from its fight with Rāwan. It is fabricated out of bamboo and the torso with newspaper, parts of which have been ripped off its body by Rāwan. A dialogue between the dying Jatayu and Rām begins. Jatayu mimes the Pundit's narrative, telling of his valiant attempt to stop Rāwan from carrying Sita away.[2]

Jatayu dies and the funeral rites are performed by Shri Rām. He covers the body with old newspapers and lights camphor around it on the grass as the Pundit chants the relevant chaupais from the text. The pieces of camphor and dry newspaper ignite. Rām uses his arrow to remove one of the camphor pieces, burning too close to the 'dead' bird performer. The cremation sends Jatayu's soul to heaven. Shri Rām and Lakshman proceed south in search of Sita.

Meanwhile, Sita, on her way to Lanka scatters her jewelry in the forest, hoping that this will help Rām to locate the direction of her flight. Tassa begins. Its rhythm accompanies Rāwan on his onward journey to Lanka.

Hanuman and his band of monkeys are now making their appearance for the first time in the 'grong' as part of the story. Hanuman, played by Sundar Jookoo, is a physically big man of 5' 10". He is dressed in red: red short pants, t-shirt, garland, waist band and wearing a mouth extension mask. In his right hand he carries a golden mace or *Mukdar (Gadda)*, the characteristic weapon of this warrior.

At the 2012 Ramleela, on the day that this episode is performed (Day 6, at 8.45 pm), there was a short intermission, a break in story, to introduce the Mayor of Chaguanas, Mr. Orlando Nagessar. He addressed the audience, the management team of the Ramleela and the performers, promising the Felicity Ramleela group a pavilion and a building to house their Ramleela paraphernalia by Ramleela 2013. He also promised that: "negotiations are on the way to make Green Park a Ramleela Centre … but for other festivals also. If not, another location nearby will be located …"

While the Mayor talked, many in the audience were taking a welcome break patronizing the food court and its array of local finger foods: corn on the cob and corn soup - $10.00 per 16 oz. cup; large hot aloo pies at $5.00 each; saheena at $5.00 each; phulouri - $5.00 per small brown paper bag; and paime $5-6.00 each. Everything came straight off the fire to the purchaser. There was an ice cream stall selling home-made ice cream with local flavours: sour sop, peanut, coconut and vanilla. The cones were $4.00 for two scoops; a small cup cost $6.00 and medium size, $8.00. Freshly squeezed, ice cold sugarcane juice was $10.00 and $15.00 per bottle.

The politicking over, the Mayor departed. Then all those who contributed to the Ramleela were publicly acknowledged by a member of the current Ramleela administration. The evening's episode ended at 9.30 pm. with the twenty three performers and four tassa drummers performing the closing ārti.

Day 8: Kishkindha Kanda and Sundara Kanda

The search for Sita: Encounter with Bāli and Sugrīv and the Burning of Lanka

The rains have not stopped. Today, it rained heavily for much of the day. The short periods of sunshine could not dry the ground. There is mud everywhere. Where the mud has not already covered the surface the grass is shiny green and slippery. The performers must exercise extra caution in their movements this evening. This sappy dirt, however, has not prevented the stage crew from continuously reconfiguring the performance area, in keeping with the rapidly unfolding story line. Additional colourful buntings have been strung over the 'playing' area, forming a canopy above the performers' heads. Strings of multicoloured electric lights - red, blue, green and yellow - are strung on the jhandis which dot, as well as support, the peripheral barrier. The maidān is now significantly more forested than on the previous days, reflective of the changing countryside of Bāli's and Sugrīv's kingdom, and the lush vegetation of these pristine forests of Kishkindha. A large clump of trees represents the hermitage of Shabri, the old female devotee of Rām who had waited decades to be in his presence. Another clump of trees on the south-western side, just west of Lanka, represents *Ashokvātika*, the grove of Ashoka trees where Sita is being kept captive by Rāwan.

The ārti begins shortly after 7.00 pm.[3] This is followed by the standard performance format of the initial circumambulations of the 'grong' by the performers with their signature dancing movements. At 7.20 pm. the Princes, Rām and Lakshman, continue their search of Sita. They are attired in immaculate orange costumes: Dhoti, *kamarband*, a sash across the chest falling at the waistline, garlands of *rudrāksha* beads around their necks, on their wrists and arms and ghungroos strapped on their ankles. Their faces are immaculately made-up, using the local brand of Sasha cosmetics. They are armed with golden bows and arrows. Instead of the usual crowns, their hair is tied in knots atop their heads. They are, after all, living in exile.

Rām and Lakshman search for Sita

The Pundit informs his audience that simultaneously in Lanka, Rāwan is visiting Sita in Ashokvātika expressing his feelings, his intense love for her, and begging her to be his queen. Wearing simple attire in sober colours with no jewelry, she "reprimands him for his misdeeds. He in turn, gives her one year to reconsider his offer". Queen Mandodari, with the etiquette and protocols befitting noble birth and regal upbringing, sends a full set of royal attire for Sita to wear. Sita returns it with her compliments, saying that since her husband is dressed as a hermit she will continue to wear the simple and appropriate attire. Queen Mandodari, touched by Sita's love for her husband, begs Raja Rāwan to return Sita to Rām to avoid his (Rāwan's) impending doom. He refuses to listen to her, scoffing at her advice.

Meanwhile, as Rām and Lakshman search for Sita they are caught by the outstretched arms of an ugly *rākshas,* Kabandha. It has no head; its mouth is on its belly and eyes on its chest. They cut off the arms of Kabandha thus releasing him from the curse that had transformed him into this demonic being. However, before he dies he advises them to visit the old lady Shabri, and to gain friendship with Sugrīv, now living on the Rishyamooka Hill. Rām and Lakshman then proceed through the forested ground to Tambour (Rishi Kut

Mountain), passing through lakes and mountains. As they enjoy the scenery, Nārad muni travelling with his characteristic Veena, passes by, observing and taking note of the entire scenario. Nothing escapes his attention.

The scene shifts to Shabri. Living in her forest hermitage, she has been waiting patiently for many years, praying for a vision, a *darshan* of Shri Rām. On their arrival at her ashram she is overwhelmed with joy. The Pundit tells his audience of Shabri's, "love and devotion to Shri Rām. Being devoid of sight she picks fruits from her garden, tastes them to ensure that they are sweet, and then feeds them to her beloved Rām. Lakshman declines her offer of fruits... She is blessed by Shri Rām and ascends to the heavens." Rām and Lakshman stay a while and then continue their search for Sita.

Outside the performance barriers there is a constant stream of people entering the maidān, gingerly picking their way around the patches of mud to get a ringside view of the evening's 'play'. There is also a constant beeline from the audience area to the food court. The stalls are crowded with patrons making brisk purchases and hurrying back to view the unfolding story.

Another sub-story is introduced by the V*yas*, that of Sugrīv and Bāli. Sugrīv a former ruler of the forest kingdom of Kishkindha, by strange circumstances is beaten and driven out of his kingdom by his brother Bāli. Seeing Rām and Lakshman in the vicinity of Lake Pampa, approaching the mountains, Sugriv sends his companion Hanuman to investigate the presence of these two strangers there, to ensure that they are not Bāli's spies. He is suspicious of all strangers.

Hanuman belongs to the forest tribe of *Bānars* who look like monkeys. The son of the god of the wind, Pāwan, and Anjana; he has the capability to transform himself at will into different forms. He assumes the form of a Brahmin - wearing lemon dhoti, orange *angwastram* and is bare headed as he approaches the strangers. The brother informs him that they are sons of King Dasarath and are in search of Sita. Realising who they are, he reveals his true identity, Hanuman. There is a rapid switch of performers and the new Hanuman appears to the visitors. He now wears a golden crown, red and yellow knee-length short pants, waistband, with a red angwastram and carrying his battle weapon, the *mukdar* or mace. He embraces the princes and escorts them to Sugrīv.

Sugrīv shows Rām the jewels that Sita had dropped while in Rāwan's chariot on her way to Lanka. Sugrīv then relates to Rām his present circumstances and his predicament. The Pundit narrates the story: "One day a demon challenged the two brothers, Bāli and Sugrīv. The demon, Mayabi, disappeared into a cave. Bāli instructed Sugrīv to wait at the entrance of the cave as he pursued the demon into its lair. Sugrīv waited six days. On the seventh day, blood gushed out of the cave. Sugrīv felt that Bāli had died and blocked the entrance of the cave, to prevent Mayabi from emerging. He returned to Kishkindha with the news of Bāli's death and became ruler of the kingdom. Bāli subsequently returned, accused Sugrīv of treason, and drove him out of the kingdom…"

After listening to Sugrīv's story, Rām and he swear everlasting friendship, promising to assist each other in resolving their problems. Shri Rām assures Sugrīv that he will kill Bāli and restore the throne to him, but Sugrīv is doubtful about the strength of Shri Rām and his capability to undertake the act. To demonstrate his prowess, Shri Rām releases one arrow from his bow which cuts down seven trees. In fact, as Rām fires the arrow, a string that held the seven leafy twigs upright is released by a stage hand. They all snap at the same level and collapse. Sugrīv is convinced of the capability of Rām. Shri Rām now advises Sugrīv to challenge Bāli in battle so that he (Rām) can ambush and shoot him (Bāli).

During the battle between Sugrīv and Bāli, Rām shoots Bāli, mortally wounding him

Sugrīv challenges his brother Bāli to a duel. Bāli accepts the challenge and rushes out at Sugrīv; the two brothers fight fiercely. It is a violent physical encounter with accompanying battle rhythm of the tassa drums. Sugrīv is experiencing the worse of the battle, being tossed and thrown around the 'grong'. He returns to Rām for an explanation of his delay in killing Bāli. Rām explains that he is unable to distinguish one fighter from the other. Shri Rām provides a flowered mala to Sugrīv to identify him. The battle resumes. Rām is hiding behind a tree - a shrub that was planted during the day. At the opportune moment he shoots at Bāli, mortally wounding him.

Rām emerges from the bushes and Bāli accuses him of cheating, but Rām responds by pointing out to Bāli the injustice of his (Bāli's) act to his brother, driving him out of the kingdom and coveting his wife. Bāli pleads for forgiveness. Bāli's wife, Tara, arrives with their son Angad and they tearfully fall at his (Bali's) side. Bāli requests Rām to protect Angad while instructing Angad to serve Shri Rām.

The 'Ayodhya' palace is now transformed into Sugrīv's kingdom in Kishkindha. With his newly regained self-esteem and kingdom, Sugrīv forgets about his promise to help Rām locate Sita 'after the rains ended'. But the rains have long stopped, with no sign of Sugrīv. Lakshman is dispatched to instill fear in Sugrīv for not adhering to his promise. Lakshman goes and achieves his purpose. Sugrīv apologises for his lapse and with his army, they return to Rām.

At about 9:08 pm., there are approximately three thousand, five hundred people behind the barriers and forty-five players in the maidān. Some other players are dressed in the garb of the local carnival characters of *jab-jab*. These *jab jabs* are really not part of the main characters of the storyline but performers on the fringe, loitering on the periphery of the 'grong', engaging the audience in comic relief.

Army divisions are dispatched by Sugriv to the four corners of the land. Hanuman leads one division southwards. Shri Rām gives Hanuman his ring so that on locating Sita he can assure her that he (Hanuman) is his (Shri Rām's) messenger. Hanuman's battalion comprises, Nal, Neel, Angad, Jāmbavan and many more warriors. They arrive at the southern sea shore, encountering Sampati, the older bird brother of Jatayu. With a remarkable vision, speaking though a face mask, Sampati informs Hanuman that Sita is in Lanka in Rāwan's grove of Ashoka trees, *Ashokvātika*, and is guarded by fierce demonic beings.

Hanuman flies to Lanka in search of Sita

The story flawlessly enters the fifth book of the Ramcharitmānas' text, the *Sundara Kanda*. The audience is told that: "Hanuman expands himself and leaps across the ocean towards Lanka, but he has many obstacles to overcome in crossing the ocean before reaching his destination. On the way he politely refuses Manik's offer to rest. Then he outwits Surasa. He encounters Singhika, who opens her mouth and draws him in. Hanuman kills her, escapes and reaches Lanka. At the main gate he confronts Lankini, the guardian Goddess of Lanka, defeats her and enters the city." The Pundit transports his audience to Lanka: He narrates: "It is morning in Lanka. Hanuman is in the bedroom of Vibhishan, the brother of Rāwan. Vibhishan awakes with the incantation on his lips, *Jai Shree Rām*! They speak. Vibhishan explains that he is a devotee of Shri Rām but since he lives in Lanka, whose ruler is hostile to Rām, he has to be very cautious of his behaviour." Vibhishan informs Hanuman that; "Surviving in that current environment is like the 'tongue between teeth,' it can be bitten any time."

Hanuman then proceeds to locate Sita. He finds her in *Ashokvātika*. He climbs up into the tree under which Sita is seated and drops Shri Rām's ring in front of her. She is startled at the sight of the ring and more astonished as he presents himself to her.

Hanuman assures her that Shri Rām will rescue her without delay. She entrusts her bracelet to him to take to Rām. With Sita's permission, Hanuman ravages the garden of Ashokvātika. Half of the trees in the grove are uprooted in his overwhelming display of strength. The destruction is performed to the rhythm of live tassa drumming.

The news of Hanuman's presence in Lanka reaches Rāwan who sends Indrajit to quell the disturbances. He finds Hanuman and hurls his *Bramaastra* weapon at him which enwraps him. Hanuman actually allows himself to be caught and brought to Rāwan's

Hanuman locates Sita in Ashokvātika

court where he informs Rāwan that he is Rām 's messenger, and advises him to seek refuge at Shri Rām's feet. Enraged at his actions and advice, Rāwan orders him to be killed. Vibhishan, the younger brother of Rāwan, advises caution, indicating that it is unethical to kill a messenger. Then Rāwan orders that Hanuman's tail be set on fire. As his tail is being lighted, Hanuman shrinks in size, freeing himself of the rope bindings.

The scene shifts. Several activities are taking place simultaneously in various parts of the 'grong' or in quick succession. Rāwan goes to visit his queen Mandodari, to inform her that he proposes that Sita be his second wife, under her administrative watch. She disregards his statements, not even looking at him. Meanwhile Sita is being harassed by her *rākshasi* guards. It is now 9.25 pm. The audience is still engrossed in the Pundit's chanting from the text and his explanations in *Trinhinglish,* the colloquial dialect.

The audience has grown even larger. It is packed 9-10 persons deep at the outside periphery of the barrier; approximately 5,000 people. They have come to see the burning of Lanka. There is no visible sign of security, no police presence, and no concern is expressed at their absence. There are no signs of rowdy or inconsiderate behaviour, no pushing, shoving, rude or foul language. No alcohol or meat is either sold or consumed on the ground. The audience is totally disciplined. This is the behavioural norm in Felicity for all of its village activities, the major ones of which are Ramleela, and Divali.

An announcement is made on the microphone by a member of the stage management team, asking parents to keep their kids away from the barriers for fear that they may collapse from the pressure of the crowd and thus cause harm to those leaning on them. They are also advised to be cautious of the open flames that will be used in the ensuing scene. The tassa drums change their rhythm to that of battle tempo. There is much excitement and animated action in the maidān. Hanuman's tail is lit and he is set free in Lanka. He jumps from building to building causing everything to burn. Actually, on the southern side of the playing field, bamboo is stuck to the ground and paper is placed around it. Hanuman's tail grows into a long lighted rope. Holding the rope in his hand he wields it at his enemies and at the bamboo and paper props and sets which represent the buildings. The sets begin to burn. With rapid speed Hanuman seems to have multiplied himself, creating many Hanumans - many monkeys enter the maidān and with their tails on fire they assist in burning the city. The appearance of many Hanumans in this context has 'bent' the text to create theatrics in Felicity. Five, 10-12 feet long staves, one end wrapped in sack cloth, soaked in kerosene, are lighted. 'Hanumans' run down the 'grong' wielding the flaming staves around their bodies, setting fire to Lanka. The 'monkeys' chase the Lankan guards around the maidān with the long staves, flaming at the tips.

In the 2012-2016 versions of the scene, another activity is added. Huge balls of flames are blown into the night sky from the mouths of some of the monkeys, bānars, filled with methylated spirit. This flame throwing, also a familiar scene in the Trinidad Carnival, but a relatively new addition to this Ramleela scene, lights up the sky above the maidān. In 2008 I had seen this activity in the Ramleela of Sahabganj in Ayodhya, India, which has been in existence for approx. 150 years. By a strange twist of fate, that specific Ramleela was introduced there by Mungal Singh, the son of an indentured Indian, a Trinidadian by birth. With his brother Adhar Singh, they had been taken back to Kanpur, India with their father Bhagwansingh after he had served his indentureship in Trinidad, leaving the rest of his family (9 sisters and mother) here.[4] I had suggested to the Ramleela organisers the introduction of the flame throwing in the scene. The rest is now history.

Hanuman burns Lanka

Open flames are burning everywhere. Demons are scampering. Hanuman is on a rampage. The Pundit loudly pronounces over the microphone to his audience; 'Don't say Superman, say Hanuman'. In local Indian folklore, Hanuman is superior to the comic strip heroes, Superman and Batman; after all he is the son of the God of the Wind (*Pāwan putra Hanuman*). The clothing of some of the Lankan guards catch fire, but they are wearing fire resistant clothing. They roll on the wet grassy turf of the maidān, quickly extinguishing the individual blazes. The booming thunder of the tassa drums contribute to the tremendous excitement by both the performers and the audience, each contributing to that of the other.

Burning of one of Lanka's guards

This action scene of the burning of Lanka, of excitement and suspense goes on for 15 minutes. It brings the action out of the text of the Ramcharitmānas on to the field of play in Green Park. It provides its own context; a local village interpretation of this ancient tale, performed in present time. It is happening now. Past time has become present, sacred time. While the present space is Felicity, which establishes the environment for the reinterpretation of the story, it simultaneously materializes the story. It merges physical distances, extended time, amplified sound, light and darkness, aggression and fear expressed by the people of Lanka to the burning of their beautiful city that, according to legend, is partly burnished with gold. This fear, combined with excitement, is similarly expressed by the audience.

While the whole of Lanka, almost the entire Ramleela 'grong', is set ablaze, there is no Fire Brigade in sight, making it extremely dangerous to the health and safety of all, players and audience alike. The players are too involved to consider the ramifications of something going wrong. The audience is too engrossed, screaming and laughing at the fleeing demons of Lanka escaping the open, flames which had spread to almost three quarters of the maidān. Thankfully, nothing goes awry. The stage management crew, with efficiency, management effectiveness and experience has been able to contain the actions of this scene within the performing area of the maidān. There have been no casualties on this day, during this episode, for as long as can be remembered over the decades.[5] The scene ends around 10.20 pm.

With sweat glistening on the bare bodies of some of the performers, the entire cast of forty-three players[6] ends the evening's performance with their customary parikrama around the 'grong', doing their signature Ramleela 'dance'. The closing prayer, ārti and final benediction are performed at 10.30 pm. Within a short period of time the maidān is empty of both performers and audience.

ENDNOTES

1. In the same episode of 2012, Rāwan wore a rich white and silver long-sleeved top and a silver shining dhoti stitched like a pantaloon down to the ankles, a multicoloured cape draped over his shoulders and dropping to the calves, golden crown, and white mask over a cloth covering his head and neck. Personal obs. by author.
2. This scene was performed at the beginning of day 8 in the year 2012 because the rain had brought a premature closure to the day's play on day 7. Personal obs. of author in 2012.
3. In 2012 the ārti began at 7.35 pm. with twenty seven players, four tassa drummers and the Pundit. The puja took about twelve minutes for all players to perform ārti at the centre of the field. Personal obs. of author in 2012.
4. Satnarine Balkaransingh, Ph.D. Dissertation, 2010. P97.
5. Personal Interviews with members of the management team of the First Felicity Ramleela. This scene has taken place over the period 2007-2016, the full duration of the field work for this publication.
6. Personal observation by the author on 20th October 2007.

Chapter Thirteen

DAILY PERFORMANCE: DAYS 9-10

DAY 9: *Lanka Kanda or Yudh Kanda*

A bridge is built over the ocean, to Lanka; Rām's army crosses into Lanka; Rāwan kicks Vibhishan out of Lanka; Sita gives her jewelry to Hanuman to bring for Rām

This evening the episode of Rām and his army entering Lanka to engage Rāwan in the war for Sita's release is to be performed. It will be the turning point in Lanka's administration. Thirty coloured flags; 12 red, 6 yellow, 5 silver, 4 gold, 2 black and 1 orange are fluttering from these barrier flagpoles, spaced at regular intervals. They surround the tall pivotal flagpole flying the tricolour pennant; red, yellow and white. Nineteen miniature red flags flutter from the base of this *mool jhanda*. Two miniature mountains, fabricated out of bamboo and crepe paper, form part of the props.

The maidān is decorated, similar to what Nobel Laureate, Derek Walcott, had seen and described, more than two decades earlier, 'as a new gas station'[1] with flags and buntings radiating from the central flagpole to the smaller poles, planted and tied to the barrier separating audience from performers. Walcott happened to be at the Felicity maidān on one of the days (possibly a Saturday just as this one) when the Leela was being performed.[2] He described the early stages of the construction of the effigies which, according to local tradition, would be erected annually for the final battle, the victory and the flaming end of Rāwan. Walcott described the scene thus:

> *Under an open shed on the edge of the field, there were two huge armatures of bamboo that looked like immense cages. They were parts of the body of a god, his calves or thighs, which, fitted and reared, would make a gigantic effigy. This effigy would be burnt as a conclusion to the epic…*

Walcott continued his description of the scene at the Felicity Ramleela:

> *Drummers had lit a fire in the shed and they eased the skins of the tables[3] nearer the flame to tighten them. The saffron flames, the bright grass, and the hand-woven armatures of the fragmented god who would be burnt were not in any desert where imperial power had finally toppled but were part of the ritual evergreen season that, like the cane burning harvest, is annually repeated, the point of such sacrifice being its repetition, the point of the destruction being renewal through fire.*

This evening the weather is inclement, the sky is heavily overcast. There is a small audience. The performance begins at 7:25 pm., much later than its scheduled commencement time. There are twenty five performers on the field, two musicians to accompany the Pundit's singing and chanting - one dholak, one dhantāl player - and four tassa drummers. The approximately one hundred and fifty people on the ground are moving between the food court and the audience area. It has taken twelve minutes for the ārti to be completed.[4] Pundit Yankatessu commences the evening's 'play' by explaining the loving relationship between Shri Rām and Hanuman, and the absolute devotion of Hanuman for Rām. He chants: "*Jai Rām, Shri Rām, Jai Jai Rām...*"

The Felicity Ramleela 'Grong' is being prepared for the evening play

The story has progressed to the sixth book of the Tulsidas's version of the Rām story, known as *Lanka Kanda* or *Yudh Kanda.* The narrative is centered primarily in Lanka, where a war is about to be waged. Hence the naming of this section as *Yudh Kanda. Yudh* means 'war'. After his burning of Lanka, Hanuman returns to 'Sita Mata' and they converse. The action is dramatised. She gives her jewellery to Hanuman, explains her predicament with Rāwan and asks Hanuman to inform Rām that if he does not rescue her in one month's time she will 'destroy herself.'

Sita gives her jewelry to Hanuman to take to Rām

With this information Hanuman departs Ashokvātika and Lanka to return to Shri Rām. On returning to the seaside camp where his monkey and bear troops are awaiting him, they proceed to meet King Sugrīv, Rām and Lakshman. Hanuman presents to Shri Rām, Sita's bracelet with her request for an early release from confinement in Lanka. Shri Rām affectionately thanks him for his efforts with an embrace. They hold detailed discussions of Hanuman's trip to Lanka and the various activities that transpired there.

Plans are now made for crossing the ocean. Rāwan's spies inform him that Shri Rām, Lakshman and Sugrīv and their army have reached the opposite seashore. Trijita the ogress, and Sita's guard, informs Sita of the news. But Queen Mandodari has great misgivings. She approaches Rāwan, pleading with him to return Sita back to her husband. She argues that: "If one monkey could come and create so much destruction, no one, not even Lord Shiva - your patron deity - could save you from Rām's arrow". This episode is enacted on the raised platform of Lanka's palace. Rāwan laughs, a mighty bellowing sound: "Ah haa, haa, haa, haa." The Pundit delivers the sound through the microphone as Rāwan mimes it. Rāwan then proceeds, with a majestic, arrogant stride, to his royal chamber. In effect he descends the stairs, to the 'grong' and summons his war council. His military commanders all dressed in military attire and in full battle readiness, support their King's impending war and their anticipated victory over Rām.

But his brother Vibhishan intervenes and pleads with him (Rāwan) to return Sita back to Shri Rām. Against the background of intense appropriate drumming, Vibhishan dramatically falls at the feet of Rāwan, imploring him to reconsider his impending actions. Rāwan is not in any mood for such advice. He literally kicks Vibhishan - who falls on the ground - and orders him to leave Lanka immediately. With four of his ministers Vibhishan flees - he actually performs the Ramleela 'dancing' movements as he moves away - to the camp of Shri Rām where he introduces himself (to Rām) as the brother of Rāwan and requests refuge 'at Shri Rām's feet'. Rām accepts Vibhishan as a friend and assures him of his installation on the throne of Lanka after Rāwan's defeat.

Rāwan with his war council

Strategic intrigue continues. Rāwan dispatches Sukh, one of his trusted advisors to meet and dissuade Sugrīv from maintaining loyalty to Shri Rām. Sukh goes to Sugrīv and tells him that both he (Sugrīv) and Rāwan are Kings and, as such, he should earn Rāwan's friendship instead of risking his life with Rām. This pleading is unsuccessful. He is captured as a spy and brought to Rām who instructs that he be released to return to Lanka.

Vibhishan then advises Shri Rām to invoke the God of the sea (Varun Devta) to allow the army a safe passage across the ocean into Lanka. This invocatory incantation is performed and they wait, but after three days there is still no response. Angrily, Lakshman strings his bow to shoot at the sea 'to dry up its water'. Varun appears and advises Rām to perform worship to Lord Shiva and then commence to build a bridge across the ocean.

It is 9:40 pm.; there is a break in the narrative. The action in the maidān stops temporarily. Mr. Saith of the Ramleela management committee makes the daily announcement of persons and groups who have contributed to this year's Ramleela production. Play resumes and the leaders of the army perform the required rituals to build the bridge across the ocean. Shri Rām instructs the in-house architect and engineer, brothers Nal and Neel to commence the construction of the bridge. The army of monkeys and bears - under the supervision of Nal and Neel - break rocks, uproot trees and carry them to the sea shore to construct the bridge. The uprooted trees are actually shrubs planted as props. The construction commences on the western side of the maidān, within the performance area to the rhythm of the Tassa drums. Finally, the bridge is completed. Its surface is constructed out of bamboo and covered with black cotton cloth. Rām fashions a *Shiva lingam* out of sand and worships Lord Shiva. Then with Sugrīv and his *banar* army of monkeys and bears - to the accompaniment of the Pundit's chanting and explanation and a military rhythm on the tassa ensemble - cross the man-made bridge over the ocean, into Lanka. They encamp in its orchard groves.

Rāwan, on hearing that Shri Rām and Lakshman have crossed the sea bridge, summons his magician, orders him to prepare a head resembling Rām's, and with his *maya* (illusion). This is done, the head is delivered. Summoning up all his dramatic ability, as King and warrior, Rāwan takes the head, smeared with blood, to Ashokvātika. He informs Sita that her husband has been beheaded, presenting the head to her as evidence. Sita gasps at the head but refuses to believe Rāwan.

The evening's play has gone far beyond its scheduled closing time; it is now 10:11 pm., the group dance is performed and Pundit Yankatessu conducts the closing ārti and mangalam, terminating the evening's episode at 10:30 pm.

Day 10: Lanka Kanda or Yudh Kanda

Mandodari pleads with Rāwan; spies in Rām's camp; Angad as ambassador in Rāwan's court; battles between opposing forces; final encounter between Rām and Rāwan; Vijay Dashami

Vijay Dashmi in Felicité

(Victory on the tenth day)

Indentured Indians pioneering village theatre, Raghu's Leela,
Chanting and interpreting verses of this ancient saga
Of the legend of Prince Rāma of Kosala,
Battling demons and armies scattered all over India,
To rescue beautiful Sita from Raja Rawan of Lanka.

Today the staccato rhythm of the booming Tassa
Drowns out the audible roll of a distant thunder,
Cumulus clouds mingle with crimson nimbus, Ashwin weather
Conjuring images of mystic lakes of molten lava
In the evening sky over the Felicité Ramleela.

Even the egrets in precise squadron formation
Glide overhead stealthy, like a dark bomber battalion,
Rama's air force scanning the scene of today's conflagration,
Riding the air currents to their secret destination,
A foreboding omen of King Rawan's destruction.

T'is a tale of valour embodying an ancient culture,
An epic story that predates Christianity,
The legend of Sita and Prince Rāma of Ayodhya
Brought by audacious adventurers across the Kali Pani,
And blossoming for a century in this soil of La Trinite.

This is possibly one of the most anticipated days of the eleven - day saga of the Felicity Ramleela.Today Rām and his army of *bānars* or forest tribes will engage in several skirmishes with mighty warriors of Lanka, see the fortunes of war rise and fall and finally triumph in battle over Lanka's ruler, Raja Rāwan. The text of this evening's narrative continues to be chanted from *Lanka Kanda* or *Yudh Kanda.*The 'grong' has been subjected to a fresh sprucing up. The grass has been freshly mowed and is spotlessly clean, notwithstanding the thousands of feet that have trampled on its surface over the last 9 days, some evenings trudging through rain, mud, slush and garbage produced from the food area. However the maidān is spotlessly clean every succeeding day of performance.

This evening the 'grong' continues to look like Walcott's 'new gas station'[5] with flags and buntings radiating from the central or *mool Jhanda* to the smaller flagpoles tied to the barrier. A profusion of coloured pennants fly on the flag poles; red, yellow, silver, gold, black and orange spaced at regular intervals, fluttering in the evening's breeze. They form an aerial, elliptical pattern surrounding the tall, pivotal tricolor one. The miniature red flags continue to fly from the base of this central *jhanda.* Two miniature mountains, fabricated out of bamboo and crepe paper, are added to the props. Two tall and imposing effigies have also been erected. They 'stand' at the southern corner of the 'grong', dominating the immediate environment. Some years, only one effigy was erected.

In 2014 the stage hands and ground technicians, with the assistance of a mechanical lift, had worked feverishly, from morning, to complete the assembly and erection of these last set of props; the two effigies 'planted' just east of the palace of Lanka. The smaller one, 19 feet tall, with a portly frame, pudgy face, cup-shaped ears and googly, protruding eyes was that of Kumbhakaran, the warrior brother of Rāwan. His body was 14 feet tall with the head and crown measuring another 5 feet in height. As in previous years the effigy was supported by a bamboo skeleton, crudely covered with papier maché paper, and painted green and pink. The pink colour was supposedly that of his skin, or maybe the artist was just asserting artistic license. In 2015 however the effigies were different; less pudgy looking and more slim. Kumbhkaran was painted red and blue. The blue colour is supposedly that of his skin, or maybe the painter was again asserting artistic license.

The other effigy, similar in design and structure, stood 44 feet tall; the body 32 feet, the head 8 feet; with a crown of 4 feet but with ten heads - the main one being fierce looking with piercing, green laser-beam eyes and visible upper teeth. It had saucer-shaped ears, a moustache curving upwards, a black 'goatee' beard, with sword and shield in its hands. The crown was of green lamé dotted with multicoloured gems, bright red *tikka*, with two hanging balls for earrings. His face, shoulder armour and waist band were painted yellow and green with the rest of the costume, blue. Each year the effigy is presented with different colour combinations. It is hoisted in an upright position a short distance away, east of Kumbhakaran. This is Rāwan, the main antagonist of this epic drama.

This year the commencement of construction of these effigies had begun approx. 3 weeks before the actual start of the Leela. The armatures of what were to be the effigies were built separately on a wooden and bamboo superstructure, framed out of bamboo and wire, then assembled and hoisted erect in the maidān. This construction was undertaken in the 'community' centre, situated on the southern periphery of the ground, between the savannah and Boundary Road.

From mid-afternoon, entire families in the village, some carrying umbrellas and portable chairs begin converging on the Green Park Savannah. They are arriving early to secure a good vantage point in anticipation of the excitement of today's episode of the Leela. The anticipated excitement is exactly what Nobel Laureate Sir Vidya Naipaul had experienced as a child - having been born and living in his ancestral home, *The Lion House* in Chaguanas, and to which he alluded in *Literary Occasion* when he attended the Leela:

> *One of the first big public things I was taken to was the Ramleela, the pageant-ry-play based on the Rāmayāna... It was done in an open field in the middle of sugarcane, on the edge of our small country town. The male performers were bare backed and some carried long bows; they walked in a slow, stylized, rhythmic way, on their toes, and with high quivering steps; ... The pageant ended with the burning of the big black effigy of the demon king of Lanka. This burning was one of the things that people had come for; and the effigy, roughly made, with tar paper on a bamboo frame, had been standing in the open field all the time, as a promise of the conflagration. Everything in that Ramleela had been transported from India in the memories of people. And though as theatre it was crude... the Ramleela had given reality, and a lot of excitement, to what I had known of the Rāmayāna*'[16].

Today, decades later, greater numbers of spectators and devotees of Shri Rām continue to make this pilgrimage to see the Ramleela. By 5.30 pm. the pennants of the jhandis - both festive and prayer ones - with their myriad colours are flying in the gentle evening breeze as the sun continues its descent into the western horizon. The western sky is ablaze with the bright yellow-orange-red cloud mix of our tropical twilight. This evening they are the harbinger of the fiery conflagration that is to follow. Animation is intense. The parking areas are being filled with vehicles of every description viz. cars, maxi-taxis and sport utility vehicles (SUVs), old and new, representing a wide cross-section of local socio-economic status. At 6.30 pm. the audience enclave, the entertainment area of chair plane and merry-go-round and the food court are all full. Over 9,000 people are already in the maidān.

Outside the performers' enclosure, the spectators - the young and young-at-heart - are parading their raiment, 'strutting in their finery'. Their levels of sophistication differ, varying widely from simple attire to village understanding of *haute couture*. The fashions range from the gaudy; *jagmaga* saris, salwār kamise and kurtas with slapdash make-up, to that of elegance; smartly cut, well fitted and aesthetically pleasing urban sophistry.The fabrics, designs and brand names of the clothing being sported also reflect both village simplicity and urban sophistication. Fab India, Nino Mantelli and Aman Chikan compete with Banana Republic, Gap, Van Heusen, Tommy Hilfiger, Nike and Polo. Egyptian cotton brushes shoulders with Indian cotton. georgette, rayon, chiffon, lamé, silks and Indian dungaree - now rebranded as 'jeans' and 'Levis' - compete with one another. Even if these village beaux and belles did not consider Trinidad, or the world as such, they certainly treated the Ramleela ground as a stage.

This evening the Green Park maidān is a veritable catwalk, the youths its models, their attire competing with those of the Ramleela 'players' now resplendent in all their glory. Only the intent and purpose of the two sets of 'performers' differ. Inside the sacred space (the 'grong') the fabrics which the swarūps and pātras are wearing include cotton, satin, lamé, spandex and silk to represent the regalia of the epic being interpreted and also to ensure costume durability from rough and long use.The warriors of both armies are dressed in all their military garb of legendary fame. The army of Shri Rām is adorned in splendid attire; flashing bright colours of gold, green, white and red, mix and match. Rām and Lakshman are both wearing armless breast plates of golden fabric and matching green dhotis, with golden crowns. Their battle ornaments are also of gold. So too, are the quivers on their backs, plastered over with crepe paper and filled with thin bamboo arrows. They carry long bows covered with crepe and reflector paper which will bounce the light beams from the overhead flood lights. It is modern technology of an imagined, ancient warfare. Hanuman has also donned a new costume - an emerald (or is it blue?) waist band tied tightly over a shiny, salmon coloured, short pants dropping to his calf. This is the characteristic length of Hanuman's pants. He wears a golden necklace with a golden crown and a thick, coloured, plastic mala around his neck, falling to his waist, and carries his mukdar.

From Lanka, Rāwan and his warriors are all dressed in new battle gear; breastplates and long-sleeved armour, long capes flowing from shoulder to ground, long baggy dhoti pants, and large golden, blue and green crowns with white gloves on their hands. Today, they have shed their face masks of the previous days, appearing with only the masks of heavy, facial make-up. There is, however, no conflict here between tradition and modernity, creativity and the carnivalesque. Rather, they are morphing into a contemporary, theatrical, folk performance - very Trinidadianesque - what may be referred to as *deshbheda,*[7] belonging to or uniquely characteristic to our Trinidadian aesthetic.

The archers of Rām's army on the battlefield

Today the tassa ensemble has also doubled its complement of percussionists and accompanying instruments; dhols (bass), tassas (kettle drums hung from the shoulders and played with thin sticks, ball-shaped at the ends) and jhanj (brass cymbals).

Rāwan with a section of his army on the battle field, without face masks

It is 6.45 pm. The performers line up under the tall, central flagpole and the evening's puja begins This long line of dazzlingly attired performers complete the ārti at the sanctified, consecrated bedi and immediately commence their signature Ramleela 'theme' dance, separated into the conventional two sections, the battalions of Rām and Rāwan. The tassa ensemble is booming, its rhythm whetting the appetite, anticipating the excitement of the evening's drama. The armies move in their usual anti-clockwise directions on opposite sides of the field, then cross in the middle, engage each other briefly, then return to their respective camps. The Pundit provides a synopsis of the previous day's episode to the audience. He recounts that:

> *The army of Rām having bridged the ocean had crossed into Lanka and was encamped on its sea shore… In a desperate attempt to convince his captive, Sita, to accept him, Rāwan got his sorcerer to make a head similar to that of Rām's and sent it to Sita, so she will believe that Rām had been beheaded. She refused to believe the hoax...*

Now playing his harmonium and accompanied by his musicians, Pundit Yankatessu chants directly from the Rāmcharitmānas, Gita Press publication, and translates for both the audience and performers. Queen Mandodari again begs her husband, Rāwan, not to fight with Shri Rām, advising him instead to surrender and return Sita to him. The scene is being dramatized. But Rāwan, so full of arrogance and ego would not listen to anyone's advice. His disdain is carried in his arrogant laughter; the Pundit utters a bellowing, guttural laugh over the microphone: "Hah Hah Hah Hah! Instead Rāwan dispatches two spies, Sukh and Sarana, to the camp of Shri Rām. Disguised as monkeys, they enter the camp but Vibhishan captures them… Shri Rām forgives them and sends them back to Rāwan with the information they have gathered."

The Pundit continues his chanting from the selected script of the Rāmcharitmānas. In his *Trinhinglish* delivery, he informs his audience that Shri Rām is taking the opportunity to admire the capital city of Lanka. With his entourage, Rām and Lakshman circumambulate the entire 'grong' with their 'dancing 'movements to the accompaniment of tassa drumming. They look over the heads of the audience, as if admiring the architecture and aesthetic physical beauty of the city of Lanka and its people. In the process, the spectators of the drama have become the citizens of Lanka. The architecture of the buildings on the periphery of the maidān is Lanka's architecture. Sacred and ancient time and space merge and become temporal time and space. Fast forward the scene. King Sugrīv and Rāwan see each other and enter into a brief skirmish. Sugrīv disengages and returns safely to his 'group', but Rām cautions him that it is not advisable for "a King like him to take such a risk".

Shiva and Parvati enter the 'grong'. Shiva carries the *trishul*, the 3-pronged trident in his left hand with his right hand outstretched in a gesture or *mudra* of 'blessing'. Parvati is at his left side. They move with elaborate steps, in slow motion, as if walking on air. Undisturbed, they circumambulate the periphery of the performance space, figuratively viewing the scene from their heavenly abode, *Brahm Loka,* mere witnesses to the evolving scenario, to the *karma* of the period and to the people involved.

Shri Rām, now exhibiting compassion, feels that Rāwan deserves a last chance. He dispatches Angad - the son of Bāli and heir to the throne of Sugrīv - as an ambassador to Rāwan's court with the message to return Sita to Shri Rām and seek his forgiveness. Rāwan receives Angad in his court, which is conducted in midfield. Rāwan listens to Angad's message but makes a counter offer to Angad; that he will restore his (Angad's) rightful throne left by his father, Bāli, to him and that he should kill Shri Rām to avenge his father's death. Angad replies that his father's dying wish was for him to serve Shri Rām, advising Rāwan to surrender instead.

Angad assumes his warrior's character. Stamping his foot and planting it firmly on the ground, Angad challenges Rāwan's men to lift it. Amid intense drumming all the strong warriors at the court attempt but fail. Rāwan approaches to try but Angad removes his foot, telling Rāwan that he should: 'Fall instead at the feet of Shri Rām, and not at my foot.' Angad departs and returns to Shri Rām. He actually crosses the field. Mandodari enters and in miming actions – as the Pundit narrates - again appeals to Rāwan to listen to the advice of his elders but to no avail.

The scene shifts to the battlefield. To the accompaniment of tassa rhythm many warriors of Lanka are killed, including the mighty Khar. Then Lakshman engages in a fierce battle with Prahasta, one of Rāwan's sons and military generals, and slaughters him. The Pundit maintains the interest and tempo of the drama. Above the loud drumming, he informs the audience that the news of the sad fate of Khar, Durum and Prahasta have reached Rāwan's court. Makaraksha, Khar's son, says that he can only perform his father's last rites if he is allowed to bring back Rām's head. With Rāwan's approval, Makaraksha enters the battlefield, challenges Shri Rām and is defeated. All around the 'grong' warriors are performing multiple roles; battling, falling, rolling over dead, then getting up and continuing the war in a different role.

Rāwan now acknowledges that this is his war and that he should end it. With a majestic flair he enters the battlefield and to the thundering rhythm of the drums he engages Lakshman in battle. Disengaging from him, he then attacks Shri Rām who completely disarms him and advises him to leave the battle field as it is unethical in war to fight an unarmed opponent. Rāwan retreats in humiliation. Then in a tactical, strategic move, Rāwan dispatches an entourage with drums and food to go and awaken his sleeping, warrior brother, Kumbhakaran.

The talents of Kumbhakaran are legendary and well known by the Felicity Ramleela followers. These include his ability to sleep for 6 months of the year, his gargantuan appetite and his capacity to fight. Rāwan requires

Kumbhakaran's assistance to defeat Rām and his army. The tassa drum ensemble accompanies the entourage to Kumbhakaran who is lying supine on the grassy turf, centre stage, blissfully asleep. They stand over the sleeping warrior, trying every possible thing to awaken him. The decibel levels of their drums and jhanj rise slowly and progressively with kettle drums, bass drums, and crashing cymbals until they are thundering into the ears of the sleeping warrior. This clatter and noise awaken Kumbhakaran. The Pundit explains the action on the field. Now with percussions silenced, Kumbhakaran eats prodigiously. Having eaten, both brothers Kumbhakaran and Rāwan converse. Kumbhakaran advises Rāwan that he was wrong to kidnap Sita but that he will nevertheless defend him by fighting Rām.

He prepares for battle. The tassa drummers move into full battle rhythm. Kumbhakaran, with sword and shield in hand, makes a circumambulation of the 'grong'. Nārad muni, continues his circumambulations on the periphery of the ground in his 1- 2- 3-4; 1- 2 -3-4 step, his kartaal in the right hand, and the large tanpura – a droning 4-string instrument – substituting for the Veena, resting on his left shoulder, as he observes and chronicles the unfolding story, Rām's Leela. This is Nārad muni's only role in the cosmic realm i.e. being an interplanetary traveler, a messenger of the Gods, chronicling the history of the cosmos. Pundit-ji also points out to his audience the roles that the other cosmic beings such as Indra, Vishnu, Shiva and Parvati play in the unfolding saga.

On the battlefield, Vibhishan (Rāwan's estranged brother) tries to convince Kumbhakaran to follow the path of a righteous life or Dharma. Kumbhakaran replies that his dharma is to fight for his brother. He engages in battles with Sugrīv, then Angad and finally with Shri Rām who fires off a firecracker 'rocket' at Kumbhakaran. It splits into bright sparks in the night sky, over the 'battlefield'. Kumbhakaran falls to the ground. The audience is informed that he has been beheaded by Rām. The drumming stops. The Pundit continues his chants from the text and translates for the audience. Then the tassa ensemble resumes with a heightened ferocity of tempo, its drums booming.

Rāwan now summons his 4 sons who are crack shots. They descend from the Lanka platform, circumambulate the 'grong' and then enter into battle, but all their offensives are aborted. Lakshman, using a thin heavily-decorated, mauve-coloured bow engages them, shooting 'rockets'. He shoots lighted fire crackers attached to his arrows into the sky. They are eventually killed by different warriors of Rām. Rāwan, now more disturbed and visibly agitated by the news of the slaughter of his 4 sons, convenes a war council. After deliberations with the council, he instructs his son Indrajit to enter battle. Indrajit goes forth with much bravery and valour but he is no match for Rām's warriors. Lakshman 'dances' down the battle field to face Indrajit who is 'dancing' towards him, armed with his magical weapon. They release fire crackers from their respective bows facing each other, but shooting into the air. The energy generated within the rhythm of battle is palpable. The audiences are visibly excited.

The opponents drop their weapon and engage in hand to hand combat. Indrajit is tossed around the battlefield; once, twice, three times. He returns each time to continue the hand - to - hand combat. They again pick up their weapons. Shri Rām, on the advice of Vibhishan comes to the assistance of Lakshman. Indrajit releases a magical weapon (another bamboo arrow). The Pundit informs his audience that: "The arrow turns into serpents which completely enwrap Rām and Lakshman. They are tightly bound and cannot move. Garud the huge bird and carrion feeder, comes to their assistance and devours the serpents, to the surprise of Rāwan and Indrajit." Then Indrajit focuses his attention again on Lakshman, circling him for another engagement. Indrajit takes aim and shoots an invisible projectile at Lakshman. He has hurled his invincible weapon, the *Shakti baan.* This war is taking place on both the physical and supernatural plane. Lakshman falls, rolling on his back on the grass. Rain did not fall today, so the ground is much firmer than on the previous days. There is no danger of dirtying the costume on the green grass. He rolls again. Lakshman's badly wounded body finally rests on its back, unconscious.

The *Vyas* keeps up a constant chant, interpreting and narrating as the action continues to unfold rapidly on the 'grong'. Hanuman rushes to Lakshman, picks him up and carries the almost lifeless body, placing it at the feet of Rām. Rām is crying, wailing and wondering what he will tell Lakshman's mother, Sumitra, and his wife, Urmila, who will be awaiting their return to Ayodhya. It is an agonizing situation and a pathetic sight. The Pundit chants the respective verses, massaging the pathos out of them as the scene is enacted with much melodrama. Hanuman is dispatched to locate *Sushen Vaidya,* a Vedic doctor residing in Lanka. Hanuman hurries there, picks up the doctor - a young boy -

and runs with him back to the scene of the emergency. The Vaidya examines the unconscious warrior and advises that the *Sanjeevani* herb, a miracle-healing plant from the Himalaya mountain, must be brought urgently to make a potion to heal Lakshman. Hanuman again sets off on his Ramleela 'jump', 'flying' to the Himalaya to find the herb to heal Lakshman. He reaches the mountain - a small mountain peak fabricated out of bamboo and covered with crepe paper - searches on it for the herb but is unable to locate it, so he lifts up the whole portion of the mountain on which the herb grows and commences his return trip to Lanka.

As he flies through the air space of Bharat, Rām's brother and current caretaker administrator of the kingdom of Ayodhya (in Rām's absence), he is mistaken by Bharat for an enemy flying through Ayodhya's air space. Hanuman is shot down by Bharat. All of this is played out on the 'grong'; the chanting to the accompaniment of the harmonium and the English narration, over the sound of the tassa.

When questioned, Hanuman reveals his identity and explains his mission to return immediately to the battle field with the *Sanjeevani* plant to restore Lakshman's health. Bharat apologises. There is much hugging. Bharat sends him off on the head of an arrow - a fire cracker arrow - at the speed of the wind, and he lands on the battle field. In the open glare of the audience Lakshman is swiftly treated. He revives, immediately regains his strength and returns to battle, much to the amazement of Indrajit.

Pundit Yankatessu announces a short interval to allow the Mayor of Chaguanas - in whose jurisdiction Felicity and its Ramleela falls - to address the audience. Mayor Orlando Nagessar has come to attend the Vijay Dashmi - Rām's victory on the 10th day. The Mayor welcomes his audience and informs them about proposals of the Borough to convert Green Park into a Ramleela venue with pavilions and adequate covered spaces to house costumes, decorations and a Ramleela archive, all familiar sounding promises. After his address we talk briefly. I propose that the venue be named the "Felicity Festival Grounds". He suggests we talk later with the constituency representative in Parliament and current Chairman of the People's Partnership Government, Mr. Jack Warner. We agree to follow up.[8] (On this day, a few years earlier, in 2007, Mr. Nagessar, Mr. Basdeo Panday, the then Leader of the Opposition party, and Mr. Jack Warner who was also the then FIFA Vice President and former representative of the constituency, were present.

Fast forward to 2015, the former Prime Minister Mrs. Kamla Persad Bissessar has come to the Ramleela. Her ruling party had lost the general elections a few weeks earlier and she is the leader of the opposition in Parliament. She is also asked to address the audience. So too was the Indian High Commissioner to Trinidad and Tobago, Mr. Gauri Shankar Gupta. Mrs. Bissessar speaks and then asks for a group photo of the cast. The action stops to facilitate her request. But many in the audience can be heard 'steupsing' and making comments of irritation and sarcasm. Mrs. Bissessar had 'never visited the Felicity Ramleela during her 5 years as Prime Minister,' even though it was rumored that her government had given a handsome grant in 2014 for the production of the Leela.

Effigies of Rāwan and his brother Kumbhkaran dwarfing the cast of first Felicity Ramleela. Also in photo (middle) is the Leader of the opposition in Parliament, Mrs. Kamla Persad - Bissessar with Indian High Commissioner to Trinidad and Tobago, H.E. Gauri Shankar Gupta. 2015

At 8.00 pm., the crowd is bursting at its seams, having grown to approximately 15,000 people, standing 10-12 deep, around the barriers. The maidān has close to thrice the capacity of the entire village. As the story rapidly unfolds, the 'grong' has become the battlefield of Lanka. The excitement is palpable, and still rising. Local humorous, carnivalesque characters on the fringe in the Ramleela add to the excitement of the evening.

The drama resumes. Rāwan and Indrajit proceed to the temple of Nikumbhila to perform a tantric yagna (a magic ritual) for Rām and Lakshman to die in the battlefield. Hanuman notices the hurried performance of the tantric puja and physically positions himself between Rām and Lakshman and the puja, thereby absorbing all the negative energies being flung in their direction; fire is flung in their directions to the accompaniment of the rolling tassa and its booming bass drums as this ritual is performed.

Vibhishan, the estranged brother of Rāwan, hurriedly runs over to Shri Rām and advises that Indrajit will be invincible if the Yagna is allowed to be completed. To avoid this eventuality, a quick discussion is held among the three and Lakshman creates a diversion. He signals Indrajit, calling him to battle, so as to disrupt the Yagna. The drums are beating in battle tempo as a fierce battle ensues. Each warrior circles and engages the other, shooting pyrotechnic arrows into the sky, even as they continue the Ramleela movements on the battlefield. Warriors, singly and in groups, are fighting. The whole 'grong' is the battlefield. Pundit-ji announces that: 'Lakshman releases the *Indrastra*, a devastating weapon, completely severing the heard of Indrajit'. On the 'grong' he falls dead.

Rāwan is now desperate. He goes to his brother, Ahirāwan, the master illusionist who lives in *Patal Lok*, the non-physical lower regions of existence or underworld; it is conceived of as 'Hell' by people of the 'Book'. Rāwan beseeches him - Ahirāvan, who is also adept at performing human sacrifice to lesser beings of the underworld - for assistance in destroying Rām and Lakshman. Ahirāwan, disguising himself as his noble brother, Vibhishan, enters the opponents' camp under the cover of darkness and kidnaps Rām and Lakshman. Quoting from the script, chanting the poetic verses, the Pundit informs the audience that:

> *Rāwan's ploy works. Hanuman, finding Shri Rām and Lakshman missing, searches high and low - he runs around the 'grong'- and locates them in Patal Lok or the nether world, just about to be sacrificed. They are however being offered food and drinks as the sacrificial rituals are being performed on them.*

The brothers sit on a bench in front of a glowing fire, prior to their being sacrificed. The explanation continues:

> *Hanuman negotiates with the guard - the gatekeeper - then enters Patal Lok. He shrinks his physical size, consumes the food and then grows in gigantic proportions with five faces, Panchmukhi.*

A huge mask costume, worn by another performer, enters the 'grong'. Roles are switched. He is portraying the five-faced Hanuman *(Panchmukhi)* with his various weapons. Panchmukhi kills Ahirāwan, returns to his natural state, as Hanuman, and escapes Patal Lok with the brothers. The audience claps.

Panchmukhi Hanuman in Patal Lok

Hanuman battles Ahirāwan in Patal Lok

The three warriors, Hanuman in the middle, his arm around each as if supporting them physically, perform a parikrama around the 'grong' and rejoin the army of Rām to continue the war.

At 9:35 pm., there is a short intermission. It is a welcome break for both the 13 member tassa drummers who, with the heavy drums slung across their necks and shoulders have been performing non-stop since the evening's play began. The 50 'players' are also tired, thirsty and sweating profusely. Sitting flat on the

Hanuman rescues Rām and Lakshman from Patal Lok

grass, bottles of water are consumed. A member of the Ramleela executive makes public announcements over the microphone, recognizing two female elders of the village for their dedicated support to the Ramleela for over two decades. They are each presented with a hamper. Four awards are also given to past players for contribution towards the first Felicity Ramleela celebrations; Mulchan Paltoo (aka Robin), Amarnath Raghoo (aka Poison), Balarama (Aka Vijay) and the fourth, 'Laventille'. Medals are also distributed to deserving performers, past and present. The stage manager appeals to the audience standing next to the towering effigies of Rāwan and Kumbhakaran to move to a safe distance away in order to avoid being burned by the impending flames when play resumes.

Performers enjoy a brief intermission. The food court is heavily patronised.
Photo: S Balkaransingh, 2015

Play resumes with Rāwan's wife, Mandodari, going into the palace's waiting room with a tharia filled with flowers and chandan (sandal wood paste) to do ārti to her husband before he enters battle.As she stands in front of him, the thali mysteriously slips and falls from her hands. She recognizes that something is amiss. It is a bad omen. She implores him not to go into battle. He scoffs at her premonitions even as he hides his anxiety and apprehension.

Rāwan enters the battle field to the rhythm of the 'phintra hand' of tassa drumming, a characteristic Ramleela drum rhythm and upbeat tempo. The full complement of *dhols* or bass players is repositioned, facing north. They are in one line, one behind the other; their dhols hanging from their necks, across their shoulders. The tassa drummers - their kettle drums also suspended from their necks - form a parallel line with the dhols. The jhanj or cymbal is positioned at the top of the line. Now they are all aligned in battle formation for the final conflagration. This is Rāwan's penultimate battle with Rām. Rām's army is arrayed in semicircular formation. The archers move off in double file in an anti-clockwise direction, wielding their battle armaments. Rāwan's army in black costume, and today without their usual face masks, is equally arrayed. They are in full battle formations on the other side of the 'grong' but also circumambulating in an anticlockwise direction. There are approx. 50 combat warriors.

The Vyas, establishing the gravity of the occasion, tells his audience that: "Rāwan laughs arrogantly and boasts of his strength to Rām."He belches out a deep, guttural, haughty laugh into the microphone. *Ahh, Hah, Hah, Hah.* The action is mimed by Rāwan on the field. Amid the warlike thunder and tempo of drumming, a fierce battle begins. From luminous bows, arrows of fire crackers are aimed at one another and then released upwards, exploding into the night sky. Rāwan uses all types of weapons against Rām. Shri Rām counters the weapons. Many warriors engage in close physical combat, in hold and release. With the enhanced battle rhythm of the drummers and the voice

A young warrior of Lanka's army defends his King

of the Pundit rising to a crescendo as he chants (accompanying himself on the harmonium) and narrates, the audience is charged, their adrenalin flowing. The energy is tactile. Warriors are engaging in their separate battles around the 'grong'. Fire arrows are flying from bows into the night sky, their fire tails

Narad muni (with understudy) passes in front of Raja Rāwan

blazing in multicoloured sprays of lights, often too close for both players' and audience's comfort. But no one bothers. The audience and performers are too engrossed in the intense din and clatter of the combined chanting, narrating, drumming and frenetic individual battles throughout the 'grong'. The rhythmic drumming and dance movements faithfully maintain their mood and character of the scene.

The audience, now grown to between 15,000-17,000, is 'hungry for blood', anxious to see an arrow piercing Rāwan's body as he fights on the battlefield. With the drums booming out their battle rhythm the energy and excitement are contagious. Again the Pundit pleads with the audience to move away from the south-western barriers; yet they push nearer, closer, tighter - like sardines in a can - to get a ringside view of the intense action, now rising to a climax. Both armies circumambulate the field in varying battle formations; arcs, semicircles, parallel lines, all engaging and disengaging in intense combat as they maintaining the Ramleela rhythmic 'dance' movements. Sweat pours down their faces, glistening and flying from their bodies. The child performers are following closely on the heels of their adult mentors. The battle is intense.

Mortal Rāwan edges closer to his symbolic self (his gigantic effigy dominating the scenery) until he is directly under it. The imposing size of the effigy casts a shadow of fear over the battlefield. It is a visual image of an insurmountable warrior which Rām, merely 5'8" tall, has to conquer. The effigy's laser-beam eyes flash the mood of the warrior King. Meanwhile, Narad muni (with his understudy) passes in front of Rāwan whose image even dwarfs Narad's size. Each time Rām shoots an arrow and cuts off Rāwan's head, another one grows in its place. This continues until Vibhishan inches up close to him (Rām) and whispers. He actually informs Rām as to what part of Rāwan's body is most vulnerable and thus where to aim at in order to strike the final blow. Rām strings an arrow into his bow, places the weapon at his forehead closes his eyes for a few moments, endowing it with divine powers. He then takes aim at Rāwan's midriff and shoots.

The arrow bounces back. Rām's lighted arrows are unable to pierce the papier maché exterior of the effigy. The audience is holding its breath. The drumming has increased to rapid tempo, the drummers' hands swinging in synchronicity, dhols and bodies swaying, beads of sweat, like pearls, flying in the night light, beating a mesmerizing rhythm that both speaks of and accentuates the current carnage on the battlefield.

Tassa drummers (dhol, tassa and jhanj) maintain the battle rhythm

Finally one flaming arrow finds its mark at Rāwan's navel, i.e. the navel of the effigy. Mortal Rāwan, still under his effigy, and enacting the emotions of the scene – having received a mortal wound - totters. He regains his composure and quickly moves away from the effigy. It has caught fire. Flames are leaping in the air. Kumbhakaran is also burning. The crowds nearer to the effigy are scampering away from the intense heat emanating from the crumbling effigies, even as the drummers pound their goat skin drums in rapid tempo. It is a thunder of tassa in Felicity.

Some of the mature and older members of the audience, the devotees of Rām, the *Rāmanandis* - or those who live and experience the *anand* or bliss of Rām - are metaphysically experiencing shifts in their realities, back and forth, from ancient time to present time. Their Felicity of Trinidad continues to shift and slip through the door into Lanka of ancient time. Their psychic doors of perception are ajar as they travel back and forth, ancient into modern time and place. Walcott's view, as a writer with an artistic, psychic perception was smack on target when he spoke of the Felicity Ramleela in 1992. For these members

Rāwan's effigy goes up in flames

of the audience, this evening's episode of the annihilation of Rāwan is not theatre; it is faith leading to the experiencing of a separate reality. This section of the audience, through their devotion or *bhakti* is experiencing their separate ecstasies and epiphanies. The heat of the flames is burning their impurities of religious doubt, renewing their faith. Their very beings are experiencing a spiritual cleansing and religious awakening.

At another level, on the spiritual plane the actors, Rām and Lakshman, have completely become the instruments of divinity, the swarūps of God. The heat and golden glow of the flames on their faces and sweating bodies have totally morphed them into living mūrtis, ephemeral beings, bronze images of transcendental forms of the *Isht* devatas, divinities at the personal level. Theatre is consolidating faith and vice versa.

Meanwhile at the physical level the ground crew in the maidān is busy manipulating the ropes which fastened the effigies to the earth, allowing them to fall safely within the designated area.

Mighty Rāwan, the once supreme ruler of Lanka now crashes to the ground. The regal, honest and noble Mandodari - Rāwan's gentle and loving queen - weeps at the loss of her husband and her children, her entire clan, lying scattered on the battlefield before her very eyes. For Mandodari, this war is her catharsis; absolute pain, yet relief from a haughty and arrogant ruler who was drawn to his death, like a moth to a flame. It is a terrible karma to bear. For the devotees of Rām, on the other hand, who seek all that is wholesome and dharmic or righteous, they have experienced *darshan*, seeing the miracle play of the Lord before their very eyes. Good has prevailed. Their very beings have been washed clean. This final scene, the burning of Kumbhakaran's and Rāwan's effigies, actually constitutes a combination of these warriors' destruction in battle, including their last rites and cremation.

At 10:45 pm. Pundit Yankatessu, with his live accompanists, chants the closing ārti and mangalam as the massive audience commences its outward trek. The thirteen tassa drummers and fifty players stand peacefully in benediction under the *mool jhanda* in centre stage as the audience begins its homeward journey, dispersing quietly and in an orderly manner; no chaos, no confusion, as if their departure had also been choreographed and rehearsed, and its actual implementation is now managed by an unseen hand.

ENDNOTES

1. Derek Walcott, "Fragments of an Epic Memory", delivered on 7th Dec 1992.
2. Walcott.
3. Derek Walcott was obviously referring to the 'Tassa' drums and not the 'tablas'. The Tassa drum is part of the Tassa ensemble comprising the Dhol or bass, Tassa or kettle drum and Jhanj or medium size, brass cymbal. The ensemble is an indispensable part of the Ramleelas musical accompaniment.
4. Author's personal observations on that day.
5. Derek Walcott, "Fragments of an Epic Memory"…1992.
6. Naipaul 7.
7. This word was used by Prof. Molly Kaushal at the First World Conference on Ramleela in Trinidad in July 2013, in her Keynote address entitled: "Ramleela: Play, Performance or Divine Grace?"
8. At the time of this book going to press, there was no visible follow-up implementation to the Mayor's promises. In retrospect, the Mayor's address on that evening appeared to be just local politicking, with no real attention paid to the support of the Arts, to the survival of the country's cultural traditions or of its invaluable heritage.

Chapter Fourteen

DAILY PERFORMANCE: DAY 11

Day 11: Lanka Kanda or Yudh Kanda

This final evening's episode of the Ramleela is significant, both in the story and in the life of the village of Felicity. Rām installs Vibhishan, the brother of Rāwan, as King of Lanka and undertakes his return journey to Ayodhya for his own coronation. Journeys have formed a salient part of this epic drama. With a wide brush of his imagination, and in keeping with the theme and intent of Valmiki's original story line, Tulsidas has taken his devotees on long journeys through kingdoms, hermitages of *rishis, sadhus, sadhvis*, verdant fields and forests of pristine beauty, as well as dark, uninviting jungles infested with demons. His narrative has taken his readers and listeners through expansive landmasses, making them familiar with some areas of the ancient land of Bharat Varsha (India). The directors of the Felicity Ramleela have also conformed to this story line and converted the ground daily to reflect this changing landscape.

Today, one such long journey - the last in the final day of this Leela - is about to be undertaken. It is Rām's return from Lanka to Ayodhya. Both the return journey and Rām's installation on the throne are compressed into one evening's episode. While the story is centred in ancient India in pre-Vedic times i.e. thousands, possibly hundreds of thousands of years ago, in the *Treta Yug,*[1] the action takes place in present time in Felicity. Today's journey is important in that it offers the audience yet another opportunity - but in this case a more personalized and close-up opportunity - for participation in the Leela itself. The journey becomes an actual procession.

It is 6.30 pm. The episode is late in starting. This has now become a norm rather than the exception. Heavy road traffic congestion prevents the performers from reaching home from work in time and preparing themselves for the evening's performance. The savannah is wet from the intermittent and sometimes heavy showers of rain during the last week. This evening the ground is sodden and sappy with a sticky, clayey mud which is at least two to three inches thick in some parts. This is particularly so around the periphery of the performance area, from where the spectators view the Leela, and in front of the food stalls. On the south-eastern side of the 'grong' a football game is winding up for lack of natural light.

The food and methai stalls are in various states of readiness for the evening's human traffic. In preparation for the brisk sales, large pieces of cardboard and other old wooden planks have been placed in front of some of these stalls, directly on top of the mud to facilitate the anticipated steady flow of customers. I am introduced by a member of the Ramleela executive to the owners and managers of these fast-food outlets catering to the palates of those who have come to attend the Leela and its mela, and who have a penchant for local finger food. This particular row of stalls of varying size are covered with old galvanized iron sheets and enclosed by combinations of plywood, old wooden laths and other used boards.

The aroma of the highly seasoned, frying savories; baiganee, kachorie, phulouri, saheena, aloo pie, pepper roti and various other traditional finger foods pervades the atmosphere and stimulates taste buds. These street foods are being served almost directly from the frying pots filled with boiling oil, straight to the customers on pieces of brown paper and tissues. Laced with homemade *achār, kuchela, chatney* or hot pepper sauce, the food is washed down with soft drinks and canned juices in various local flavours viz. mango, passion fruit, carrot, guava and combinations of these. Bottled water - a recently introduced consumer item, and presumably a better product than the purified local tap water - is also on sale. Children have gravitated to the home-made ice cream stall, serving local fruit flavours. Village commerce at the micro level is flourishing.

During the past few days whenever there was a lull in the action on the field, the vendors became busy. When the drama in a particular episode was intense and captured the attention of the audience, they themselves became spectators, taking turns to run out to the railings to 'take in' their favorite scenes and hurry back to 'help out' in the stall. The women, dressed in *salwār kamise, saris*, some in jeans or skirts, are attired as spectators. Some wear aprons only when they are 'over the pot', frying fresh portions of foods. There is no visible difference in appearance and attire between the stall operators and the daily Ramleela audience.

Paime, originally a product of the First Peoples of Trinidad (Kairi) is a favourite delicacy. It is made from corn meal mixed with sugar and dry, grated coconut, essence, bay leaf, all rolled in banana leaf and held together by a string tied around the leaf, keeping the ingredients in place. The string is a dry straw of about one meter in length, stripped from the same banana tree. This tied package, the size of the palm of an adult hand, is then boiled in a large pot, cooled and served at room temperature. It makes a very delicious and substantial snack. Today, as I am formally introduced to the paime sales lady, she smiles and refuses to accept my few dollars as payment for her paime.

The evening's puja is about to begin. The 'gods', actors and new players assemble under the central *jhanda.* This area, consecrated as holy ground twelve days ago, continues to assume its role as sacred, religious space. In the process, it has become spiritual space in the metaphysical realm. For these brief moments each year at this particular time, worlds coexist side by side and even overlap. Geographic delineation of boundaries blurs.

With the ārti having been performed and the opening signature Ramleela dance movements completed, the *Vyas* advises the audience that:

> *Today is possibly one of its most important days in Felicity (in its cultural life). It is the last day of the Leela. Today, you will see Rām performing the coronation and installation of Vibhishan as King of Lanka in a magnificent ceremony. Now with the newly installed King's permission, Shri Rām will dispatch Hanuman to Ashokvātika - where Sita has been in captivity and now awaiting her release - to inform her of the good news. We will witness Sita's visible pleasure at both her release and her reunion with her husband. She will then accompany Hanuman back to the waiting party and there she will perform the Agni Pariksha, the purifying fire ceremony.*

He continues his narration: "…On entering the fire the m*aya* or illusionary form of Sita is burnt away and the real or pure Sita emerges."

The installation of the new King of Lanka takes place. Sita is then presented to and is embraced by Shri Rām. It is an act of jubilation as Shri Rām performs homage to Agni Dev. The scene unfolds rapidly. Shri Rām must take leave of King Vibhishan and Lanka and commence yet another long journey to his kingdom of Ayodhya after fourteen consecutive years in exile. Pundit-ji resumes his narration, reading from his text:

> *Rām's function has been successfully undertaken... he has destroyed Rāwan and his evil administration; installed Vibhishan, Rāwan's just and honest brother, on Lanka's throne and thus his task is completed...The time has come for Rām with his army of victorious warriors, including mother Sita and Lakshman, Hanuman and all of his army of monkeys to leave Lanka... and return to Ayodhya where his brothers Bharat - functioning as king ad interim - and Shatrughan await him to have him installed on that throne for the commencement of Rām Raj, the reign of Shri Rām ....The Royal entourage; Rām, Sita, Lakshman, Hanuman and their army of victorious warriors, retainers and followers, are preparing to depart Lanka....*

On the grong the departing group is assembling. Vibhishan offers his *Pushpak Viman* (his flying machine) as return transport to Ayodhya but this gesture of goodwill is politely declined. The entourage commences the departure from Lanka at the southern end of the maidān. The audience is much smaller than that of the previous day. Yesterday approx. 17,000 spectators witnessed the death and immolation of Rāwan. Today (2015) is Monday, the first working day of the new week. The audience is approximately 2,000. In 2012, on this day a surprise dignitary had arrived to view the proceedings i.e. His Excellency Malay Misra, the Indian High Commissioner to Trinidad and Tobago. He was accompanied by his Cultural Officer, Mrs. Sunita Pahuja. They were invited to accompany the procession on its way to Ayodhya, through Felicity. They settled instead for enjoying the ambience of the grounds and savouring the finger foods, some freshly parched popcorn and bottled water, and conversing about the history of Felicity and its Ramleela.

The icons, actors and spectators, now intermingle and begin to pick their way out of the muddy savannah, around the puddles of water, heading to the western entrance of the ground on to dry land and the asphalt-surfaced single lane, *Clarke Road.* Each member of Rām's entourage is handed a lighted earthen deya with a cotton wick floating in coconut oil, placed on a flimsy paper saucer. In the other hand, they receive two lighted, smoking sandalwood incense sticks i.e. *chandan* agarbatti. By this action, spectators are being transformed into pilgrims as part of Rām's entourage as he symbolically makes his way from Lanka to Ayodhya, through the roads of Felicity. Now on the dry road and away from the mud, the royal entourage is rearranged into various sections. The heroes are in front, followed by their victorious army contingents. Then follow the close supporters (now converted to pilgrims), on foot, carrying their hand-held lighted deyas and smoking incense. Motorcars, vans, pick-up trucks, motorbikes and youths on bicycles follow in that order. This moving procession shows glimpses of the 'tableau' format, referred to in India as *Jhaki* Ramleela.

On the hood of one of the motor-cars are mounted two funnel-shaped megaphones or 'mikes' - the public loud speakers. These 'funnels 'are reminiscent of the days of advertising the release of new 'Indian' movies and of announcements of village bereavements. Children used to run after the 'mike' vehicles to pick up the handbills that were thrown out, and which provided the details of the cinema advertisements. Today, a tape recording of the Pundit's chanting of the relevant *chaupais* and his narrative description of the return journey are being amplified through the two funnels. On the open tray of a pickup truck, a few vehicles behind the mike vehicle, is the tassa ensemble of drummers - dhol, tassa and jhanj. With decibels clashing from both vehicles, the amplified recorded musical chants and the tassa drummers, this medley of sounds compete for attention. Neither gives way to the other.

The procession passes one of the village mandirs

The procession, having been formed into Trinidad carnival-type sections, travels south along Clarke Street turning east into Boundary Street; then north into Cacandee road. As we walk through the pathway, there is a noticeable air of village cleanliness, both on the roads and the compounds of the homes and business places. No garbage is visible outside the gates, waiting for the garbage collectors, as is the norm on other days. The whole village is clean. The procession now occupies the full breadth of the roadway.

The icons at the head of the procession move gracefully on the asphalt road, executing their characteristic hop-skip-skip dance steps. Their ankle-bells tap out 'ching-ching-ching' sounds as they 'dance' to the rhythm of the tassa. Their long and brightly decorated bows and arrows move in synchronised harmony with the body movements, as if choreographed by a guru from the spiritual realm.The flickering flames of the deyas in the hands of the processioners cast eerie glows on their iridescent faces, creating ethereal forms and ephemeral visions. It is a glorious sight; a marvelous feeling. Rām's return journey with his battle-scarred, weary, yet jubilant warriors has become a mystic event. Spirituality, metaphysics and religion have taken on a contemporary presence.The journey from Lanka to Ayodhya is being made in Felicity, along its roads, in present time with the spectators of the previous days of the Ramleela also becoming today's procession of pilgrims, of Rām's well-wishers, nay his loyal friends.

A traffic police detail had already put measures in place, diverting vehicular traffic away from the procession route, allowing for its unhindered movement. Notwithstanding this, there is a minor traffic jam on the main thoroughfare of Cacandee Road.

As the animation of this march proceeds through the village in its strident pace, more onlookers join in. Foot and bicycle supporters are added to the rear of the procession, all excitedly keeping pace with the music. The residents of the village, in the path of the procession, emerge from their houses. Children are visibly excited at the pageantry and colour; others observe the procession from a distance. Some welcome them with palms clasped prayerfully as they pass. Others, particularly the older folk, position themselves strategically to receive the *darshan* of Rām and Sita and their entourage. The high frequency sounds of *khols* - the drums of the Hare Krishna chanters forming part of the procession - invoke a familiar jubilant, devotional atmosphere. Old ladies cover their heads with their *orhnis;* small transparent veils. With heads bowed and hands clasped together in pious salutation they offer their *pranams*, the traditional *namaskar*, as the swarūps pass in front of their houses accompanied by the combined, amplified chanting and drumming.

The villagers of Felicity and all those thousands who have been converging nightly from outside of Felicity for the last ten days are being transformed today into pilgrims - by their act of participation in this procession. They have automatically become subjects of Rām's spiritual realm and devotees of God. It is said that anyone who walks in the footsteps of or treads the beaten path of Rām becomes a pilgrim. This is the spiritual role into which the Leela has cast them. Temporal time has merged into spiritual time. Here this sacred and spiritual time and space, the religious and the secular are merging smoothly and flawlessly.

By this process, Felicity - the small insignificant town, west of the Borough of Chaguanas - is also being transformed into a sacred ground of epic proportions. The web of the Leela simultaneously transforms this village space into theatrical space and pilgrim site; the holy ground upon which

The 'dancing' procession back to Ayodhya has become a tirtha (pilgrimage), through the streets of Felicity

God is traversing and hence blessing. This procession being performed with devotion (by many) becomes a pilgrimage, a *tirtha,* an instrument for the transformation of the village and its occupants into devotees and blessed pilgrims. Never mind that Felicity is almost twelve thousand miles away from the original venue (India), separated by oceans of water. Moreover, it is eons apart from the supposed occurrence of this legend, and miles away from that different yet familiar culture in which this legend had its genesis. Over the last 100 years Felicity, like the thirty-six plus other Ramleela venues in Trinidad, annually becomes the playground of the Gods and icons, sacred space of the spectators cum pilgrims and theatre of the people, all working together in communal fraternity to produce this spectacle.

This ritual thus takes on an air of importance, redefining the pathway being traversed, converting it into religious site and sacred landscape. By this annual act, possibly in its centennial year, the Ramleela continues to redefine and alter the spiritual space and social status of Felicity. Moreover, in the pluralistic society of Trinidad where Felicity is still considered possibly one of the last remaining bastions of a unique 'Indianness' and 'Hinduness', this procession is an indicator of prestige and a consolidator of social structure and identity. For the ordinary Indo–Trinidadians of this central region and the devoted villagers of Felicity, their First Felicity Ramleela has instilled reverence into their landscape.

This *pradakshin*a is not simply a physical, processional event, a sacred circumambulating of a greater part of the village. The energy generated and emitted in the reproduction of this culminating episode of the Ramleela alters the spiritual crust of Felicity. To the older folks, this annual circumambulation has reaffirmed the physical and spiritual boundaries of the village, distinguishing the 'insiders' from the 'outsiders'. It also reconsolidates the prestige of the village and affirms its cultural status within the historical hierarchy of Trinidad Ramleela.

Moreover, this pradakshina secures, and will protect the village with a spiritual armour against negative energies or 'evil forces' emanating from outside. There is also another, much wider, metaphysical implication. The electromagnetic energies generated here will connect with the positive energies of the other 36 Ramleelas taking place simultaneously throughout the country into a larger sacred environment, converting the entire national landscape into energized, spiritual space.

As the procession moves along its designated path, there is evidence of the commencement of preparations by the villagers' for the impending festival of Diwali. Truck-loads of freshly cut, long bamboo poles have already been deposited along the roadsides. Each household participates as a worker in this hive of collective activity to ensure that the entire village will be ablaze with the Diwali lights, a few days later. On Diwali night, there will be processions of spectators on the roads, in and out of the village. These thoroughfares will be veritable moving car parks. Foreign tourists and local residents, the outsiders and the insiders will mingle to view the Diwali celebrations, as the entire village is illuminated with thousands of lights, and the villagers emerge from their homes in attire reflecting a riotous display of styles, designs, colours and fabric, an annual modeling stage of traditional and modern Indian and western clothes.

But enough of Diwali, Rām's return to Ayodhya tonight in this folk drama is also being welcomed with a different festival of lights; lighted deyas in the hands of the processioners as their faces convey emotions of *bhakti,* of devotion, happiness and joy. The procession has grown to about 150 feet long as it is joined by more followers on foot and on bicycles. This evening, the procession is late in keeping to its time schedule. It makes a detour, cutting out a few hundred yards from its usual route. Annually, it proceeds in front of the Felicity Shiv Shankar Mandir on Cacandee Road with its attached Primary Hindu School, turns west into Balkissoon Street, travels a short distance down the street and turns left again into Nolan Street. Today it turns west into Maha Sabha Street and travels south, in a quicker pace, turns into Nolan Street and travels down that street. By this time the parade has been on the road for more than an hour; covering approximately one and one half km.

On the outskirts of 'Ayodhya', it is joined by more villagers; devotees and citizens of the kingdom who, on hearing the din and clatter of drums heralding Rām's return, have come to the city's border to meet and greet them and to accompany them back to the palace. It is a day of jubilation, the end of the period of constant roaming of Rām and Lakshman as stateless citizens; the humiliation of Sita and the restoration of her impeccable character. Finally they are returning to their home where Rām will rule in peace and there would be no more war, thus re-establishing the essence of the name, *Ah Yudh* - the absence of war - or 'Ayodhya', the place of peace and contentment. Rām will restore justice and usher in a period of prosperity during his rule, a period of Ramrajya.

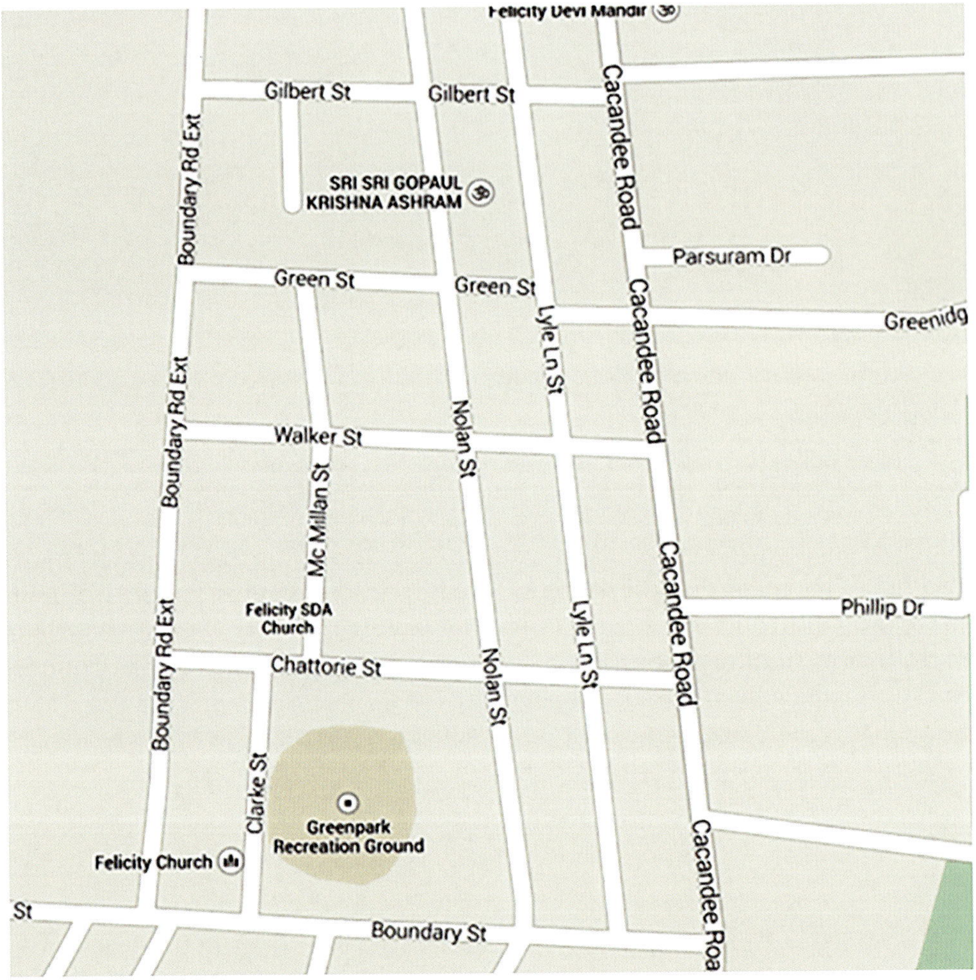

Map 6: The procession route of Rām's return from Lanka to Ayodhya: From Green Park through Felicity village and back

The people of Felicity continue to emerge from their homes to witness the event. With the flames of dozens of deyas still flickering in the hands of their bearers, amplified music and live drumming, the procession has become a *Jhaki Ramleela* - a processional theatre of Ramleela. It turns right into Chattorie Street, travels west down that Street and turns south into a short street which leads into the northern periphery of the Green Park Recreation Ground. The procession has completed an inner circumambulation of a major portion of the former village, now expanded in all directions due to population growth. Hanuman, the forerunner to the procession (disguised as a Brahmin initially - a shawl is wrapped around him - and then in his form as Hanuman - as the shawl is removed) brings the glad tidings to Bharat at Nandigram. Rām's arrival at the palace is imminent. There are happy expectations mixed with anxiety. Bharat hurries to the palace and prepares for the royal welcome.

The procession approaches the northern entrance to the 'grong', which now represents the gates to the kingdom of Ayodhya.[2] It has taken about one and one half hours to cover approximately three kilometres. It approaches the grong between the Pundit's *singhasana* and the decorated northern platform, the Ayodhya palace. Its entrance is lit with a row of oil-filled deyas, about 15-20 feet long.The audience in the maidān; those who were awaiting Rām's return, is invited to join the welcoming party, the *Milan*. They join in to greet Rām and his entourage. By this act, they have been converted to citizens of the realm of Ayodhya, welcoming their King back to his throne. The huge welcoming party excitedly waits at the gates of the royal palace of Ayodhya, now decorated with palanquin, royal banners, royal icons and colours - all shining in the night light, enhancing the spectacle. The party is headed by brother Bharat and Rām's 'mothers'. There is a din and clatter of amplified music, drums, people and lights from the advancing entourage. Then they merge with the lighted deyas and lively, happy, amplified, appropriate Bollywood music. Village drama continues to assume the veneer of musical pageantry.

Bharat (in white) welcomes Rām back to Ayodhya

The procession enters the sanctified ground. This is the same spot from where the exiles had departed, 14 years ago, in different circumstances. Bharat welcomes the returning party, embracing, Shri Rām, Lakshman and others. The traditional Indian injunction of small brother not being allowed to embrace elder sister-in-law is discarded in this Trinidad melting pot of emergent, new values. Bharat embraces his elder sister-in-law, Sita. Shri Rām advises Bharat to forgive his mother, Kaikeyi, for her role in calling for his banishment and the resultant pain she had caused, both personally and collectively.

The tassa continues to play a festive 'hand'. The taped music competes for airplay. There is much *parchaying*, waving of lighted deyas

Ārti is performed to the returning party: Rām, Sita and Lakshman

around the visages of the honoured guests. With much fanfare the heroes; Rām, Lakshman and Sita, walking in slow motion with stylized movements, as if on air, ascend the throne. Guru Vashishta crowns Shri Rām as King and Sita as his Queen. The coronation of Shri Rām takes place amidst music, dancing and other celebrations. A dance item is performed to film music. A local dancer, Rampersad performs a Ganesh Stuti (*Deva Hu deva Ganapati deva, Mangalam Ganesha...*). More *parchaying* is done to the royal party. Another dance is performed in the Kathak classical dance technique but to a Bollywood musical track (above the ongoing rhythm of the tassa). The dancer, performing on the wet soggy grass, interprets the lyrics of the song which extol the valour of Shri Rām. Hanuman stands guard. The tassa ensemble has moved from their previous position on the mid-eastern periphery of the ground. They are positioned on the edge of the grass, close to the Ayodhya pandal, continuing to beat a festive welcoming drum hand as the Pundit chants from his text. These activities are all occurring simultaneously.

The victors are welcomed with dance

The evening's episode comes to a fitting conclusion with Rām and Sita sitting on the royal throne in Ayodhya. They are surrounded by Rām's three brothers, Hanuman, his advisors and courtiers in tableau formation.

To the accompaniment of the pundit's chanting: *Aarati Shri Rāmāyana je ke jai…* (Salutations to Shri Rām), the rest of the cast perform ārti and the final benediction to the tableau - a change from worshipping on the *āsana* in the middle of the 'grong'. The final prayer, *Twamewa Mata, Chapita twamewa…* (Oh god you are my mother and my father…), is collectively chanted from all around the savannah with piety and a tone of sadness.

L-R; Sitting-Hanuman, Rām, Sita & Lakshman
Standing -Shatrughan, Bharat, Nārad muni and his understudy

At 9.45 pm. the audience, like sparks radiating from a single energy source, reluctantly departs in all directions. Slowly, members of the management team and the cast of performers assemble to collectively provide to the Vyas-ji, a fitting *cēdhā* or gift of appreciation (contained in the traditional, large, brown-paper handle bag) in keeping with established protocols. In turn they receive the blessings of Pundit Yankatessu and gradually, almost reluctantly depart from the maidān. Tomorrow, the renters of the various stalls and clean-up crew will restore the maidān to its former condition as village playground, until the following year, God willing, when it will be again converted for yet another enactment of the Leela of Shri Rām.

ENDNOTES

1. The Indian concept of time, from a historical, archaeological perspective is calculated according to a specific, mathematical formula. This formula identifies the ages, eons or *yugas: Sat, Treta, Dwapar and Kal Yuga.* Each Yuga comprises thousands of millennia. For further info on this topic see: W.J. Wilkins, *Hindu*

Mythology, Vedic and Puranic (Delhi: Rupa Co., 1975) (York: Vintage Books A Division of Random House, Inc., 1999)364-371.Also see Swami Shri Yukteswar, Giri. *Kaivalya Darsanam: The Holy Science* (California: Self Realisation Fellowship, 1984).

2. Personal observation over several years, but specifically in 2013. Reconfirmed by author with executive member, Gewan Nanack in October 2014.
3. While the law terminating the Indian Indentureship system was enacted in 1917, the system legally ended in 1920.The last contracted labourers had their contracts terminated in 1920.

Chapter Fifteen

TRINIDAD RAMLEELA: AN ENGINE OF GROWTH FOR COMMUNITY DEVELOPMENT AND SOCIO-ECONOMIC DIVERSIFICATION

Today, the descendants of the original East Indian migrants - the fourth, fifth and sixth generations – are registering their presence in many ways on the cultural landscape of Trinidad and Tobago. They continue to introduce and to consolidate their philosophies for living, their religious creeds, literary works, rituals, festivals and traditional performative folk forms on this soil. Their values, norms of behaviour, work ethic, artistic expressions, religious, and other secular, cultural practices reflect, to a great extent, not only their traditions, but determine the legacies that are laid down for future generations, providing forward, backward and vertical linkages. In Trinidad and Tobago's plural, mosaic society, its traditions facilitate an appreciation and understanding of one another's histories, creative and performative urges, lifestyles and ambitions.

The year 2017 is very significant for the twin island Republic of Trinidad and Tobago. It marks 172 years of the arrival of the first sailing ship, 'Fatel Rozack'; and 100 years of the arrival of the last ships (the "SS Ganges" and "SS Mutlah") bringing Indentured immigrants from India to these shores. The law terminating the Indian indentureship system was enacted in 1917.[12]

Oral history also suggests that this year (1917) may actually be the 100th year of the commencement of the first Felicity Ramleela. This however, cannot be confirmed in the absence of documentary evidence.

The Ramleela has not only survived but grown significantly. This is evident in terms of its open air performances, the length and duration of the production, the quality of the story telling, the dramatic enactments, the quality of props, decor, costuming, stage management, the fringe activities that contribute to the event and the overall growth in audiences. On the evening of the immolation of Rāwan, the audience numbers between 15,000-17,000 people, crowding every available space on the grounds and in the buildings overlooking the park.

While the actual performance of the Leela has remained the pivot around which everything revolves, there are many separate and distinct worlds orbiting the central event. These include the commerce, bazaar, fashion, entertainment and worship; spectators who become devotees and worshippers, performing ārti for gods and shouting, with much verve and passion, *Hara Hara Mahadev* and *Shri Rām Chandra Ki Jai,* on cue. There are the merry-go-round and chair plane rides, the cotton candies, the homemade ice creams, paper windmills and, on some days, open space for kids to run and engage in rough play. These 'worlds' overlap and coexist in their own 'space'; each having their unique life and their own centre, yet demonstrating some measure of mutual exclusivity within the same physical space. It is more than the initial religious folk theatre; it is a *jhamela,* a carnival of happy fusion and exciting confusion.

The whole *mela* atmosphere attracts the young and old, the religious and the secular, the leaders and the followers. The politicians, both at community and national levels, rub shoulders with the artistes, vying for the attention of the massive audiences as they strut their few minutes on the stage, under the neon lights. In Trinidad's currently violent society, unsafe and unpredictable, the Ramleela ground is a haven of freedom and safety for the family. The maidān temporarily becomes the convergence zone of much socio-economic, political and village gossip, and even match-making. In this melting pot of Felicity the First Felicity Ramleela festival is a catalyst for community integration. The bond between the villagers, performers and their environment are consolidated in a reciprocal process and relationship. Here, individual human relations are welded within the village and its folk theatre, each contributing in continuously consecrating the space, understanding and recognising the energy of this consecrated place and becoming an indivisible part of the spirit of Felicity.

The Felicity Ramleela is really a complete village, theatrical happening. It is participatory entertainment, carrying its fair share of satire, burlesque, humour, music, rhythm and movements. It promotes interracial and intra-social collaboration, highlighting village cohesion. From the socio-economic perspective, it fosters growth and development at the household and community level. Almost all of its various preparatory activities – the various artistic inputs in the production, design, fabrication of costume and effigies, music, sound, lighting, the food fairs and entertainment at the periphery - are usually sourced within the geographic boundaries of the village. The villagers take responsibility for their own activities, laughing at their own foibles, celebrating their triumphs, and learning by trial and error. Here, the youths grow through mentoring and by following the elders.While the majority of the audiences are the villagers themselves, country-wide spectators are accommodated.

This annual village event promotes the concept of the common man aspiring to maintain the legacy and the essence of Indian art - as conveyed through both the oral and folk tradition - and indeed all art and their beauty. This event also celebrates that spark of divinity contained within all of us, regardless of religious, racial, creed, social status and gender biases.

At another level this process assists the villagers to develop collective leadership and administrative capability, self-motivation, and professionalism - commencing from the grass roots level. In the process, the village spawns and nurtures its art forms and its cadre of home grown social workers, project planners, managers, and leaders. But this is not to say that this view is unique to Felicity alone. It represents the role, function and *modus operandi* of various other Ramleelas existing within this tiny Republic of Trinidad and Tobago.

And if we are to now personalize the point and ask a very relevant question such as …, "what are the descendants of the original East Indian to Trinidad, doing to enhance, to promote, and to influence the development of T&T?" Using the empirical evidence of this folk festival, the response is, "a significant amount." This has been achieved with very little State intervention, funding or public fanfare but with quiet dignity, honour, pride and self-respect, and with possibly a certain amount of élan and bravado. Yet this collective contribution has not deteriorated into conceit, obnoxious arrogance or self-righteousness.

Ramleela as socio-religious consolidator

The Ramleela has been an equalizer even within the Indo-Trinidadian social structure, breaking down caste, class, gender, age, religious differences and secular, political barriers. Regarded initially as a festival of and for 'Hindus', Ramleela now draws the attention and interest of all faiths and races within the community, whether it is at the spectator or participant level. People of all social sectors are now welcome and included. Anyone can aspire to be and actually achieve the distinction of playing any character role in the production, subject to ability and commitment, provided that they abide by the identified rules and disciplines.

The daily worship or ārti ritual, before and at the end the Leela, is performed by all characters involved in the production. This has further contributed to removing the socio-economic barrier of caste and class. The construction of the effigies especially that of Rāwan, brings together a significant mix of artisans and village helpers.

Changing roles of women and youths in the Ramleela

In the early days of the Ramleela, the cast of performers were all male. The role of Sita was played by a young Brahmin boy, dressed as a female. Men would fill the roles of the queens and other female characters. The Indian society then had relegated their women's roles to being socially submissive, modest, shy, well respected and conservative. Their dancing, acting, even speaking in public was not openly encouraged. Very few women would be brave enough to even voice their opinions to their husbands and family. The roles of females in this Leela were thus confined mainly to providing behind-the-scenes assistance i.e. cooking and preparing the prasad daily for the puja, stitching of costumes and helping to do the performers' facial makeup. This was the direct consequence of the patriarchal, male dominated, Indian society. Since the 1970s, wide and sweeping changes within the country and more so in the Indian community through literacy, education, and increasing socio–economic independence resulted in the changing roles of women, even in the Ramleela. Today, they are equal partners in the production, both on stage and in the planning and preparation for the event.The sanctified area of the performance continues to be the *shala* for only those who will undergo the disciplines and the prescribed abstinences, and are considered 'worthy' to take an active role in the Leela. Women have claimed their equal place in the Leela and are now a part of this 'worthiness'.

The youths have also become an integral part of the production. They assist in preparing their own costume jewelry, armaments and weaponry. Their contribution significantly reduces some of the financial costs of the production that the Ramleela administration has to find annually, to produce this folk drama. They derive their disciplined training from the adult performers - learning through mentorship, on-the-job training and emulation. Moreover with the continuing trend of deglobalisation, the radicalisation of youths and the growth of intelligent, dynamic, passionate youths, the Ramleela and its narrative provide the environment for advancing a new kind of revolution with which they can identify; it is a cultural revolution with a positive value system and an enhanced perspective for development.

Influence of the language of the epic on the local linguistic landscape

Up to as late as the 1950s the text (the Rāmcharitmānas), was chanted in Awadhi and explained using a mixture of the dialects of Bhojpuri, Hindi, and some Trinidad English *(Trinhinglish)*. Currently, selected parts of the text continues to be chanted in Awadhi - referred to in Trinidad and Tobago and the Caribbean as Hindi - and interpreted in*Trinhinglish*, for enactment. Some words from this mixed fare have entered local jargon, enhancing the unique Trinbago vocabulary. People now name their sons after many of the heroes of the story but the spelling and pronunciation have significantly changed. Rām is spelt as 'Ram'; Lakshman as 'Lutchman', 'Hanuman' as Hanooman. The word Ramleela is spelt Ramleela and even Ramdilla in Trinbago's evolving dialect of English. An interesting observation is that no female in our country within the Indo-Trinidadian community, so far, is named Manthara, or Shurpanakha, two supposedly evil-minded female characters within the realm of the dharma or righteous living. Both females had royal connections; one a servant in the royal household, the other a sister of the King. However when chambermaid Manthara's character is closely analysed, one finds that she was really a very logical, strategic thinker, advancing a cause, a political argument, for dynastic ascension for socio-political control. Additionally, the messages contained within the text of the Ramleela have been incorporated into local dialect in parables and euphemisms. The name Rāwan - or Rawan as it is spelt and pronounced in Trinidad and Tobago - is used in political jargon to refer to a wicked and devilish person. Hanuman, the son of the god of wind (Pawan) is considered superior to the western comic strip folk hero, Superman.

Changing the timing and context of the Leela to suit local environment

The Ramleela itself has undergone many incarnations in the local presentation. The production timings have shifted to suit changing socio-economic circumstances. The physical form and format of the presentation has also moved from the previous simple 'maidān' or savannah type enactments, to various versions of stage designs and stagecraft; props, décor and sets. So too have the narration.While maintaining the essence of the text, the performances have been tailored to suit the local context, introducing humor and other paraphernalia to enhance the production. The modus operandi of the performers has also changed. Creative skills are developed and showcased in areas such as costume designing and fabrication, in makeup and face painting.

The Felicity Ramleela story and its enactment, as much as the Felicity story itself, is multifaceted, multidimensional, porous, yet organic, equally a synthesis as it has been a catharsis. It is as much reality as perception, and *maya* or illusion. There is the indomitable spirit of those devout spectators, Rām's devotees who come day after day, year after year to witness the unfolding of this timeless story. For them, this is not just village or street theatre. It is Leela, God's play. It is faith contained in their very consciousness, embellished and infused with its own energy. The electrically charged atmosphere of melodious chanting by the Pundit combined with music, movements and actions, costuming and lighting create and deliver emotions, moods or flavours of actions and reactions or *rasa (*all accentuated by dance and music). These in turn create dynamic, multiple actions and reactions. In the process the spectators cum devotees receive grace or *darshan*. They have neither time nor interest in questioning whether Rām is an historical or mythic character. They come annually to witness the destruction of the evil King Rāwan by Sri Rām, the incarnation of God, supreme reality itself. Good has conquered evil, the annihilation of the *adharmic* or unrighteousness that was the antithesis of cosmic law. Attending the annual Leela renews their moral and ethical values, simultaneously providing catharsis and then grace. These annual treks to the maidān have become part of their consciousness, part of their very DNA.

To the secular spectator, the folk drama creates an exciting atmosphere of the melodramatic with other elements of entertainment. These moods are also influenced by fabric and costumes - colour combinations, body, head gear and armour - props and sets. It presents a judicious mesmerizing mix of sounds, sights, smells and tastes all compactly delivered in one venue; a place where they and their families can roam and mingle within an atmosphere of safety and comfort, in all-embracing village hospitality.

Attending the Leela annually also appeases the nostalgia of past experiences of this theatrical, village spectacle; the attractive costumes, mesmerizing drumming, battles incorporating pyrotechnic displays, street foods and sometimes the mud – a consequence of thousands of feet trudging on wet ground for several days during the annual rainy season. In between, and at the end, there is the anxious anticipation of fire, the exciting crackle of bamboo, wood and papier-mâché shooting into the night sky, consuming the symbolic, mortal remains of Rāwan and his brother Kumbhakaran. The annual experience is simultaneously exciting, bewildering, disturbing, exhausting and yet, satisfying.

The First Felicity Ramleela showcases the whole gamut of human emotions and thoughts ranging from the mystic realm, the occult, magic and illusion, to farce. There is indeed the presence of the comic element in the enactment which is a necessary aspect of an engaging dramatic work. This story forms a collective memory of the Leela at different levels; at the individual, family or village memory. These memories are stored through the spoken words as narrative, sung in poetic verses or dramatized in this local folk theatre tradition, Ramleela; going back 100 years.

What may appear to some spectators as purely a secular, simple village drama is simultaneously interpreted by others from the perspective of devotion and reverence. It is faith personified, *bhakti*. It is worship in action, puja in animation. In this regard, people do not attend the First Felicity Ramleela performance or any other Ramleela in Trinidad simply out of curiosity. There is something more to this annual event, beckoning its adherents to the performance space, the anticipation of the forthcoming events.

This folk pageant incorporates many different aspects of the life of Felicity and its peoples, as indeed the other Ramleelas do to the several villages in Trinidad where they are performed. The central theme always remains Leela, or play in epic proportions. It does not conform to the strict definition of western theatre: The audience does not enter an auditorium, where the lights dim and you are requested to turn off your cell phones or refrain from eating and drinking. It does not separate or quarantine the performers from their audience. Instead, the audience becomes participants and pilgrims in this journey to identify with the divine. But it remains intensely theatrical, a passionate play and display of village artistry. This festival incorporates the sacred and the profane dimensions of artistry, the satirical and the burlesque, incorporating self-help, micro enterprises and a culturally healthy lifestyle.

This Ramleela festival is an ideal example of holistic, village life – moving from simple bazaar or mela and theatre to a study in modern village relationships, its interactions with the various sections of the community, with the changing gender issues, socio-economic and technological innovations within the evolution of our arts. It is also a study in local leadership which cumulatively, has manifested in a gentle, benign and peaceful, God loving community. Most of all the community looks forward to each day's production despite the otherwise hectic schedules of school, of work or at home. The Ramleela satisfies the thirst for involvement and engagement in our local arts.

In this regard, one must commend the ability and artistic grit of the early village Indian peasants - these seemingly 'uneducated coolies' coming from the agricultural hinterland of the Indian subcontinent - to adapt an ancient epic tale and stage it on the village greens of their erstwhile, new 'hostile' environment. These simple peasants established a legacy of artistic creativity, an annual spectacular pageant in the open-air which never ceased to mesmerize the audiences. Many of those who came as mere spectators were swallowed up in the drama's hypnotic, transportive element, making them pilgrims and vessels for consolidating faith. Greater still, the villagers continue to transform the concept of theatre into sacred theatre, a passion play, transporting its audiences to sacred time and place. This is difficult to comprehend, even today. What is even more mind-boggling is that while the Trinidad society in the 20th century promoted its western artistic expressions and could stage its best productions, for possibly 3-5 days, the village Ramleela was conducted in epic proportions and spectacle for 11 consecutive days. After 100 consecutive years it continues this theatrical marathon with minimal State patronage (State support began only in the 1990s, and even then in a very limited way). This is the audacity of the village folks of Felicity, maintaining their folk pageant within the context of Leela, the Leela or story of life.

Using our multicultural asset for socio-economic diversification

Trinidad and Tobago has been built on migrant labour and shared cultural values, each grouping introducing their unique traditions, heritage and art forms. This evolving society has created its own complex of dynamics and differences; religions, races, creeds, shade of colour, and classes. The layers of differences superimposed, one on top of the other, do create challenges for formulating policy prescriptions for governance and management. These challenges however, are themselves advantages for community development and overall socio-economic diversification. The commonalities must be harnessed to forge that unity within the multicultural diversity of this Antillean Caribbean nation.

ENDNOTES

1. Hugh Tinker, *A New System of Slavery: The Export of Indian Labour Overseas, 1830-1920* (London: Oxford University Press, 1974) 364.

GLOSSARY

Adikaavya	First poem, referring to the Rāmayāna which was written in metric verse
Adhyatma	A 14th century (AD) version of the Rām story
Ahimsa	Non-violence
Aji Lamo	A folk theatre of Arunachal Pradesh, India
Amrit	The nectar of immortality; ambrosia
Anand	Bliss
Ankiya Nat	A folk theatre of Assam, India
Anubhava	The expression of an emotion (Bhava/Rasa), which is the consequence of a motivation. Vibhav is the motivation with anubhava being the consequence of the motivation
Aranya Kanda	The third book of Valmiki's Rāmayāna. It deals with Rām as a forest dweller in the wilderness and the circumstances leading to Rāwan's abduction of Sita
Ārti (arti, ārtē)	The waving of a lighted lamp, deya, agarbatti (incense sticks) or camphor on a thali (tharia) in a circular, clockwise motion in front of a deity or revered person with respect and devotion
Asura	A demonic being
Avatār	Incarnation, usually of the Divine/God
Axis mundi	Symbolically, the "hub" or "navel" of the universe as it is conceived in the world view of a particular culture
Ayodhya Kanda	The second book of Valmiki's Ramayan dealing with the circumstances surrounding Rām's exile, Bharat's entreaty to him to return, and Bharat's return to Ayodhya as *protem* ruler

Bala Kand	The first book of the Valmiki Ramayan which narrates the birth and adolescent life of Rām
Baraat (barāt)	A Bridegroom's procession or party in a Hindu wedding
Bedi	A temporary altar constructed - at Hindu religious ceremonies - with a base/foundation of either dirt or leaves of the banana tree, and elaborately decorated with a *yantra* (mystic symbol), flour, rice and other ingredients
Bhava	Emotive expression produced mainly from facial features
Bhang	The intoxicating hemp (cannabis sativa or *ganja*) consumed as a drink or mixed in preparations of cooked food and methai (confectionery)
Bhagavad purana	Hindu religious text based on the life story of Lord Krishna
Bhagwatmela	Performing Tradition from Tamil Nadu, India
Bhajan	Devotional song
Bhakti	Hindu religious orientation of devotion to God through pure love
Bhakta (m); Bhaktin (f)	A devotee of God
Bhojpuri	A living language, originating from the States of Bihar (western region) and Uttar Pradesh (eastern regions) of India and spoken in Trinidad.
Bhoomi Puja	Worship of the earth as sacred ground
Boudh Ramleela	Folk theatre of Odisha (Orissa), India
Brahman	Godhead
Brahmin	The first or highest category within the Hindu caste or varna system. The Pundits and *purohits* (priests and acolytes), educators and administrators belonged to this caste
Caturasra	A rectangular stage
Cēdhā	A gift for religious or spiritual work performed

Chalisa (Chālisa)	A forty-verse song composition, usually dedicated/chanted to specific deities
Chamar	Belonging to the fourth category or *Shudra*, within the Hindu caste system. *Chamar* is a sub-caste: leather (*chamra*) worker within the Shudra caste
Chao (Chho)	Dance drama of Bengal and Odisha, India
Chatti	Hindu ritual performed on the sixth day after childbirth
Chela	Disciple or follower. Also referred to as *shishya*
Chhand	A six- line lyrical verse usually found in Hindu religious texts, especially the Rāmayāna
Chowpai (chaupai)	Four line lyrical verse usually found in Hindu religious texts
Chautaal	A type of folk song, performed during the Holi/Phagwa festival
Chulha	Earthen fireplace, constructed either on the floor or on an elevated platform
Daheja	A system whereby members of a village assist one other at weddings or village events by contributing money, foodstuff and manual assistance
Dame Lorraine	A masquerade character in the Trinidad and Tobago carnival
Darshan	Sanskrit term meaning 'viewing'; an auspicious 'sight' of a deity or sacred object; the beholding of an apparition of divinity
Dasavatar	Ten incarnations of God, on earth
Dasarath	King of Ayodhya, father of Rām
Deva or Devata	A lesser or demi god
Dhantaal (dandataal/ dhantāl)	*A* percussion instrument; a thin, iron rod about three feet long, tapering at the top and rounded at the bottom. It is struck by a smaller, U-shaped piece of iron. It is used for keeping rhythm

Dharma	The Hindu complex of religious and social obligations (a sense of duty or right action, morality and virtue); a righteous way of living a full and fruitful life, based on truth, purity, compassion and charity. Dharma is one of the four-fold paths. The others are: *Artha* (acquisition of wealth & prosperity); *Kama* (the fulfilment of desires); and *Moksha* (aspiration to salvation or ultimate, supreme bliss)
Dharmacharya	A learned person and spiritual guide, leader or upholder of the dharma by action and example; a distinguished person
Dharma Shastra	Holy writ; code of law
Dharti Mata	The term used for 'Mother Earth'. The earth is always referred to as 'mother' since she brings forth/produces the harvest. She is also referred to as 'Goddess'
Dholak	A double-mouthed hand drum made of wood with the mouths covered by skin
Dee	A local or village deity believed to be the protector of one's landed property
Dīpa Vaṁśa	The oldest historical record of Sri Lanka
Divali Nagar	Literally, a "Divali Village". In Trinidad, however, it refers to an annual event, at a specific location, observed just prior to the Festival of Lights, showcasing various aspects of Indo-Trinbagonian culture
Doddatta	Performing tradition of Karnataka, India
Doha	A lyrical couplet
Doob (Dub)	Nut grass
Ganja	Marijuana
Gandharva	A celestial musician in Hinduism and Buddhism; it is also a term for skilled singers in Indian classical music

Garara	An Indian dress worn by women comprising a full- length skirt, s waist-length (or shorter), firm-fitted bodice with a two and one half yard, long shawl
Ghanta	A thick brass gong struck with a wooden mallet
Ghat	Flight of steps leading down to a river
Guru	A preceptor, mentor, teacher or spiritual guide
Havan	The ceremonial fire into which oblations are poured during Hindu religious ceremonies
Hawan kund	A vessel in which the 'sacrificial fire' is kept
Itihaas	Story
Imam	*A* Muslim religious leader
Jahaji bandal	The small bundle that each Indian indentured immigrant carried as he/she disembarked from the ship. It contained their total worldly possessions wrapped in cloth and slung over their shoulders or carried on their heads. The 'bundle' was also suspended with a stout stick over their shoulders
Jahaji bhai	*S*hip's brother. A relationship that was established aboard the ship transporting Indian immigrants. These relationships usually sustained long after the indentureship period ended
Jal	Water
Jati	An occupational sub-group within the Hindu caste system
Jhaki	The bramble of the bamboo grass, with the accompanying leaves
Jhaki (Jhanki) Ramleela	A form of presentation of the scene in 'Tableau ' format
Jhamela	Confusion
Jhanjh	A pair of medium-sized brass cymbals

Jhandi	A consecrated flag or pennant (*pataka*), flying usually atop a bamboo pole or flagstaff
Jhopry	A temporary structure
Janak	King of Mithila, father of Sita
Jātra	Folk theatre of Bengal, India
Jutha	Pollution of food or drink, contaminated by a person's mouth or saliva
Kaajal (Kājal)	The soot of the deya - which burnt either pure coconut oil or ghee - collected by leaning a clean spoon over the flame. *Kājal* is applied to the eye lids/lashes both for medicinal and cosmetic purposes
Kali/Kāli	Hindu Goddess; the "terrible" form of the female force or *Shakti,* responsible for the destruction of evil
Kamarband	A waist band
Kangan	A thick bracelet. In the Hindu wedding ceremony it refers to a ceremonial thread attached to certain charms tied around the wrist of the bride and the groom to ward off "evil or negative forces". It is removed after the wedding ceremony
Kartik Nahaan	(Nahān) A ritual bath during the month of *kārtik*, the eighth lunar month of the Hindu calendar
Katha	A story. The telling of a story, either through narrative, verse, music or dance movements or a combination of these; ceremonial recitation of stories from a sacred text
Kathakali	A Classical dance drama from Kerala, India
Kishkindha Kanda	The fourth book of Valmiki's Rāmayāna, dealing with Rām's search for Sita, the forging of alliances with Hanuman and other forest dwellers in order to locate Sita, and plans to visit Lanka
Kharaw	A wooden sandal

Koodiattam	A performing tradition of Kerala, India
Krishna Janamasthami	Birthday of Lord Krishna
Krishna Leela	The depiction of the life story or divine play of Lord Krishna
Kshatriya	Warrior caste, the second caste within the descending hierarchical classification of the Hindu caste system
Kuchipudi	Classical dance drama from Andhra Pradesh, India
Kumbhkaran	The brother of king Rāwan
Kurta	A loose, flowing tunic-like top, usually with long sleeves and length varying from thigh to mid-calf
Kutiyah	A small, hut-like structure usually made of rudimentary material
Langot	A male undergarment
Langot	A piece of cloth used as a truss
Lawa	Hindu pre-wedding, fertility ritual performed exclusively by women, which often includes very sexually suggestive singing and dancing.
Leela/Līla	A technical term of Hindu theology meaning play, interaction or sport, usually of God as in Ramleela or Krishna Leela
Lota/Lōtā	A brass water pot or container
Lohbān	Incense
Mahabharata	An ancient Indian epic
Mahakavya	A great poem
Maidān Ramleela	Open- air playground in which Ramleela is staged
Majeera	Very small, brass cymbals
Mala	A garland of flowers
Manch	A raised stage, such as proscenium stage
Mandir	A Hindu temple

Mangalam	Benediction
Mantra	A sacred Hindu verse which is rendered through a chant
Mārīcha	The uncle of Rāwan, a sorcerer
Mela	A bazaar with food (cooked and raw vegetables) games and other entertainment
Mool Jhanda	Root or main flagpole with a pennant at the top
Murti	Image or statue of a deity
Nakkatiya Ramleela	A processional form of Ramleela
Natya Shastra	An ancient Indian treatise on dramaturgy
Nau (m)	A male who assists in the organization and performance of many of the Hindu rites and rituals, especially in the life-cycle rituals
Nāuni/Nauni (f)	Female equivalent of a *nāu*; the wife of a *nāu*
Nau Raatam	Nine-day period dedicated to the worship of the female aspect of the Divine
Nav graha	Nine planets within Hindu astrology which are propitiated
Neemakharam	An ungrateful person. Literally means 'not worth the salt' which one has eaten from a person
Neota	Traditional form of Hindu invitation to weddings, *yagnas* and *pujas* and other festive occasions; usually delivered by the village *nāu/nāuni*. It consists of a verbal invitation accompanied by the ritual of giving of rice to the invitees as a symbol of the invitation. The *nāu/nāuni*, in turn, is sometimes given a token sum of money, more in a ritual context than for any financial purposes
Om	A sacred sound, the vibrating sound of the universe
Pagal samundar	Crazy Sea (ocean)
Pancham	Fifth

Panchāyat	A group (usually five- from the word 'panch') of village elders who, based on a combination of intelligence and social, economic and religious status, is entrusted with the responsibility of resolving both family and communal disputes
Panchaiti Yagna	Communally sponsored and organized religious worship
Panth	Religious sect or group
Parchay	To worship, to welcome a guest by performing ārti
Parikrama	The circumambulation of a geographical area
Pataka	A pennant or pennon
Pathshala	Localized village school engaged in the teaching of Hindi and aspects of Hindu religion and culture
Patra (Pātra)	An actor
Payaasam	A sweet dish, consisting of boiled, sweet rice, dry nuts and raisins
Phagwa	Hindu festival celebrating the reaping of winter harvest and beginning of the spring season: Observed with much revelry, singing, dancing, partaking of confectioneries, and the dousing of persons with both dry colours and coloured water
Pitambar	Yellow, usually the colour of Sri Krishna's dhoti
Pradakshina	Ritual circumambulation of an object of veneration
Praja	Traditional Indian patron-client relationship
Prasad	Consecrated food, or food eaten after being offered to God
Pūja (puja, Pooja)	Religious worship, usually conducted by a Pundit
Pujari	One who performs Hindu rituals

Pundit (m); Pandita (f)	In Trinbagonian usage, a Hindu priest or knowledgeable person
Punditai	The practice of the Hindu priesthood
Purana (purāna)	Sacred ancient writings in Sanskrit on Hindu mythology and folk lore
Putul Naach	Dance of 'rod puppets'
Rakshas (Rākshas)	Demons or demonic beings
Rāmayāna (Rāmayan)	The story of Shri Rām
Ramleela	The divine play, depicting the life story of Shri Rām
Rām naumi	The birthday of Lord Rām
Ramraj (Ramrajya)	Utopian rule of King Rām, depicted in the *Ramayan*
Rang manch ka puja	The sanctification of the stage or performance venue
Rang Manch ka puja	Worship of the stage
Rasa	Emotion or flavour
Rasadhari Khayal	A folk drama from Rajasthan
Rehal	Wooden book stand used for holding the Hindu religious texts in place and open, during recitation
Sadhana	Worship
Sadhu (Sādhoo)	Male religious mendicant. In Trinidad, the term refers to a man who is particularly devout and knowledgeable on certain Hindu matters
Sadhuain	Female equivalent or the wife of a Sadhu
Sanatan Dharma	The generalized, orthodox form of Hinduism which evolved in India and was brought to Trinidad; literally translated as "eternal religion" based on the principles of love and truth
Sandhya	The evening prayer; worship at twilight or at the junction of day and night/night and day
Sankalph	Worship performed for a specific purpose
Sant	A holy person

Satsang	Religious occasion involving recitation from the holy texts and the communal chanting of devotional songs; not necessarily conducted by a Pundit
Shankh	Conch shell which is blown
Sharam	Shame or disgrace
Shiva lingam	A phallic symbol representing Lord Shiva
Shloka/Sloka	Two or four-line lyrical verse
Shrota	Literally, an audience, but popularly perceived to be the person taking an active part in the performance of sacred rituals
Shurpanakha	The sister of Rāwan
Sewalla	A Shiva laya, a place Shiva is worshipped
Singhasana	The "seat of the lion", the throne. In the *Yagna* setting it refers to the consecrated, elevated area upon which the Pundit sits and conducts the readings. In the Ramleela it can also refer to the place where the Pundit stands and delivers his discourse while directing the performance
Sindoor	Vermilion applied in the middle parting of a woman's hair as a symbol of marriage
Sita	Appeared from the furrow of the earth; daughter of King Janak of Mithila, wife of Shri Rām, mother of two sons (Lava and Kush)
Skhamba,	The metaphysical pillar that connects the three worlds (heavenly, earthly and nether).It is identified as the centre of the universe
Smriti	Developed, expounded, preserved and transmitted through memory
Sonnatta	Performing tradition from Karnataka, India
Sortha	A type of lyrical couplet
Stuti	Two or four-line prayer
Sudra	Lowest of the four Hindu castes/varnas
Supāri	Betel nut
Swang	A Ramleela folk drama

Swarūp/swaroop	The form, appearance and physical features of the earthly manifestation of God. He or she is a person who becomes the character to be portrayed
Taal	Rhythmic cycle of time beats
Taittirīya Upanishad	One of the sacred scriptures of Sanatan Dharma
Terayattam	A Ramleela folk drama of Kerala, India
Tholu Bomalattam	A form of Shadow theatre of Andhra Pradesh, India
Tryasra	A triangular stage
Upanishad	One of the 3 constituent parts of the Veda or book of knowledge.It comprises of commentaries; part in verse, part in prose. The commentaries extoll 2 basic ideas to achieve moksha or salvation; one through merging with the Godhead; the other through action (Karma Kand), or through knowledge (Gyan Kand)
Vaishya	Belonging to the mercantile or farmer caste; third in the orthodox Hindu caste system
Vanvaas (banbas)	Exile to the wilderness
Varna	Terminology applied to one or any of the four major castes in the Hindu caste system
Vastra	Clothing or raiment
Vedas	Hindu sacred scriptures comprising four volumes considered to have been divinely revealed; they are Rig, Yajur, Sama and Atharva Vedas
Vias (Vyas)	Title given to the Pundit presiding at a *Yagna* or *Katha* – after Vyas deva, the legendary compiler of the Vedas
Vibhav	An expression of the face or the body, resulting from a thought or motive
Vikṛṣṭa	A square stage
Visharjan (visarjan)	Ritual of immersion

Yagna	A series of religious rites and ceremonial, scriptural readings, usually spanning a period of three to fourteen days in Trinidad
Yakshagana	Performing tradition of Karnataka, India
Yantra	Mystic Hindu Symbol

List of Abbreviations:

D.L.P : Democratic Labour Party

P.N.M : People's National Movement

BIBLIOGRAPHY

1. Ahye, Molly. *Golden Heritage: The Dance in Trinidad and Tobago*. Trinidad: Heritage Cultures Limited, 1978.
2. Askari, Syed Hasan. and Qeyamuddin, Ahmad. Ed. *The Comprehensive History of Bihar. Volume II, Part 1*. Patna: Government of Bihar, 1974.
3. *The Comprehensive History of Bihar. Volume II, Part 2*. Patna: Government of Bihar, 1974
4. Baker, Hans. *Ayodhya*, Netherlands: Institute of Indian Studies, University of Grogenheim, 1986.
5. Balkaransingh, Satnarine. *The Shaping of a Culture Rituals and Festivals in Trinidad compared with selected counterparts in India, 1990-2014*. UK: Hansib, 2016
6. Bezbaruah, M.P. Chief Ed. *Fairs and Festivals of India. Vols. 111, 1V and V*. New Delhi: Gyan Publishing House. n.d.
7. *Bhagwatpurana.*
8. Comins, D.W. *Note on Immigration from India to Trinidad.* Calcutta: ... 1893.
9. Dalrymple, William. *City of Djinns- A year in Delhi.* London: Flamingo, 1994.
10. Forrest, G.W. *A History of The Indian Mutiny 1857-58. Volume 1*. New Delhi: Asian Educational Services, 2006.
11. *A History of The Indian Mutiny 1857-58. Volume 2*. New Delhi: Asian Educational Services, 2006.
12. *A History of The Indian Mutiny 1857-58. Volume 3*. New Delhi: Asian Educational Services, 2006.
13. French, Patrick. *The World Is What It Is. The Authorized Biography of V.S. Naipaul.* London: Picador, 2008.

14. Gooptar, Primnath. *The Ramleela of Sangre Grande: Celebrating 25 years of the Sangre Grande Ramleela Committee, 1990-2015*. Trinidad: Caribbean Print Technologies Ltd., 2015.
15. Jain, Rajendra. *Ramleela - In Ballet.* Delhi: B.R. Publishing Corporation, 1994.
16. Kapur, Anuradha. *Actors Pilgrims Kings and Gods The Ramleela of Ramnagar* - Calcutta: Seagull Books, 1990.
17. Keyne. H J. "Report of Archeological Survey of India 1862-63 vol.1", p 321 in *A Visitors' Handbook to Lucknow (1875)* and re-published in Aakshi. Ayodhya Shoda Sansthan, 2003.
18. Klass, Morton. *East Indians in Trinidad: A study of cultural persistence.* U.S.A.: Waveland Press, Inc., 1988.
19. Kingsley, Charles. *At Last: A Christmas in the West Indies.* London: Mac Millan, 1873.
20. La Guerre, John. Ed. *Calcutta to Caroni.* St Augustine: Univ. of The West Indies, 1985.
21. Murali, Atlury. Ed. *India in the Caribbean.* New Delhi: India Empire Publications, 2015.
22. Myers, Helen. *Music of Hindu Trinidad - Songs from the Indian Diaspora.* Chicago: The University of Chicago Press, 1998.
23. National Ramleela Council of Trinidad and Tobago (magazine); 2007.
24. Pattanaik, Devdutt. *Myth = Mithya, A Handbook of Hindu Mythology.* New Delhi: Penguin, 2006.
25. Pathak, Vishuddhanand. *History of Kosala, up to The Rise of the Mauryas.* Delhi: Motilal Banarsidass 1983.
26. Prasad, R. C. (Ed and Translated into Hindi and English) *Tulsidasa's, Shri Rāmacharitamānasa (The Holy Lake of the Acts of Rama*). India: Motilal Banarsidass, 1990.
27. *Ramleela 1991.* National Ramleela Council, Trinidad: A Sanatan Dharma Maha Sabha of T&T Inc. publication, 1991.
28. *Ramleela 1992.* National Ramleela Council, Trinidad: A Sanatan Dharma Maha Sabha of T&T Inc. publication: 1992.
29. *Ramleela 1993.* National Ramleela Council, Trinidad: A Sanatan Dharma Maha Sabha of T&T Inc. publication, 1993

30. Ramsingh, Hardeo. *The History of Felicity Village (1838-1996) Trinidad*: Self-Published,1996

31. Richman, Paula. Ed. *Many Rāmāyanas: The Diversity of a Narrative Tradition in South Asia.* Delhi: OUP, 1994 (California: University of California Press, 1991).

32. Sachchidananda, Ganapati. *God Word Vol II . Excerpts from Speeches*, Mysore: 1998.

33. Sattar, A. (Abridged and Translated), *The Rāmayāna-Valmik.*; Delhi: Penguin Books, 1996.

34. Schechner, Richard. *Performative Circumstances, from the Avant Garde to Ramlila.* Calcutta: Seagull Books, 1990.

35. Schechner, Richard. *The Drama Review: The Journal of Performance Studies.* Ed. Special Expanded Issue Trinidad and Tobago Carnival. (Guest Ed Riggio, Milla, C.) Vol. 42, Number 3 (T159), 1998.

36. *Sri Rāmacharitamānasa.* Gorakhpur: Gita Press, 1976).

37. Singh, Rajendra. *Ramaayan Quiz Book.* Delhi: Ocean Books Pvt. Ltd., 2003.

38. Singh, Sherry - Ann. *The Rāmayāna Tradition and Socio-Religious Change in Trinidad. 1917-1990.* Unpublished PhD Dissertation. University of the West Indies, St Augustine, Trinidad 2005.

39. Sookdeo, Neil. *Freedom, Festivals and Caste in Trinidad After Slavery - A Society in Transition.* USA: Xlibris Corp., 2000.

40. Thapar, Romila. *Ancient Indian Social History - Some Interpretations.* New Delhi: Orient Longman, 1978.

41. Tully, Mark. *No Full Stops in India.* Delhi: Penguin, J992.

42. Verma, Ram. *Before He was God, The Rāmayāna, Reconsidered, Recreated.* Delhi: Rupa &Co, 2010.

43. Vertovec, Steven. "Hinduism and Social Change in Trinidad." PhD Dissertation, London, 1987

44. Wilkins, W.J. *Hindu Mythology, Vedic and Puranic.* Delhi: Rupa Co., 1975 York: Vintage Books A Division of Random House, Inc., 1999.

45. Yukteswar, Giri Swami Shri. *Kaivalya Darsanam: The Holy Science.* California: Self Realisation Fellowship, 1984.

Newspapers, Journals and leaflets

46. *Times of India Lucknow.* Sunday October 5, 2008.
47. *Times of India Lucknow.* Monday October 6, 2008.
48. *Census of Population of India (2001)*, Government of India publication.
49. Printed information from Mahant Jai Ram Dass of Ayodhya; Authority on Ramleela.

APPENDICES

APPENDIX 1

RAMLEELAS OF TRINIDAD &TOBAGO AND THEIR GEOGRAPHIC LOCATIONS

1. Antar Jyoth Mandali - Jerry Junction. Orange Field, Carapichaima
2. Brahma Gyaan Ramleela - Esmeralda Road, Cunupia
3. Bluebirds Sports And Cultural Organisation - Rochard Road, Penal
4. Brickfield Shiv Mandir - Brickfield Village, Waterloo Road, Carapichaima
5. Caroni Hindu Group - Seewala Street, Caroni
6. Cedar Hill Village Youth Social And Cultural Org. - Cedar Hill Village, Princes Town
7. Dow Village Ramleela And Cultural Org Inc. - Railway Road, California
8. Felicity Youth Ramleela Group - 54 Maha Sabha St., Felicity
9. First Felicity Ramleela And Cultural Group - Clarke St. Felicity, Chaguanas
10. Gyaan Deepak Kirtan Mandali - Chotoo Street, Aranguez
11. Gyaan Jyoti Mandali - Hummingbird Savannah, Madras Road, Cunupia
12. Hindu Prachar Kendra - Gilibia Trace, Raghunanan Road, Enterprise
13. Kashie Vishwanath Mandir - Penal Rock Road, Penal
14. Knox Street and Environs Sports and Cultural Association - Robins Recreation Park, Knox Street, San Fernando
15. Krishna Rāma Mandir - Guaracara Recreation Ground, Williamsville
16. La Pastora Action Group - Arnold Dwarika Recreation Ground, La Pastora, Santa Cruz
17. Longdenville Hindu Mandir - 67 Nelson Street, Longdenville, Chaguanas

18. Mc Bean Ramleela And Cultural Group - Lower Mc Bean Recreation Ground, Southern Main Road, Mc Bean, Couva
19. Om Shakti Mandir - Aranguez Park, San Juan
20. Param Dhaam Ashram - Latchoos Road, Penal
21. Pandavas-Palmiste And Environs Drama And Visual Arts Society - Palmiste National Park, SS Erin Road, Phillippine, San Fernando
22. Pierre Road Ramleela Committee - Pierre/Tahadille Recreation Ground, Pierre Road, Charlieville, Chaguanas
23. Rio Claro Ramleela Committee - Clearwater Village,Rio Claro
24. Sanatan Brahma - Reform Junction, Gasparillo
25. Sangre Grande Ramleela Committee - Sangre Grande Hindu School, Rousseau St, S/Grande
26. Satya Drishti Temple - Papourie Road, Lower Barrackpore
27. Shiva Gana Organisation - Campoo Shiv Mandir
28. Sri Ram Indian Cultural Association - Matilda Road, Princes Town
29. Soledad Ramleela Committee - Cedar Road, Claxton Bay
30. St. John's Trace Ramleela Committee - St. John's Trace, Avocat, Fyzabad
31. Sukh Shanti Bhakti Mandali - Warner St, Freeman Road, St. Augustine
32. Swaha Divya Ashram - 5 Mowlah Road, Preysal, Couva
33. Swaha Hindu College - Sangre Grande
34. Swaha Sri Ram Dham - St. Lucien Road, Diego Martin
35. Tarouba Ramleela Committee - Tarouba Road, Marabella
36. Tulsi Manas Mandir - Swaha Hindu College, Sangre Grande
37. Tunapuna Hindu School Ramleela - Pasea, Tunapuna

Source: *The National Ramleela Council of T&T, list of Ramleela groups in 2015(Website- http://www.nrctt.org); verified by author with NRCTT Secretary, Chimandath Maharaj.* The names of the Ramleelas are listed in alphabetical order.

APPENDIX 2

ESTIMATED COST OF PRODUCING A MAIDĀN(SAVANNAH) RAMLEELA IN TRINIDAD AND TOBAGO (TT) FOR A 10-11 DAY PERIOD WITH A PRODUCTION CAST AND CREW OF APPROX. 60-75 PERSONS: 2015 PRICES IN TT$.

ACTIVITIES TT$

1. **SCRIPTING**

Research, Script and printing of script copies	1,000.00

2. **CONSTRUCTION AND FABRICATION OF PROPS &SETS**

Construction of 3-4 stages (basic materials)	2,500.00
Construction of effigy of Rāwan (materials & Labour: 40-45')	12,000.00
Construction of Effigy of Kumbhakaran (material & Labour: 30')	8,000.00
Other Props (boat, plough, deer, horse, bows, arrows, swords, shields, etc.)	10,800.00
Misc. and Labour Charges (honoraria)	5,200.00
Ground Prep, décor of the performance area (flags, buntings, shrubsetc.)	5,000.00

3. **COSTUMES**

Costumes for main characters: Rām, Lutchman, Sita, Rāwan 5X4:	50,000.00
(Cotton cloth, satin, beads, dust (gold, silver etc.) laces, trimmings, wire, stitching, crowns etc.	
Costumes for 45 persons (45X3)@ $1,000.00	45,000.00

4. **MUSICIANS' FEES**

Tassa drumming (transport [2,000] & fees [8,000.00])	10,000.00
Musicians for Vyas (daily performances-honoraria for 4)	5,000.00

5.	**RENTALS**	
	Electricals & lighting; spot and basic effect	2,600.00
	Public address system	10,000.00
	Portable toilets (4)	8,000.00
6.	**PUBLIC RELATIONS & MARKETING**	
	Banners	4,200.00
	Posters	
	Fliers	
	Public announcements etc.	
7.	**REFRESHMENTS**	
	75 persons (performers, technicians and organising committee) for 11 days @ $20.00 per person per day (water &prasad etc.)	6,500.00
	Honorarium to Pundit/ Story Teller/ Director	5,000.00
8.	**MOBILISATION AND DEMOBILISATION**	
	Assembly, dismantling, transport and return of facilities to original state.	8,000.00
	Post production get-together	10,000.00
9.	**TOTAL**	**$208,800.00**
10.	**CONTINGENCY - 10 %**	$2,088.00
11.	**GRAND TOTAL**	**$210,888.00**

Source: This cost estimate has been prepared by the author from actual expenditure patterns of three maidān Ramleelas over a three year period 2013-2015 i.e. the Sangre Grande Ramleela, Pandavas of San Fernando and the First Felicity Ramleela. The estimated costs were based on a production cast of approx. 60-70 persons and a performance duration of approx. 10-11 days compared with another stage (manch) Ramleelas. In order to reduce costs, where possible, and make the production a reality, some of the cost items are sponsored and labour is provided 'gratis' through 'sweat equity'. The production becomes a labour of love and devotion (bhakti).

NB: This estimate does not include *honoraria* to any of the actors/actresses in the Leela. Their stage contributions are done *gratis* by them for the entire 10-11 day period. Some Ramleela groups do, however, have a post-production awards and recognition 'get-together' which is heavily subsidised by the performers themselves.

APPENDIX 3

MANAGEMENT COMMITTEE, MAIN PERFORMERS AND TECHNICAL CREW OF THE FIRST FELICITY RAMLEELA AND CULTURAL ORGANISATION, 2010-2017

Officers 2015 and 2016-2017

President:	Rance Kanhai	Sundar Jookoo
Vice- President:	Gewan Nanack	Gewan Nanack (2016)
Secretary:	Kisha Bachu	KishaBachu
Treasurer:	Kelvin Saith	Kelvin Saith
Public Relations Officer:	Sundar Jookoo	Kishan Beharry
Grievance Officer:	—	Shivaram Ramoutar
Trustees:	Keith Bharath, Shivaram Ramoutar & Varendra Saith	

Pundit/Vyas/Sutradhār - Budharat Yankatessu

Main characters (Swarūps and Pātras) 2010- 2017

Shri Rām	-	Deon Daly/Shivaram Ramoutar
Lakshman	-	Shivaram Ramoutar/Randy Santoo/Vikash Ramoutar
Bharat	-	Denish Ramkalawan/Randy Santoo
Shatrughan	-	Varoon Nanack
Sita	-	Valini Nanack/ Abhilasha Sahabir
Dasarath	-	Fareed Hosein
Kaushalya	-	Kajal Sahabir
Kaikeyi	-	Abhilasha Sahabir/Trisha Sonny
Manthara	-	Jamie Ramkissoon/Shivana Jookoo/Ian Harrison
Guha	-	Anesh Ramoutar
Kewat	-	Avinash Rambaran

Vashishta	-	Raj Pulchan
Vishwamitra	-	Narie Dev
Sugriv	-	Anesh Ramoutar/Satchin Ramoutar/Sarwan Ramoutar
Hanuman	-	Sundar Jookoo/Satchin Ramoutar
Narad muni	-	Hansraj Nanack/Satish Mahabir/Dennis Ramjass
Shiva	-	Tiffany Ali/Persad Pulchan
Parvati	-	Jamie Ramkissoon
Rāwan	-	Sirju Ramoutar/Ramesar
Ahirāwan	-	Harry Persad (Uncle Golly)
Shurpanakha	-	Naresh/Devika Pulchan/Danielle Balroop
Mandodari	-	Danielle Balroop/Namita Singh
Kumbhakaran	-	Anil Nanack
Vibhishan	-	Varendra Saith
Indrajit	-	Vikash Ramoutar/VarendraSaith/Shiva Ramoutar
Mārīcha	-	Varendra Saith
Jatayu	-	Micky Birbal/Dhol Birbal
Sampati	-	Dhol Birbal
Angad	-	Satchin Ramoutar

Stage Management and Technical Crew

Stage Crew	-	Kelvin Saith, Sundar Jookoo, Varendra Saith, Karrisa Britton, Shivram, Vikash, Anesh and Sirju Ramoutar, Gewan Nanack and Keith Bharath.
Sound system	-	Natty Sounds (Natty Ramjass)
Tassa Drum ensemble	-	Saraswatie Shooting Stars & Backroad Boys Tassa Group

Info Source: Rance Kanhai, Gewan Nanack, Kelvin Saith, Varendra Saith, Shivaram Ramoutar and Sirju Ramoutar.

INDEX